THE NEW AND REVISED CATALOG OF
AMERICAN ANTIQUES

THE NEW AND REVISED CATALOG OF
AMERICAN ANTIQUES

by William C. Ketchum, Jr. Photography by John Garetti

GALLERY BOOKS
An Imprint of W. H. Smith Publishers Inc.
112 Madison Avenue
New York City 10016

TO THE AMERICAN COLLECTOR

Prepared and produced by Rutledge Books, Inc.
25 West 43rd Street, New York, New York 10036

Fourth printing 1984

**Published by Gallery Books, a division
of W.H. Smith, Inc.,
112 Madison Avenue, New York, New
York 10016.**

ISBN 0-8317-6315-9

Page 1. Rear: Chest pine; New England, ca. 1850; $250–325. *Center:* Bannister-back side chair; Connecticut, late 18th century; $275–450. *Right:* Candle stand, pine and maple; New England, ca. 1820; $650–900. *On floor:* Woven rag rug; New York, ca. 1860; $85–125. *Pages 2–3.* Weathervane, copper and tin, old paint; New York, 1890–1910; $3,750–5,000. Horse and rider vanes are less common than those featuring the horse alone. *Left:* Fine Victorian bed, pine and oak; late 19th century; $450–600. Typical of the high-quality factory-made furniture from Grand Rapids, Mich. *On bed:* Diamond quilt in blue, tan, and white; New York early, early 20th century; $250–325. *Bottom left:* Six-board chest, pine; East, late 19th century; $200–350. *Pages 6–7.* Footed blanket chest, grain painted; East, mid-19th century; $600–900. *On chest:* Horse and rider push-pull toy; East, late 19th century; $750–1,000. Arrow-back Windsor rocker, pine and hickory, yellow paint on black; East, mid-19th century; $600–750.

CONTENTS

INTRODUCTION

It would be nice if there were no need for antiques price guides. There was such a time, but it was long ago. The memoirs of early collectors tell of snatching Shaker chairs from village dumps, rescuing decoys from woodboxes, and offering modern factory china to farmers who happily exchanged it for sgraffito-decorated pottery plates. While not all these stories are literally true, of course, they do reflect a time when collectors were few (and, generally, very wealthy) and antiques were abundant. Alas, such is no longer the case.

Today, the collector army is legion and the demand insatiable. This condition has had two results: prices for all kinds of antiques have risen steadily over the past few decades; and the definition of what constitutes an antique

has been expanded greatly. There was a time, for example, when the only American glass of interest to antiquarians was early pressed and free blown; bottles in general were ignored. Now, bottle collecting in all its facets is one of the most popular American pastimes.

It is likewise in all other fields of antiques. Although the legal definition still requires an object to be at least one hundred years old to qualify as an antique, the popular idea of an antique admits to the fold objects that are considerably younger—sometimes as young as twenty or thirty years. This expanded definition has come about partly because of the rise in prices: as certain kinds of antiques have become inaccessible to the collector of average means—for whom this book was

written—he has turned his interests to new, and younger, fields.

These changes have presented serious problems, as well as opportunities, for the average collector. As has been indicated, certain areas—silver, pewter, and eighteenth-century furniture, for instance—are largely closed. Few examples exist outside museums and large private collections, and when examples do come on the market, their prices are prohibitive. Yet these are the very areas in which prices have over the years become relatively stabilized and predictable. The collector may not be able to pay for it, but at least he can figure out pretty much what it will cost! The "new" antiques or collector's items—objects less than a hundred years old—are something else again.

Opposite: Victorian oil painting; 73,500–6,000. *Center:* Sugar bucket, pine and hickory; $50–65. Double-drawer chest, pine, gray paint; $135–185. *Bottom:* Floral hooked rug; $60–75. All, East, 19th century. *Left:* Two-drawer Empire work table, fine grained paint; East, ca. 1840; $1,750–2,000. *On table at right:* Excellent gooseneck teapot, toleware; New England, ca. 1830; $1,200–1,400. *Bottom:* Hooked rug, rag on burlap; East, late 19th-early 20th century; $200–275. *Below:* Tilt-top candlestand, pine and hardwood, with inlaid checkerboard and green legs made from tree roots; East, mid-19th century; $1,200–1,500. A real piece of folk furniture, rare and choice.

Many of them, such as advertising materials or candy bottles, were not even considered worthy of collecting a decade ago. And their prices fluctuate widely from region to region, day to day, and show to show. Without some sort of guide to current prices, the antiques collector soon becomes confused and bewildered.

Much of the confusion about the prices of antiques exists because people tend to overlook the unique nature of the business. And business it is, although some dealers see it more as a holy pilgrimage. Antiques shop proprietors are business people—they buy and they sell. But their work differs in one very important respect from other retail operations. When an antiques dealer sells a piece of pottery or an oak rocker, he cannot just ring up the wholesaler and order another. It may be weeks or even years before a comparable piece comes his way, and he may pay more (or, possibly, less) for

it than he paid for the first. There are no fixed wholesale prices in the field; and since the dealer's asking price to the public is to a great extent based on what he himself has to pay, his price must inevitably vary from time to time. Similarly, unlike the usual retail situation, many antiques come to the seller in a damaged condition. If he must make repairs or pay someone else to do so, that too must be figured into the ultimate price.

Nevertheless, certain pricing standards have developed that make it possible to determine the range within which a given antique will be sold. At its simplest, this general rule prevails: a given antique object is worth whatever a person will pay for it. This standard is most evident at auctions. When a piece goes up at auction, it is usually unique—that is, another similar piece is not likely to be sold at that auction. All present have a chance to indicate what they will pay. In the usual course, several people will start to bid. As the price climbs, most will drop out, indicating that the object has now passed what they perceive as its value. One of the remaining bidders will eventually prevail, and the price that he pays will fix the value of the object at that place and time.

However, anyone who has spent much time around auction barns knows that the next time a similar (or identical) example comes up, it may sell for far more or far less than its predecessor. There are a variety of reasons for this. Sometimes it's a matter of personality. Two competing bidders gripped by "auction fever" may become so caught up in their personal duel that they push the price far beyond the value of the item. The presence of serious collectors can also create an unnatural situation. When dealers bid, they must keep in mind how much they themselves can ultimately sell the piece for. When the price is bid up too high, their margin of profit disappears and they drop out. This is not true of the collector who buys only for himself. He will go as high as is necessary (and as he can afford) for a desired addition to his collection. The size of the crowd present at an auction; the auctioneer's knowledge (if he isn't aware of an object's value, he won't push it); the absence or presence of insiders paid to bid up prices—all these can have a major effect on auction prices. So auction prices alone are a poor guide to value.

Above: View of Niagara Falls in carved wood frame, one of a set of paianted circus panels; 19th century; $1,000–1,300. *Right:* Federal grandfather clock, wood with handsome painting; Connecticut, ca. 1820; $10,000–15,000. Clocks in general are expensive; unusuallly decorated ones like this are even more so. *Opposite:* Extremely rare miniature pewter cupboard, oak, with doll-size treen dishes; New England, 1780-90; $900–1,100.

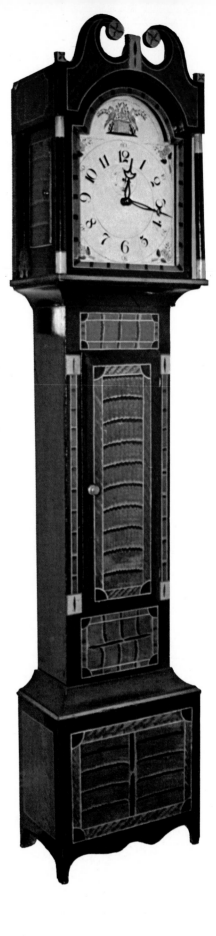

A somewhat better standard is set by dealers' prices. Since the antiques dealer must sell to survive, his prices over the long run will have some relationship to what the public is willing to pay, and hence, though roughly, he will approximate the market price. However, many factors may affect these prices. As previously mentioned, dealers' prices are greatly influenced by what the dealer has had to pay. Overhead, such as rent and electricity, are also figured into the price. Since these costs tend to be lower for country dealers than city, they tend to ask lower prices; thus, they become wholesale suppliers to city dealers, who can in turn ask more, since they deal with a much larger clientele.

Moreover, dealers—like collectors—vary greatly in their knowledge of the field. Some keep reference libraries and research any piece that is not within their area of immediate knowledge. Others, though in business for years, never seem to learn very much. These are the individuals through whose fingers slip the great buys of the decade.

A third and often very important source of accurate information on pricing is the sophisticated collector. In every area of antiques, there are collectors who have spent long years buying and studying their favorite pieces. They attend all the important auctions and visit shops on a regular basis. They are frequently far more aware of prevailing prices within their specialty than are most dealers.

In preparing this catalog, the services of all these authorities—auctioneers, dealers, and knowledgeable collectors—have been used, in an attempt to overcome the problems inherent in existing price guides. Unlike the usual practice, the prices arrived at for this book are presented not as a single figure but as a range, since, as should be evident from the foregoing discussion, it is impossible—except at the moment of sale—to pinpoint a single price for a given object. Having a range of prices at his disposal will enable the collector to determine approximately what is a fair price for any individual antique. Moreover, since "a picture is worth a thousand words," every object whose price is given is also illustrated. Anyone who has ever tried to translate the standard price-guide terminology—"crock with blue decoration, $35"—into something meaningful in terms of his own piece of

Opposite: Jelly cabinet, walnut and poplar; Pennsylvania, ca. 1840; $550–650. *On top of cabinet, left to right:* Hand-painted checkerboard, painted pine; New York, late 19th century; $125–200. Goose decoy; New York, 19th century; $250–400. Pair of Indian clubs in black paint; New England, early 20th century; $45–60. Stoneware keg; Ohio, mid-19th century; $250–325. Splint fruit-drying basket; Maine, late 19th century; $135–185. Painted boxes, birch and pine; East, second half 19th century; $50–450 each. *Below:* Empire secretary, grain-painted pine; East, mid-19th century; $3,000–4,000. An interesting piece with highly detailed painting.

stoneware will immediately recognize the value of this approach.

As a further aid to identifying a prospective purchase, considerable extra information is given for each entry. For instance, the place in which an item was made, narrowed down as accurately as possible, is cited wherever this would help to identify a piece: an early nineteenth-century chair handmade in Maine will differ in important details from one made in Pennsylvania at the same time, whereas the region in which factory-made goods

of a later period were made—political campaign buttons, for example—is of little or no significance. Similarly, the name of the maker or manufacturer is cited wherever it is known. Every attempt has been made to determine the date of a piece, the reasons for this in an antiques catalog being all too obvious.

Furthermore, each antiques area covered in the book is discussed in its own introductory text. These chapters examine such vital concerns as how a particular object was made and, by

Above: Center and right: Grained desk, pine and maple; 1830–45; $450–650. Step-down Windsor side chair; 1820–40; $125–200. Birdcage Windsor side chair; 1820–40; $250–400. *Above desk:* Primitive oil of sailing ship; late 19th century; $1,500–1,750. All, New England.

Above right: Portrait, oil on canvas; East, mid-19th Century; $1,300–2,000. blanket chest, pine and maple, green and tan graining over red; Hudson Valley, N.Y., ca. 1810; $1,200–2,000. *Right:* Map of Schoharie County, N.Y., paper; mid-19th century; $125–175. Eastlake-style sewing machine cabinet, oak; Midwest early 20th century; $200–250.

Page 16. Double-door cupboard, pine, old yellow paint; New York, ca. 1870; $250–300. *On floor, left to right:* Cricket bench, painted pine; East, mid-19th century; $35–60. Stoneware canning jar; Pennsylvania, ca. 1880; $90–130.

extension, how to spot reproductions and outright fakes; how to identify styles; how to tell whether a piece is really old; how to choose objects that the average person can afford—Art Deco silver, for instance—and what types are priced beyond his means; how to identify the outstanding items in any field; how to find areas that have attracted little attention as yet and so are worth exploring—children's board games, for example; how to form a collection of the objects that particularly fascinate you; where to look for the best buys; and how to know whether a prospective purchase is a good investment. It is hoped that these chapters will give the collector a deeper understanding of his specialty and enable him to make future purchases with increased wisdom and confidence. A bibliography is provided for those who wish to delve even further into their field.

Adding a few words of caution is also in order here. The reader is advised to take the term *price guide* quite seriously. Keep in mind that the prices quoted, though they are the best approximations available, are still only guidelines. Prices are not fixed in the antiques field (indeed, we hope they never will be), and many factors may cause the price of an object to vary somewhat from that set forth here. One of the major differentials is the condition of the piece. The prices given here are for pieces in good average condition sold at the retail level, which means, in effect, what one may expect to pay a dealer for an object that shows natural wear but is not damaged or missing essential parts. Damage, such as chips in glass or missing feet on a piece of furniture, generally reduces the value of a piece by 30 to 50 percent. The specific reduction will vary greatly, though, dependent not only upon the extent of the damage but on the buyer's attitude toward it. In certain categories—glass and paper goods are good examples—damage is difficult to repair and will dramatically lower the price. Many dealers will not even handle cracked or chipped glass, regarding it as worthless. Others will immediately devalue such objects by as much as 90 percent. Damaged stoneware pottery and furniture, on the other hand, usually fare better. Cracks and chips in a hundred-fifty-year-old stoneware jug are considered serious only if they affect decorated areas (a crack through the

design on a bluebird jug, for instance) or structural integrity (a missing spout on a teapot). In furniture, early specimens often have replaced pulls or cracked tops. If the piece has been well repaired, its original value will be reduced by not more than 25 percent.

What one is willing to pay for a damaged piece will depend greatly on how much it is needed. A collector will probably purchase an antique that is rare and not likely to be seen again even though it is no longer whole. On the other hand, an article produced in large quantity—such as a commercially made cast-iron toy—will come along again, so that if a damaged example is bought at all, it should be at a significant discount.

From this, it should be apparent that antiques prices, and price guides, are affected variously depending on the type of antique being discussed. In fact, antiques may be said to fall into three broad categories. There are, first, those objects that were at one time produced in factories, in large quantities, in essentially identical forms—lithographs, such as the popular Currier and Ives prints, or cast-iron toys from the period 1890 to 1920. Because these were made in such quantity and have survived in large numbers, they come on the market frequently. Prices may be high because of the great demand, but since the supply is so substantial, the frequent trading allows rather firm prices to be established. Any variation in these prices may be explained by the condition of the item or any one of the other factors previously discussed, but the basic prices are distinct and may be reliably set down in price guides.

A second, much larger category consists of utilitarian items that were, for the most part, made by hand according to certain uniform specifications, resulting in a surprisingly uniform appearance. For example, a dozen or so different basket forms appear throughout the Northeastern states: rectangular market baskets; covered storage baskets; wide, flat drying trays; and others, made by thousands of different local basketmakers. No two are ever exactly alike (as is true, of course, of all handmade things), but their differences are so small that they are negligible. A splint eel trap from Kentucky is enough like one from Massachusetts that the collector can readily recognize their kinship. With such antiques, sharp differences in price may be the result of differences in condition, the collector's desire for a

locally made item, or the presence or absence of decoration. Despite these, however, it is possible to determine reliably a general price range into which most pieces will fall most of the time.

The third category, generally termed *folk art*, presents a much more difficult pricing problem. Here the objects are characterized by a lack of uniformity. Paintings and sculpture are unique objects. Even though Niagara Falls, for instance, has been painted a thousand times, no two renditions are exactly alike. Anyone buying an art work old or new must recognize that there is no piece with which his acquisition can be compared exactly, so that it is next to impossible to quote a specific price without knowing the specific item. True, there are general guidelines. Primitive paintings attributed to the Prior-Hamblen School go for thousands of dollars, whereas paintings of the Victorian period—of which there are a great many, primarily landscapes—usually sell for a few hundred dollars or even less. However, within either category an individual work may sell for much more or much less than the norm. Accordingly, when dealing with painting and sculpture and to a lesser extent with uniquely decorated objects, such as painted furniture and scrimshaw, the collector should consider the objects illustrated and priced here as being simply representative of types, not as specific prices for specific works.

Finally, a word about fads. Over the course of time, certain categories of antiques have attracted inordinate collector interest, generally for a rather short period of time. During the past decade, quilts, painted furniture, decorated stoneware, tramp art, and hooked rugs have all had periods during which they were favored with intense attention by collectors. This interest is usually stimulated by a show dealing with the field, mounted by a respected museum. A book or two relating to the artifacts may then be published; and then the dealers pick up the scent. Within a few months, galleries in the major cities will feature the chosen antique, and ads in antiques publications stress the availability of choice pieces. The major characteristic of such a flurry is an abrupt upward shift in price. In some cases, these prices hold well over a long period of time (quilts are a good example) and may now be regarded as being representative of true value. In others, such as stoneware, the sharp increase is followed by a steady decline, as prices slip downward to reflect a more meaningful relationship to the object's intrinsic worth. The problem for the collector or dealer in such a situation is that he then finds himself holding pieces that are worth far less than what he paid for them and that, if he so desires, he cannot sell for any price near what he invested.

A price guide is of no help in this area, for it must reflect the prevailing prices, no matter how inflated they may be. On the other hand, collectors should be cautioned against investing in items that have experienced sudden rises in price, such as the currently popular "Nantucket" baskets, and should hold the line by refusing to buy at unrealistic figures. Remember, in fields other than folk art, rejecting an overpriced specimen does not necessarily mean losing it forever. A comparable and more reasonable piece may come along at any time. And after all, searching is half the pleasure of collecting antiques!

INTRODUCTION TO THE THIRD EDITION

The discerning collector, comparing this edition of the Catalog with the two prior ones will quickly recognize that the prices listed vary substantially in many cases and, more important, that the variances are not always in an upwards direction. During the 1970s collectors and dealers came to think of the antiques market as a continuing upward spiral with almost everything worth more today than it had been yesterday or the day before. This is no longer the case.

The sharp economic downturn of the early 1980s had a profound effect on the antiques market. One major auction house suffered severe reverses, and many dealers went under. Most of the business failure was among dealers who had dealt primarily with middle class buyers—those with incomes in the $20,000–50,000 range. These buyers, who had previously been able to spend $500–1,500 per family on antiques, were sharply hit by job losses and salary cutbacks. Many of them have still not returned to the market. For the most part, on the other hand, the upper middle class and the wealthy were largely unaffected by the recession; but a rising stock market offered them alternative investment opportunities. The cumulative result was that middle range and speculative antiques declined in price, while traditional high priced objects held their own and often advanced substantially.

Sharp economic improvements since 1983 have buoyed the market, but the recovery, as reflected in prices found in this edition, has been uneven. Furniture, both high style and painted country, has continued its upward rush. Prices above $100,000 for a fine example of 18th century cabinetmaking can no longer be regarded as remarkable. Folk painting and folk sculpture

have broken all records. Quilts remain remarkably strong and have been joined in the winners' circle by samplers, some of which have sold for over $25,000. And, now, hooked rugs and woven coverlets are attracting sufficient attention that prices in the thousands are being realized. Even such humble things as baskets and woodenware can be worth a lot of money. Swing-handled or Shaker-made baskets have joined those made in Nantucket in the $300–1,000 range, while the auction world was stunned by the recent sale of a tiny Shaker lapped oval box for over $4,000!

That's the good news. There is much that is not so good. The silver market plummeted following decline of world silver prices and has not yet fully recovered. The speculation in photographic images led to severe setbacks in the early '80s, and many feel that as a result that field is now underpriced. Prices for all but the best antique bottles have declined over the past five years, and much the same may be said of other mundane objects such as undecorated tin, granite ware, depression glass, Fiesta Ware, mass produced oak furniture and certain types of toys.

Other fields show little significant change. After a boom almost a decade ago, tramp art is essentially static. This is true also for all but the best stoneware and redware. Enthusiasm for advertising art and for posters has for the most part not been reflected in substantial price rises.

The above examples are but a portion of the entire antiques field, but they serve to emphasize the fact that the market is not monolithic. Some areas move up, others move down; and some remain little changed over a period of time. The collector or dealer who buys assuming that any antique or collectible will automatically increase in

value like a savings account will often be disappointed. This was never true even during the boom days of the late 1970s, and it is even less true today. Collectors and dealers must focus on areas of advance and buy just as carefully as they would in the stock market. There are no sure things.

Other problems discussed in the 1980 edition remain with us. Theft of antiques has increased and is now primarily the work of sophisticated professionals, as reflected in the recent hijacking of several van loads of fine antiques from major national show dealers. Owners of valuable objects must not only think in terms of substantial insurance coverage but must also decide if the risk of loss justifies the expense of elaborate security systems. Fakes and reproductions abound—especially in the fields of folk art and painted furniture. However, here the remedy is in the hands of the buyer. If every collector will educate himself or herself through reading, visits to museums and attendance at educational seminars the faker will find small market for his work. The wise buyer has little to fear from him.

And, all problems aside, the public response to this book clearly reflects the fact that enthusiasm for Americana continues unabated. The number of collectors continues to increase as does their knowledge and appreciation of these objects which form so important a part of our national heritage. It should be a source of pleasure to all of us to know that, unlike the situation even a few decades ago, no significant piece of Americana is today likely to be cast upon the garbage heap because it is "just some ugly old thing from the attic."

I.
FURNITURE: CHAIRS AND TABLES

The form and variety of early American furniture are accurate reflections of the condition of its owners. The earliest immigrants to these shores brought few possessions with them other than some boxes, a cook pot, and the clothes on their backs. But among those early arrivers were counted some skilled cabinetmakers; and as the immigrants prospered, they built homes and stocked them with a multitude of furnishings. This tradition persists today, with Americans owning greater numbers and types of furniture than any other people.

The furniture field is one of the most active areas of antiques collecting. It is ironic that whereas the resale value of modern factory-made furniture is, for the most part, essentially nil, pieces made in earlier times continue to increase in value. The price range is extraordinary. One can easily pay as much as thirty-five thousand dollars for a Chippendale highboy or as little as five dollars for a late-Victorian press-back side chair. The two pieces are worlds apart, yet they have two things in common: they both can be used, and they both will become more valuable with time.

The seventeenth- and early eighteenth-century colonial home contained but a handful of furnishings—a table, some stools, a chair or two, and a few storage chests. People often slept on the floor, and what beds there were have vanished with the passage of time. By the 1750s, these few items had been augmented by a variety of useful objects: highboys and lowboys, chests of drawers, sofas, beds, and cupboards. The basic types of furniture did not disappear, however. In fact, they increased in both quantity and kind so that today there are literally thousands of early chairs, tables, and chests available on the market. Of these, the chair was produced in the greatest number of forms.

Stools and Benches

Stools and benches were certainly the first structures intended for sitting on. A few early examples—the "joint stools" put together of seasoned oak—have come down to us. They seem far too small to accommodate comfortably the ample twentieth-century posterior; but then our ancestors—working harder and eating less than we do—were

smaller than we are. The joint stool was essentially a horizontal board joined to two or more verticals, and its form has persisted. Small stools for milking, footstools, and the backless benches of the Shaker meetinghouse all recall the former preeminence of this simple but sturdy object.

Chairs and Sofas

When we turn to the chair, we find a much greater variety of types. Few examples are available of the heavy oak Carver chair favored by the settlers at Plymouth Bay; but if one fancies ladder-backs, press-backs, kitchen chairs, or wicker, pieces can be collected by the dozen and at very reasonable prices. It is best to go about the business somewhat systematically; to do that, it is important to know something about the various types of chairs and how each was made.

The earliest American chairs—the so-called Pilgrim chairs—were built of oak, with bulbous sausage turnings made on a crude lathe. Since there are few authenticated native examples—many were imported from England and Europe—purchase of them is risky as well as expensive. By 1700, however, pine and hardwood ladder-back chairs had appeared in this country, and they have continued in production right down to the present day.

All ladder- or slat-backs—so-called for their several horizontal back splats—are put together in essentially the same way. Horizontal dowels—called "sticks," from which comes the term *stick furniture*—and slats of dried wood are inserted into holes and slots cut in vertical members, which are made of unseasoned wood. As the unseasoned, or "green," wood shrinks with age, it locks onto the unshrunken dry pieces, forming a tight bond. Until about 1860, this union was further assured by the use of hardwood pegs, which were driven into holes placed at points of stress—such as the juncture of the back posts with the top back slat. From 1860 to 1900, nails replaced pegs, and after the turn of the century, pinning disappeared completely.

While the ladder-back was seen in all homes in the early years, the well-to-do soon turned to chairs whose design was influenced by European taste. The dichotomy between native and

European-influenced styles existed in all areas of furnishings; in fact, we may characterize all American antique furniture by dividing it into two general areas: fine furniture, whose style changed periodically with the infusion of new ideas from abroad; and country furniture, which continued substantially unchanged for generations.

There are seven recognized periods of so-called fine furniture, each with its distinctive elements of style. These are:

Pilgrim or Jacobean	1630–1690
William and Mary	1690–1725
Queen Anne	1725–1755
Chippendale	1755–1785
Federal (Sheraton and Hepplewhite)	1785–1810
Empire	1810–1840
Victorian	1840–1910

The basic characteristics of all these styles were developed on the Continent and found their way to these shores through the influence of English cabinetmakers. As a general rule, the American product was more restrained and less formal in concept than its European counterpart.

We have already discussed the Pilgrim chair, whose form had remained basically unchanged since the Middle Ages. In the late seventeenth century, it was replaced by several different styles, which shared the general characteristic of an elegance previously unknown in American chairs. The William and Mary style is distinguished by cane seats and backs, elaborate carving on legs, arms, and back, and shaped or ball feet, elements rarely seen in modern furniture. Like Pilgrim chairs, however, William and Mary examples are so rare as to be unavailable to all but a few museums and collectors.

Such is not the case with Queen Anne examples. These exist in large numbers as both side chairs and armchairs, and they are great favorites with collectors. The formal Queen Anne style is distinguished from its country cousin by its curved cabriole leg and pad foot; its rural counterpart is usually found with a vaselike back splat and elaborately turned lower legs and front stretcher. Both forms are expensive, though the country pieces may occasionally be found for very little at country auctions or house sales.

One type of Chippendale chair resembles the Queen Anne except for its cabriole leg, which is generally carved and has a ball-and-claw foot. The other form is distinguished by a straight, square, or rectangular front leg. Although walnut was a preferred wood in the William and Mary period, both Queen Anne and Chippendale chairs are made of several woods, including mahogany, maple, birch, and walnut.

Federal chairs are lighter in construction and more delicate in design than those of the preceding periods. Two types are noted: the Hepplewhite, with a shield or oval back, and the square-back Sheraton. Both have tapered legs, and ornamentation—by inlay, painting, or carving—is common. Until rather recently, Federal chairs were, like other furniture of the period, of no great interest to collectors, but enthusiasm and prices have increased greatly during the past decade.

In contrast, the heavy-handed design, broad veneered surfaces, and massive proportions of Empire furniture have not appealed to antiques lovers, with the exception of examples traceable to the shops of such famous cabinetmakers as Duncan Phyfe (whose work bridged this and the preceding style). Empire side chairs may still be bought at reasonable prices, and armchairs and wing chairs can still be found for a fraction of what one would pay for their equivalents from an earlier period.

Country examples of Empire continued the trend toward painted furniture that had begun in the Federal era. Best known and most desirable are the Hitchcock chairs: slat-back, rush- or cane-seated pieces with elaborate stencil decoration. Hitchcocks bearing the original maker's label are very desirable, but reproductions are common and faking of labels is not unknown.

Typifying the baroque taste of their era, Victorian chairs were made in a wide variety of styles, too numerous to categorize. The mid-nineteenth century saw the beginning of factory-made furniture, and Victorian manufacturers were eclectic, taking design elements from many different periods and blending them freely. All styles of Victorian furniture are popular today, particularly armchairs and sofas. The country, or "kitchen," versions are generally made of pine and oak, with decorative motifs that were stamped into flat surfaces by giant steam presses; these have appreciated steadily in value over the past decade but can still be purchased reasonably, particularly in rural areas. Matched sets of four or more are an excellent investment.

While the Hitchcock and press-back chairs enjoyed great popularity in rural homes, the ladder-back was always preeminent. Some of the finest specimens were made in the nineteenth century by craftsmen of the Shaker sect, whose religious communities were scattered throughout the northeastern United States. Shaker-made chairs are characterized by textile tape rather than rush or splint seats and are often labeled. Today, Shaker side, arm, and rocking chairs command premium prices. Other ladder-back chairs are much more reasonable—particularly if they lack a seat or require stripping away many layers of old paint. Good examples can often be acquired for as little as five to ten dollars.

A second favorite chair style is the Windsor. Starting from a squat English prototype, characterized by a row of vertical dowels forming the back of the chair, American chairmakers developed an almost endless number of variations: the hoop back, continuous arm, birdcage, writing arm, arrow back, and rod back, to mention but a few. The finest Windsors were manufactured prior to 1850, but the form persisted well beyond that date. A good-looking specimen in old paint always runs well above a hundred dollars.

Far less expensive and more readily obtainable are wicker chairs and sofas They were factory-made in great numbers from 1870 on and are now very popular. All but the most elaborate can be acquired for less than fifty dollars. Watch out, though, for modern pieces just in from Hong Kong or Taiwan! These will lack the signs of wear—frayed ends or cracking paint—evident on the originals and are generally less complex in construction. Wicker fits in with most other furniture and offers an interesting field for exploration.

Tables

The earliest American tables were massive affairs—great oaken boards six feet or more long set on thick turned legs. As time passed, a variety of tables developed, but the Pilgrim style persisted in the harvest and the sawbuck table. The latter could be dismantled and placed out of the way, a practical development seen also in the chair table, whose top tilted back to reveal a handy bench. Both forms were well suited to the crowded conditions of the small colonial house. These early pieces generally lacked hinges and often nails

as well; they were pegged together like a chair, and the lift tops, where present, swung on carved wooden swivels.

As the eighteenth century progressed, with its increased standards of elegance and comfort, the number of tables in use greatly increased. The family harvest table was augmented by smaller candlestands and tea tables, whose tops often tilted aside to make more space in the room or to serve double duty as fire screens. Small rectangular work or side tables, often with drawers, were placed about the room; and in public places, tap or tavern tables resounded to the clang of pewter mugs. The drop-leaf and the gateleg tables largely replaced the chair table as a space saver.

While early tables were most often made of oak, later forms come in various woods—maple, walnut, cherry, mahogany, and poplar. They often had pine tops, which frequently wore out over the years or became lost, to be replaced by others. One of the most difficult matters in buying an old table is to determine whether you are getting the original top. To be sure, always look under the table. Nail or screw holes in odd places, signs of finish on what should be an unfinished surface, and uneven wearing are all indications that a change has been made.

The frames of these tables were occasionally nailed together; but more often they were either pegged or dovetailed, a technique in which triangular openings were cut in two pieces of wood to be joined at a right angle. When the pieces were properly matched, the joint fit perfectly and held securely without benefit of glue or nails. Tops were nailed or pinned on with wooden pegs. Like early chairs, these tables were customarily painted, since the use of several different woods in one piece of furniture created contrasts displeasing to the colonial eye. Today, much of this original paint has been lost. Since its presence always enhances the value of a piece, the temptation to replace it always exists. In recent years there have come on the market several excellent milk-base paints that accurately reproduce the early colors: "Shaker" red, for instance, or "Amish" blue. In the hands of an expert, these can be applied so as to be almost indistinguishable from the original finish.

Fine, or "high-style," tables show a progression similar to that seen in chairs. William and Mary examples are heavy, with turnip feet and applied decoration. Queen Anne pieces bear the cabriole leg and show a preference for mahogany or its American-grown substitutes, cherry and walnut. In the Chippendale period, either the knee is carved in leafy patterns or the entire leg is a plain, tapered shaft. The Federal leg is square if Hepplewhite, or, if Sheraton, round and reeded, tapering down from top to bottom. By the Empire period, the leg has become a thick block turned above and below. Carving and a variety of shapes reappear in the Victorian era.

Tops are rarely of pine in the better pieces. Usually they match the wood of the base, and they may be scalloped, rounded, cut at the corners, or, in the case of drop leaves, shaped in a half circle. Decoration is largely confined to the skirt, or valance, beneath the tabletop. This was usually just cut in a shape, such as a scroll, in the earlier periods, but it was often inlaid in the Federal era and veneered in the Empire.

Victorian tables were frequently topped with marble, a custom developed during the Empire period; Victorian pieces also employed such conceits of the preceding era as cast-iron or bronze feet and various metal fittings. Carving, which had not been prominent since the late eighteenth century, reemerged with a vengeance or was imitated in cheaper pieces by the use of pressed-wood designs. Cast-iron and wicker tables became popular, and the latter are seen in some variety, though rarely are they larger than a modern card table.

Tables are less common than chairs, and their prices do not vary as greatly. Good early examples, both high-style and fine country pieces are costly, especially when painted. Since few tables are bought for show alone, they tend to be sold for their functional as well as esthetic quality, and even plain country examples from the last century sell for over a hundred dollars. Until a few years ago, oak Victorian tables were a good buy, but their prices have now skyrocketed. Wicker is still an inexpensive substitute, and simple country dining and work tables, particularly those of the Empire period, can be found at appealing figures.

Three examples of painted country ladder-backs. *Left:* Ash, brown paint; Virginia, ca. 1900; $50–75. *Center:* Maple and hickory, blue paint; New York, ca. 1900; $75–125. *Right:* Ash and maple, old red paint; Connecticut, early 19th century; $125–200.

Tripod stool, pine, traces of old red paint; East, late 18th-early 19th century; $75–125. The earliest form of household seating.

Small bench, pine, traces of old blue paint; Maine, mid-19th century; $60–120. Typical of small benches used as milking stools and footstools.

Windsor-style tripod stool, pine and maple; New England, first quarter 19th century; $200–275.

Bench, painted pine; New England, mid-19th century; $90–135. Possibly a school bench.

Wagon seat, pine, original gray paint with yellow striping; Maine, 19th century; $250–325.

Slat-back side chair, pine and maple, old black paint; New England, early 18th century; $300–425.

Early 19th century ladder-back chairs; New England. *Left:* Pine and maple, pine seat; $65–90. *Right:* Ash and maple, old black paint; $75–100. Original paint adds to the value of this piece.

Country Queen Anne Spanish-foot side chair, maple, old black paint; 18th century; $1,500–2,200. A New England example of a popular chair.

Queen Anne side chair, balloon seat, mahogany; Massachusetts, ca. 1760; $2,200−2,800.

Lyre-back Chippendale side chair, mahogany; New York, late 18th century; $3,250−4,500.

Country Chippendale lyre-back side chair, ash and hickory, old black paint; Massachusetts, late 18th century; $900−1,500.

Country Chippendale side chair, cherry; Maine, late 18th century; $750–1,250.

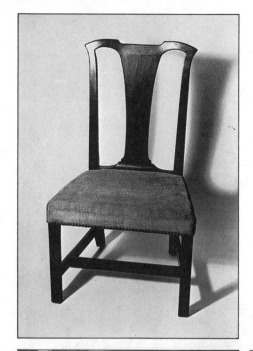

Oval-back Hepplewhite side chair, mahogany; New England, ca. 1800; $750–1,200. One of several variations on the Federal-period side chair.

Empire side chairs with cane seats, child and adult size, walnut; New England, ca. 1820. *Left:* $140–200. *Right:* $125–160.

Hitchcock-style side chair, white with green striping; New England, 1820–40; $100–165. These chairs, generally of maple, have been widely reproduced; only early examples are of interest.

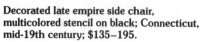

Decorated late empire side chair, multicolored stencil on black; Connecticut, mid-19th century; $135–195.

Left: Rod-back Windsor side chair; $120–175. *Right:* Step-down rod-back Windsor side chair; $175–300. Both, Maine, early 19th century; pine and maple.▼

Bow-back Windsor side chair, pine and maple; New Hampshire, ca. 1830; $300–450.

Two New England Windsors, both in ash and maple; early 19th century. *Left:* Brace-back bow armchair, old black paint, late 18th century; $1,800–2,600. *Right:* Fan-back side chair, black paint; $900–1,400.

Left: Modified birdcage Windsor, bamboo turned, black and gold paint; New England, 19th century; $245–315. *Right:* Late Windsor-style kitchen chair, pine and maple; Maine, ca. 1900; $20–30.

Carved Victorian side chair, rosewood; New York, ca. 1850; $175–325. A good example of an early Victorian chair.

One of a set side chairs in the Victorian mode, oak; Boston, Mass., early 20th century; $60–75.

Left: Late Windsor-style rod-back kitchen chair, pine and hickory, white paint; $20–30. *Right:* Empire-style side chair, walnut, cane seat; $45–70. Both, New England, 19th century.

Two late Victorian factory-made side chairs, hickory and ash; New York, early 20th century. *Left:* $45–65. *Right:* With stamped decoration, so-called press-back; $70–95.

27

Chippendale wing chair, mahogany; **Massachusetts**, late 18th century; $3,000–6,500.

Hand-carved armchair, oak; Maine, 19th century; $140–220. An extremely crude piece of the sort made from 1630 to 1930.

Hepplewhite wing chair, mahogany; New England, ca. 1800; $1,200–1,500.

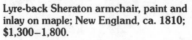

Lyre-back Sheraton armchair, paint and inlay on maple; New England, ca. 1810; $1,300–1,800.

Firehouse Windsor armchair, pine and hickory, light blue over old dark blue paint; New England, late 19th century; $75–110.

Victorian wing chair, rosewood; New York, 1840–65; $400–500. The most sought-after examples in this genre are by Belter of New York City.

Wicker armchair; Midwest, late 19th century; $225–280.

Wicker armchair, white paint; Midwest, early 20th century; $90–140.

Folding chair, birch and hickory; New England, mid-19th century; $300–450. An unusual prototype of the modern folding chair.

Ladder-back rocker, maple; New England, early 19th century; $300–425. Good arms and four slats make this a desirable specimen.

Spanish-foot country Chippendale chair converted to rocker, pine and maple; Maine, 18th century; $175–250. Conversion to a rocker greatly reduces the value of any piece.

Ladder-back rocker, old black paint; Maine, mid-19th century; $150–190.

Left: Child's ladder-back rocker, ash and maple, old black paint; $125–175. *Right:* Full-size ladder-back rocker, hickory and maple; $100–125. Both, New England, first quarter 19th century.

Rod-back Windsor rocker, pine and maple; New England, ca. 1840; $185–235.

Victorian overstuffed rocker, rosewood; New York, ca. 1860; $350–500.

Comb-back Windsor rocker, pine and maple; New Hampshire, ca. 1820; $450–525. A stylish example of a popular and hard-to-find rocker.

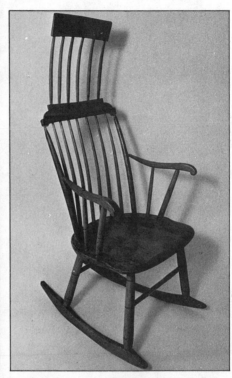

Boston rocker, pine and maple; New England, ca. 1860; $75–100. Lack of decoration accounts for the lower price.

Stencil-decorated Boston rocker, pine and maple; Massachusetts, ca. 1840; $200–275. A style that has been widely reproduced.

Thumb-back Windsor rocker with potty hole, pine and birch, old black paint; New York, mid-19th century; $100–140.

Victorian caned rocker, birch; New Jersey, late 19th century; $150–185.

Two press-back rockers, pine and ash; New York, early 20th century. *Left:* $150–185. *Right:* $75–100. Good investments in the rocker field.

Firehouse Windsor rocker, pine and hickory, old green paint; New York, late 19th century; $110–140.

Wicker rocker, white paint; New York, early 20th century; $100–125.

Victorian swivel-base desk chair, cane and oak; East, early 20th century; $275–300.

Child's armchair, pine and maple, old red paint; Maine, 18th century; $150–200.

Early infant's potty chair, pine, green paint; Pennsylvania, 18th century; $200–275. Potty chairs always sell at prices well below comparable examples with solid seats. ▼

Late Windsor-style child's armchair, pine and hickory, black paint with gold trim; New York, ca. 1850; $90–135.

Windsor-style potty chair, pine and maple, old green paint with gold striping; Maine, ca. 1860; $75–95.

Infant's high chair, pine and maple, old red paint; New England, late 18th century; $325-450.

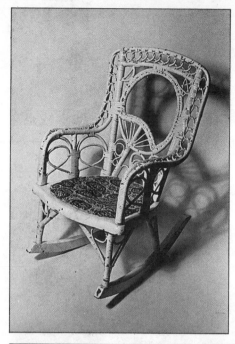

Windsor-style infant's high chair, pine and hickory, old black paint; Pennsylvania, mid-19th century; $250–375.

Child's rocking chair, wicker, yellow paint; New England, late 19th century; $250–400.

Windsor-style settee, pine and birch, old yellow paint; Massachusetts, ca. 1870; $475–550. Benches of this sort were made throughout New England for use in churches and public halls.▼

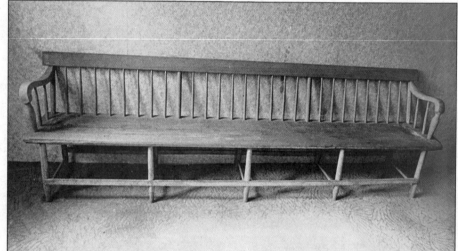

Hepplewhite sofa, mahogany; Connecticut, ca. 1800; $3,200–4,000.

Sheraton sofa, mahogany; New England, ca. 1810; $3,800–4,700.

Sheraton sofa, mahogany; New York, ca. 1800; $2,750–3,500.

Victorian fainting couch, rosewood and pine; Massachusetts, ca. 1880; $100–225.

Wicker fainting couch, white paint; Midwest, early 20th century; $350–450.

Empire sofa, the so-called Grecian couch, walnut; ca. 1820; $1,200–1,800. Much less common than the full-backed version.

Scallop-back wicker settee, white paint; Midwest, early 20th century; $375–500.

Wicker planter; Midwestern, ca. 1900–1910; $75–150.

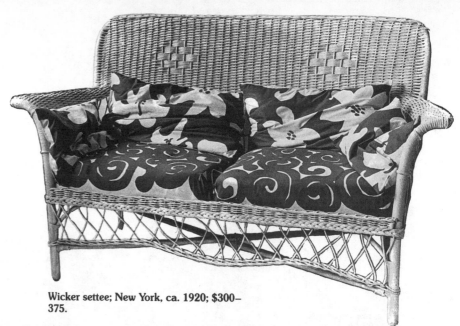

Wicker settee; New York, ca. 1920; $300–375.

Turnip-foot tavern table, walnut and pine; Rhode Island, late 17th century; $2,500–3,200.

Early tilt-top table, pine and ash; Maine, 18th century; $1,200–1,500.

Tavern table, pine, scalloped corners and green paint; Maine, 18th century; $1,100–1,450.

Tap or tavern table, pine; New York, early 19th century; $700–950.

Side table, breadboard top, pine, old red paint; New England, early 19th century; $550–700. ▼

Side table, pine, grain-painted in brown; New England, mid-19th century; $300–425.

Swing-leg tavern or tea table, pine, traces of old red paint; New York, 18th century; $900–1,200.

Queen Anne tilt-top table, mahogany; New England, 18th century; $1,300–2,000.

Sheraton-style two-drawer side table, tiger maple; New Hampshire, ca. 1810; $875–950. Tiger-maple grain adds value to any piece of furniture.

Sheraton-style single-drawer side table, pine; Maine, ca. 1820; $325–450.

Empire-style two-drawer Pembroke table, cherry and pine; New York, ca. 1840; $150–200.

Victorian spool-turned side table, pine; Massachusetts, late 19th century; $125–160.

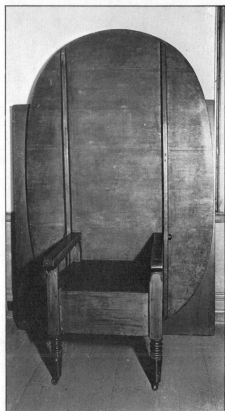

Harvest table, pine, old blue and white paint, light brown top; Maine, ca. 1860; $650–1,000.

Sheraton-style chair table, walnut; Pennsylvania, ca. 1800; $1,400–1,900.

Sawbuck table, pine, base in old blue paint; Maine, early 19th century; $900–1,100.

Queen Anne drop-leaf table, trifid-foot, walnut; New England, mid-18th century; $2,400–3,000. ▶

Queen Anne-style drop-leaf table, mahogany; Massachusetts, 18th century; $2,200–2,700.

Hepplewhite two-part dining table, mahogany; New England, ca. 1800; $4,800–6,400. An extremely fine example of a rare type.

Country Hepplewhite Pembroke table, cherry with apple top, traces of old gray paint; Maine, ca. 1820; $270–380. ▼

Country Hepplewhite drop-leaf dining table, cherry; New Hampshire, ca. 1810; $500–625.

Sheraton drop-leaf dining table, mahogany; Maine, ca. 1820; $900–1,200

Square-base drop-leaf table, pine and maple; Vermont, early 19th century; $350–475. Tables of this sort are often attributed to Shaker craftsmen.

Empire pedestal-base dining table, mahogany; Massachusetts, ca. 1820; $450–550. Empire tables continue to be undervalued. ▼

Victorian pedestal-base dining table, oak; East, late 19th century; $325–475. A very popular type today.

Empire drop-leaf dining table, walnut; New Jersey, ca. 1840; $250–400.

Chippendale-Hepplewhite transitional candlestand, mahogany inlaid with white wood; Massachusetts, ca. 1790; $1,500–2,000.

Shaker lamp table, pine and maple, old red paint; New Hampshire, first half 19th century; $1,750–2,500. An otherwise prosaic piece of furniture turns to gold when identified as Shaker.

Spider-leg candlestand, mahogany; Maine, early 19th century; $650–800.

Spider-leg tilt-top candlestand, cherry; Massachusetts, late 18th century; $900–1,300.

Hepplewhite snake-foot candlestand, pine, base in black paint and rural scene in oils on top; Maine, ca. 1810; $2,200–3,000. A fine example of country decoration.

Large tilt-top tea table, maple; New Hampshire, late 18th century; $1,000–1,700.

Empire candlestand, mahogany; New England, ca. 1830; $250–325.

Victorian candlestand, walnut; Midwest, ca. 1860; $175–235. ▼

Hepplewhite spade-foot games table, maple with burl maple veneer; New England, ca. 1800; $3,000–4,500.

Ottoman or foot rest, walnut; Grand Rapids, Mich., ca. 1880; $90–125. Pieces of this sort were very popular in the late Victorian period.

2

FURNITURE: CHESTS AND OTHER PIECES

Case Furniture

Case furniture refers to furniture that encloses a space, from an early meaning of the word *case,* a "chest." Included in the term are chests, bureaus, highboys and lowboys, desks, trunks, and cupboards. The term is used to distinguish these usually solid pieces from the group known as *stick furniture,* in which relatively slender vertical members—that is, legs—form an important part of the construction. Tables, chairs, and all other seating pieces may be called stick furniture.

The earliest American case pieces are chests that date well back into the seventeenth century. Stout of proportion and sturdy of build, they are made of oak as the base wood, with carving and applied decorative devices worked in a contrasting wood such as maple. Like the earliest American chairs, they resemble their more numerous European cousins, so if you are going to spend the money on a representative example, the transaction should be carried out with a dealer who can guarantee the local origin of his pieces.

Also like the early Pilgrim chairs, seventeenth-century case pieces rarely come on the market anymore. It's much easier—and cheaper—to buy a fine old six-board chest, a simple form that takes its name from the number of pieces of wood that compose it: one board for each of the four sides, and one each for the top and bottom. Such chests were made from 1700 on and may be found in plain pine or walnut or decorated in a variety of ways, including painted-on graining, often in red and black or yellow and brown. The choicest decoration is seen on the so-called dower chests from Pennsylvania, Virginia, and New Jersey, which often show hand-painted names, dates, and decorative motifs such as flowers and human figures. These may sell for thousands of dollars. Note that repainted or newly painted dower chests are appearing on the market. Most are so poorly done as to fool no one, but watch for those telltale signs that indicate the authenticity of an old piece: spidered or chipped paint, worn spots at points of contact, and early hardware.

Chests were usually nailed or dovetailed together, and hardware and construction methods give important clues to age. The earliest specimens—those made before 1800—will often have snipe hinges (interlocking hairpin-shaped pieces of wrought iron) and will be constructed with crude hand-shaped nails. Most pieces made after 1830 will contain square-headed cut nails and wrought-iron butt hinges. Screws will be hand-finished, with off-center slots and flat points. The presence of wire nails or modern screws and steel hinges indicates that the chest either has been repaired or is of an extremely late date.

Traveling chests—the predecessors of the steamer trunk—are found in many different forms. Some were covered with cowhide and studded with brass nails. They may be as large as a full-sized chest or as tiny as a cashbox. Smaller examples are sometimes extremely attractive, and all but the painted Pennsylvania and New England examples are greatly undervalued. Nineteenth-century travelers, particularly in the years after the Civil War, also carried pressed-tin and wood trunks, and these have recently become desirable. They may have flat or domed tops, frequently with attractive lithographs pasted inside their lids. Tin trunks may still be found for as little as ten dollars at country sales and auctions.

Cupboards, both standing and wall varieties, evolved from chests. They are popular functional pieces of antique furniture and command a good price. Originally, they were usually built into the walls of a house, so that many were destroyed or drastically altered after removal. Their most common woods were pine, poplar, or cherry, and they were almost always painted; but since that paint has often disappeared—either through wear or by some well-intentioned but ill-informed owner—those pieces that still possess a good original finish command premium prices. As with chests, the age of a cupboard can be determined by nails, construction, and hinges. Backboards were left unfinished, so that the original saw marks can be seen. These saw marks are another clue to age; straight saw cuts indicate a date before 1840, since the circular mill saw was not widely introduced before that time. Drawers should have a few big dovetails rather than the numerous uniform small ones evident in factory furniture, made after 1880.

Highboys are really an early and sophisticated type of cupboard. There are few of them available; indeed, few of them were made, for most colonists could not afford such an expensive luxury. Country-style examples are even less common than those made by city cabinetmakers. Lowboys too are costly and hard to come by, but in their later form as the bureau or chest of drawers, they are more familiar. Empire and Victorian bureaus with their lavish oak and walnut decoration and fine beveled mirrors are an excellent buy. They are still plentiful and reasonably priced and will appreciate in value, something one can't expect from their modern counterparts. A particularly good buy at present is Victorian cottage furniture—inexpensive, factory-made pieces with hand-painted decoration; they were originally used in middle- and working-class homes (hence the name *cottage*) and have a "folk" quality that goes well with modern furnishings.

The earliest desk was a mere box with a slant top, often intended simply to hold the family Bible. The form survived well into the nineteenth century, but long before that, someone had thought to put a frame or set of legs on the box and thus create the desk as we know it. A few William and Mary specimens may be found, but the earliest common types date to the Queen Anne and Chippendale eras. Any halfway decent desk of this age commands a price above a thousand dollars, but country examples such as the schoolmaster's desk are much more reasonable. These were generally made in pine and may be decorated by graining. High-style Empire and Victorian desks were much more lavish as well as considerably larger; and one type, the Wooton desk, which was custom-made for offices and countinghouses, contains literally dozens of drawers. The few Wootons on the market today sell for as much as a pre-1800 desk.

Beds

Beds did not appear to any extent before the Queen Anne period and were rare until the Federal era. Empire beds are big and cumbersome and most Victorian examples are extremely lavish except for two types, the brass and the spool-turned. Brass and brass-trimmed iron beds are extremely popular today and command a high price. They look well in the modern bedroom, but one should be aware that a large number of similar examples is being manufactured today. At present, though, these are themselves so expensive as to make it highly unlikely that they would be represented as antique.

Spool-turned furniture appeared after the Civil War and lingered on past 1900. Beds in this style may be found in pine, walnut, or maple. They are inexpensive and attractive, particularly the single beds, which may be used as couches. They may often be obtained at country sales and auctions for no more than twenty dollars.

Mirrors, Frames, Shelves, and Racks

Mirrors were rare in early American homes. Aside from the puritanical injunction against vanity, glass was expensive and was reserved for a more crucial use in windows. Until the 1750s, most people who wanted to look at themselves had to be content with a peek into the water bucket. Queen Anne, Chippendale, and Federal mirrors were reserved for the rich and

hence are elaborate and costly. More accessible to the average pocketbook is the extremely attractive walnut-veneer ogee mirror of the Empire period. Its simple lines blend well with twentieth-century decor, and its low cost causes this mirror to appear often in shops and homes. Victorian mirrors, on the other hand, are factory-made and rather plain, and the demand for all things Victorian makes them carry higher prices than they would otherwise merit.

Anyone who has purchased a modern picture frame knows how exorbitant the price of glass has become. If you have pictures to frame, look for old frames. Antiques dealers stock large quantities, usually with the original glass, for a fraction of what one would pay for a cheaply designed modern counterpart. Nineteenth-century frames, particularly from the Victorian period, were made in an enchanting array of styles; many are absolutely unique, being the handmade product of the well-bred lady's idle moments. They are fun to own and are all reasonably priced. Look especially for

the folk art frames, those constructed of the unusual materials the Victorians so delighted in—shells, pinecones, birch bark, or (from a later period) even popsicle sticks.

Wall shelves and racks are also a good buy. Shelves in various forms appeared early, and some, such as the eighteenth-century pipe racks of New England and Pennsylvania, are extremely expensive. Watch out for later reproductions of these treasures. The fakes are usually put together with modern wire nails or brads and show neither the right patina nor signs of wear an old piece should have.

Victorian wall shelves come in various forms and woods. Walnut is popular, and pine may be stained to imitate it or may be painted in a variety of fanciful colors. Some of these racks are expandable. Others may be cut with a jigsaw to produce decorative patterns, such as Masonic symbols or patriotic motifs. Hall racks for coats and hats are also common, and some may be massive, multipurpose pieces frequently incorporating a marble-topped table and brass or bronze fittings.

Chippendale chest of drawers, mahogany and flame mahogany veneer; Massachusetts, ca. 1780; $6,500–8,000.

Framed low chest, pine and oak, old red paint; New England, early 18th century; $800–950.

Pilgrim chest, oak and maple; New England, late 17th century; $11,000–15,000. An example of the earliest American chests. ▼

Footed six-board chest, pine, red and yellow graining; Pennsylvania, mid-19th century; $500–700.

Top: Small chest, pine, old mustard paint; Connecticut, mid-19th century; $65–85.
Bottom: Six-board chest, maple, snipe hinges and traces of old red paint; New York, late 18th-early 19th century; $300–450. Six-board chests in maple are rare.

Blanket chest, pine, old red paint; Vermont, early 19th century; $650–800.

Hepplewhite swell-front chest of drawers, mahogany; New Hampshire, ca. 1800; $2,750–4,500.

Empire chest of drawers, mahogany; New England, ca. 1830; $750–900. A fine chest subject to the general prejudice against Empire; hence the relatively lower price.

Sheraton bow-front chest of drawers, mahogany; Massachusetts, ca. 1810; $2,200–3,000.

Well-decorated Victorian chest of drawers, grain-painted pine; Rhode Island, ca. 1890; $230–310.

Victorian cottage bureau, pine, blue, white, and red, hand decorated on blue and gray ground; Midwest, late 19th century; $350–425.

Queen Anne chest on chest, maple, old black paint; New Hampshire, ca. 1760; $9,000–12,000.

Victorian-style bureau, oak and pine, old brown paint; New England, late 19th century; $250–330.

Hepplewhite high chest of drawers, flame mahogany; Connecticut, ca. 1800; $3,500–4,200.

William and Mary highboy, walnut and walnut veneer; Rhode Island, late 17th-early 18th century; $35,000–50,000.

Hepplewhite sideboard, mahogany; Massachusetts, ca. 1800; $9,000–14,000. All sideboards are rare enough to command a good price. ▼

Queen Anne highboy, maple; New Hampshire, late 18th century; $12,000–17,500.

William and Mary chest on frame, oak, ▲ original red and black paint; Massachusetts, late 17th century; $45,000–55,000.

Early Empire sideboard, mahogany; New York, ca. 1820; $1,400–1,650. A well-done transitional piece with traces of Sheraton.

49

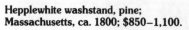

Hepplewhite washstand, pine;
Massachusetts, ca. 1800; $850–1,100.

Queen Anne bonnet-top highboy, maple;
New England, ca. 1770; $25,000–33,000.

Sheraton washstand, pine and maple; New
Hampshire, early 19th century; $350–500.

Queen Anne dutch-foot lowboy, maple;
Connecticut, ca. 1760; $22,000–28,000.

Empire washstand, walnut and walnut
veneer; New England, ca. 1840;; $250–400.

Hanging cupboard, oak; New England, late 17th century; $7,500–9,000.

Victorian commode, oak and oak veneer; Midwest, late 19th century; $225–325. Factory made but increasing in popularity.

Victorian cottage commode, pine, blue, red, and white design on blue and gray ground; Midwest, late 19th century; $275–400.

Hanging cupboard, pine, grained finish; Maine, mid-19th century; $400–500. ▼

Small corner cupboard, pine; New England, ca. 1870; $250–325.

Victorian commode, oak; late 19th century; $125–175. Another good buy in early midwestern factory funiture.

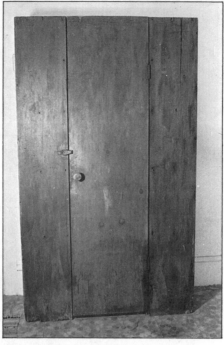

Standing cupboard, pine; New York, early
19th century; $450–575.

Cupboard, pine; New England, early 19th
century; $500–650. Probably originally a
built-in piece.

Large cupboard (7' tall) pine; Midwest, mid-
19th century; $750–900.

Open-top cupboard, poplar and pine;
Pennsylvania, ca. 1850; $900–1,400.

Cupboard, blue and white paint; New York,
ca. 1860; $2,500–3,200.

Small painted chest, pine; Pennsylvania, ca. 1820; $525–650. A dome-top lady's chest with excellent decoration.

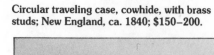
Circular traveling case, cowhide, with brass studs; New England, ca. 1840; $150–200.

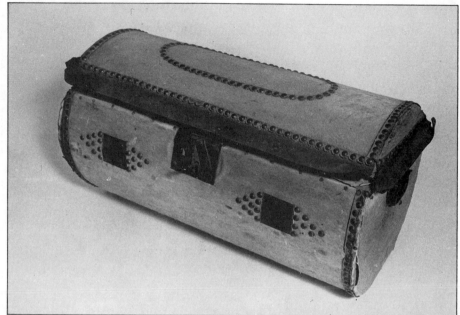

Document box, cowhide with brass studs; New York, mid-19th century; $100–135.

Child's chest, wood and lithographed paper; New England, late 19th century; $75–95.

Victorian dome-top traveling chest, painted tin and wood; Maine, late 19th century; $95–135.

Empire spice chest, walnut and walnut veneer; Massachusetts, ca. 1840; $375–550.

Federal cellarette, mahogany; New England, early 19th century; $650–900.

Tabletop or lap desk, pine; Maine, mid-19th century; $110–160.

Schoolmaster's desk, pine with black on brown graining; New England, mid-19th century; $450–600.

Schoolmaster's desk, pine and maple with traces of old red paint; New York, ca. 1870; $275–425.

Chippendale fall-front desk, mahogany; New Hampshire, ca. 1790; $4,000–5,500.

Sheraton lady's desk, mahogany; New England, ca. 1810; $2,300–3,100.

Federal fall-front desk, mahogany; New England, ca. 1800; $2,800–3,500. A transitional piece with a simple country interior.

Spool-turned desk, pine; Vermont, late 19th century; $120–160.

Victorian roll-top office desk, golden oak; Boston, Mass., early 20th century; $1,300–1,800.

Sheraton canopy bed, mahogany; Massachusetts, ca. 1800; $5,500–8,000.

Early Empire carved bed, walnut; Maine, dated 1818; $2,000–2,700.

Left: Late Federal-early Empire transitional bed, mahogany and pine; Maine, ca. 1820; $1,200–1,600. On bed is a wooden bed key used to tighten ropes that support the mattress; ca. 1820; $10–12. *Right:* Trundle bed, pine; Maine, ca. 1820; $350–425.

Victorian spool bed, old red paint; Massachusetts, ca. 1870; $300–375.

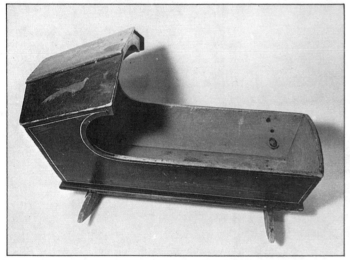

Hooded cradle, pine, stencil decoration on blue, pale blue interior; New England, ca. 1840; $650–750.

Hooded cradle, pine; Maine, mid-19th century; $150–200.

Queen Anne child's playpen with split spindle siding, pine; Maine, late 18th century; $500–750. A rare piece.

Chippendale mirror, walnut; New England, late 18th century; $650–950.

Sheraton girandole mirror, gilded pine; New England, ca. 1800; $1,200–1,800

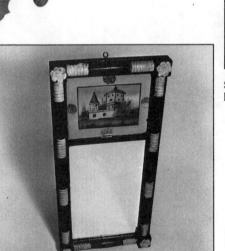

Sheraton-Empire transitional mirror, pine, black paint and gilding with reverse-glass painting; New York, ca. 1830; $250–350.

Empire ogee-frame mirror, walnut veneer on pine; Connecticut; mid-19th century; $80–110. An example of an inexpensive and attractive mirror that is readily available.

Ogee-frame mirror, walnut; New England, mid-19th century; $100–135.

Victorian decorative frame, pine cones on pine; South, late 19th century; $35–40.

Victorain wall mirror in Sheraton style with oil painting of lighthouse possibly replacing an earlier reverse-glass painting; $275–350.

Factory-made wall mirror, pine with silver paint and decorative lithographs; Midwest, early 20th century; $35–50.

Victorian saw-cut wall shelves, walnut; Midwest, late 19th century; $75–120.

Hanging shelves, oak; New York, late 19th century; $100–140.

Wall magazine rack, pine; Midwest, early 20th century; $45–65.

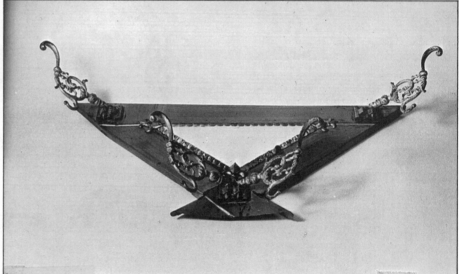

Victorian coat rack, bronze and walnut; New England, late 19th century; $75–125.

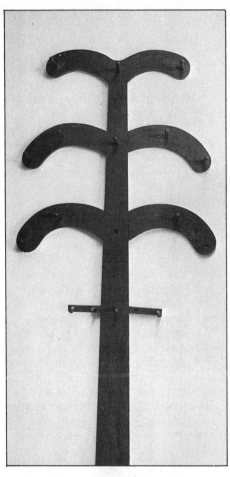

Unusual country hall tree, pine; New York, mid-19th century; $265–350. A piece of functional folk art.

Footed towel rack, pine; Maine, late 19th century; $75–110.

Elaborate mirror and vanity box, pine and walnut veneer; New England, ca. 1850; $200–275.

Melodeon, mahogany and rosewood; made by Austin and Dearborn, Concord, N.H., ca. 1840; $1,200–1,650.

61

3

FOLK PAINTING AND SCULPTURE

Many attempts have been made to formulate a precise definition of American folk art, and the boundaries of the definition have varied considerably from time to time. The pioneer collectors of folk art, in the early decades of the present century, confined their interest largely to paintings—oils at first, followed by various types of watercolors. However, under the pressure of decreasing supply and increasing demand, as well as the recognition that folk art is to be found in other mediums, the term has been broadened to include drawings, silhouettes, cut paper, and especially sculpture of various kinds.

Painting

The line between academic and folk painting is, superficially at least, rather easy to draw. The academic painter has been trained; he is aware of and employs perspective and color and size relationships in an attempt to create a faithful likeness of an object, person, or scene. The folk artist, on the other hand, is not skilled in these techniques and is not really interested in them. He does not paint what he sees so much as what he remembers, using what has been called non-optical vision; he puts down what he perceives to be the essence of his subject—the very thing sought by the modern abstract painter. Primitive or folk paintings are, therefore, likely to be flat, lacking in depth. Color is put on in blocks without much shading, and figures vary in size depending upon the artist's feeling about their importance.

With the exception of work done at women's academies, there was little of what we call folk painting prior to the very late eighteenth century. Until then, only the rich could afford paintings, and those that they owned were created by European academic painters or by Americans trained in the same discipline. With the general increase in prosperity after the Revolution, it became possible for farmers and small merchants to afford paintings. They initially sought portraits in oil, the very things that the wealthy had been commissioning previously. Since academic painters were not available to the country folk, these people turned instead to local artists, men and women who might have been sign painters, furniture decorators, or writing masters. From 1800 until the invention of the

camera destroyed their craft at the middle of the century, itinerant folk artists roamed the hinterlands of New England and the Middle West, stopping here and there and painting for all who would pay. What they created forms the core of what we now call folk art.

Buying folk art is tricky business. Portraits, the most desirable of folk paintings, are simple works, for which the artist was paid anywhere from three dollars to twenty-five apiece; today they may sell for as much as five thousand dollars or more. Some bear the signature of a known artist, such as Prior or Hamblen, and these bring a fancy price indeed. Most folk portraits are unsigned, however, and with them one plays the game of attribution. Even the faintest similarity of a given work to one signed by a known folk artist brings forth exclamations of delight and a big jump in price. But paying a lot of money for an oil of somebody's great-grandmother just because it happens to look faintly like a Prior is risky at best.

While not as popular as portraits, oil paintings of animals, ships, and landscapes all have their devotees and are far from inexpensive. There are, however, primitive oils that can still be purchased reasonably. First, there is a large group of Victorian landscapes that were done in this country, probably by copying European paintings or artist's manuals. Many are rather ordinary (but in truth, so is much high-priced folk painting), while others may contain "foreign-looking" elements such as Swiss roofs or non-American peasant costumes. Much of this work is now classified loosely under the term *Hudson River School* in an attempt to relate it to the bucolic and very expensive American landscapes done by such outstanding native painters as Church and Cole. Certainly, some of these largely unsigned paintings are of American scenes; but, more important, they all offer an area of native painting that has been largely ignored.

Oil painting was done primarily on canvas, artist's board, or wood, but specimens on other mediums are found. Victorian women often painted on velvet, and toward the end of the nineteenth century there was an interest in painting on glass and pottery. Potteries sold "blanks"—undecorated pieces of pottery—that could be painted at home. There are quite a few such

examples around, and they are often both charming and inexpensive.

Reverse glass painting—wherein the image is painted on the back of a piece of glass—was a popular technique for many years. The earliest were done with the aid of standardized designs previously engraved on the glass; but throughout the nineteenth century, freehand examples were also executed, primarily for use in clock panels and mirror tops. Reverse glass portraits are most desirable, while the late Victorian patriotic paintings of Mount Vernon, the White House, and the Statue of Liberty represent excellent buys at present.

Watercolor has been employed for many years in this country, and most early examples are by women. Portraits are relatively uncommon, and most appear to have been done by amateurs. Apparently, most professional painters and their customers preferred oils. Young women were trained, often at school, to execute two types of watercolor. The first was the theorem, which was a picture—usually of a basket of fruit or a vase of flowers—created by use of various stencils. Theorems flourished until about 1870; they have a "hard line" quality very attractive to many collectors, and they are quite expensive. Almost equally desirable are mourning pictures, which were executed in watercolor, charcoal, or a combination of either with embroidery on cloth. These memorials to dead loved ones incorporate such universal—and stereotyped—symbols as a tomb, an urn, a weeping willow or two, and the mourning survivors; they were popular from about 1790 to 1840. With such stereotyped material, it is hardly surprising that the results often seem stiff and uninspired. Nevertheless, these works were generally composed freehand and have a certain archaic charm; they are in demand, particularly if they contain identifiable elements such as a specific house or recognizable locality.

An extremely important area of watercolor is fraktur painting, the decoration of birth or marriage records, created by people of German descent in Pennsylvania and New Jersey. Examples known from the very early 1700s consist of a text lettered completely by hand (in a style similar to the sixteenth-century typeface called Fraktur; hence the name); this is surrounded by an elaborate tinted border containing angels, birds, and flowers. These first fraktur are expensive, extremely so. By 1820, however, printers were issuing preprinted frakturs to which only the decoration was added by hand; and by 1900, when the art was dying out, even the decoration was being printed. Some of the printed fraktur with freehand decoration are very well done, and they are, on the whole, a good buy. Genealogical records in watercolor also appear, as do a wide variety of landscapes and folk scenes. All are highly collectible.

Drawing and Paper Cutting

Drawing in charcoal was especially popular during the Victorian period. While most such work is on paper, some interesting examples were done on sandpaper, or "marble," as it was known, a medium that imparts an eerie quality to the picture. Charcoals on sandpaper are generally landscapes, often copies of earlier European prints or oils. As they are beginning to attract enthusiasts, now is the time to buy them.

Pencil drawings are generally small and late. A few portraits exist, mostly from the 1870s and 1880s, but much of the work consists of sketches done as preparation for oils or watercolors. Such is not the case with ink drawing. Fancy, or "flourished," work in ink, commonly known as calligraphy, was popular in Europe in the seventeenth and eighteenth centuries. Many of the motifs seen in American calligraphic drawings of the nineteenth century, presently much sought after, are derived from the earlier foreign examples. Calligraphy is closely associated with handwriting of the so-called Spencerian school, so that many pieces incorporate writing as well as pictorial elements. Larger calligraphic pieces are priced quite high at present, but smaller work, such as that found in autograph books, can be had for less. Never pass up an old autograph book without thumbing through to see whether it contains some drawings; good calligraphy comes to light regularly in this way.

Silhouettes, called in their day "shades," are simply black paper cutout representations, in which the sharp contrast of the black and white and the precision of the cutting combine to produce a very dramatic effect. While a few scenes were done, the vast majority are portraits, generally either of a bust or the full figure, usually seen in profile. Since they could be cut quickly by an expert, silhouettes were inexpensive. Until the camera preempted the field, they served as the most accessible form of family portrait. A substantial number of silhouette cutters earned a living in the first half of the nineteenth century by cutting likenesses of their customers, often adding embellishments such as tinted facial color and hair. Many silhouettes are signed by their creators. They are being made today, though, and are easily faked, so it is best to buy from a reputable and knowledgeable dealer.

Another rather unusual art form, also practiced by women, was paper cutting. Entire compositions might be created from various carefully prepared paper elements. Watercolor was often also employed in this work, and in some cases tinsel rather than paper was cut and pasted to achieve a spectacular shimmering effect. Tinsel drawings are clearly related to theorems and seem to represent a later development of that style, being generally attributable to the second half of the nineteenth century.

Sculpture

Folk sculpture, like painting, does not lend itself to ready definition. At one end of the spectrum are highly professional pieces such as the popular plaster groupings by the academically trained John Rogers, whose work is folk only in the choice of subject matter. At the other end are many different wooden figures, some crude, some not, some charming, some not, but all sharing in common the fact that they were created by nonprofessional—untrained—sculptors. Professional wood-carvers there were, of course, and in abundance. Every shipbuilding town had at least one man who could be counted on to shape figureheads and do the fancy work for the bow and captain's cabin. There were artisans who carved wooden weathervanes and others who manufactured cigar-store Indians, smaller shop figures, and a variety of ornate signs. These were all professionals, but none appears actually to have been trained as a sculptor. As a result, their work has the flat, primitive look so appealing to today's collector.

There were also legions of whittlers who formed small statues, toys, and useful objects for others or just for their own amusement. Some, like Wilhelm Schimmel of Pennsylvania, have become famous for their work. Most have vanished; only their objects remain. These vary greatly in quality. For the collector, there is also the problem of fakes. Whimsical carved pieces are very popular today, and their very crudeness makes it easy for them to be duplicated or for new pieces on an old theme to be designed. Everything from ship models to cigar-store Indians is subject to reproduction, so one must proceed here with caution.

Metal sculpture is much less common than that in wood. It is by and large the work of smiths, something they turned out in their spare time as gifts or for limited sale. Tin, iron, and copper were all used. With the exception of weathervanes, which are treated later in this book (Chapter 16), metal sculpture is not much in vogue today. Prices are on the low side, and some good buys can be made.

Though not really folk art since it was cast in factory molds, chalkware is treated as such by most collectors. During the period 1850 to 1900, a vast quantity of these plaster-of-Paris figurines were turned out in New England and Pennsylvania. Birds, animals, human figures, fruits, and vegetables may be found. They were designed to imitate fine porcelain and earthenware mantel pieces, such as those made at Staffordshire, England, and they were colored (in strong primary colors) and gilded. Originally, they must have appeared extremely garish; today, with their hues muted by time, they are interesting and attractive. Whether they are attractive enough to justify the prices asked for them is another matter. Chalkware is generally one of the more over-priced areas of antiques, these mass-produced items being offered at prices in the hundreds of dollars.

Shellwork is of interest to some collectors. Outstanding in this category are the ornately designed shell pieces known as sailors' valentines. Few were made in this country; they were, rather, souvenirs purchased by American sailing men in such places as the West Indies and brought home for display. Later, at the end of the nineteenth and in the early twentieth centuries, shellwork was made in this country for sale to tourists. It was usually mounted on a cardboard frame or box and bore a slogan such as "Remember Me" or "Souvenir of Fort Lauderdale, Florida." Such pieces are not terribly old but are low-priced and should begin to attract considerable attention.

Oil on board, *Grinning Cat;* mid-19th century; $500–1,500. A fine example of the sort of animal painting now attracting attention. Unsigned, as are most such paintings.

Oil on board in daguerreotype case, miniature portrait; 19th century; $450–900.

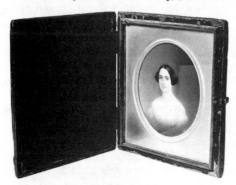

◄ Oil on wooden bowl, *Tabby Cat;* late 19th century; $500–650. Painting on wooden plates and bowls was frequent during the 1880s and 1890s.

Oil on canvas, *Sailing Ships;* second half 19th century; $1,500–4,000. Typical of the strong, well-painted marine scenes now so popular.

◄ Oil on canvas, *Winter Scene;* signed "Clara Beers, Nov. 20, 1880, Jonesville, N.Y."; $3,500–6,000. An outstanding signed primitive painting.

Oil on canvas, *Warships;* early 19th century; $1,500–6,500. An interesting primitive seascape.

Oil on canvas, *Mountain Landscape;* typical of the late-19th-century unsigned oils commonly ascribed to the Hudson River School; $250–450. ▼

Oil on canvas, *Mill Scene;* signed by Edward Bernard, active second half 19th century; $525–700.

Oil on canvas, *Woodland Lake with Deer;* Adirondack Mountains, N.Y., representative of the nature painting practiced by visitors to that area in the late 19th century; $300–500.

Oil on velvet, *Waterlilies;* Victorian still life of a sort frequently found in New England; $150–200.

Oil on velvet, *Still Life;* New York, mid-19th century; $900–1,500.

Oil on stoneware preserve jar, *Cloverleaves and Flowers;* Maine, late 19th century; $100–125. Paintings on pottery appear frequently in the coastal Maine area. They are real bargains in the folk art field.

Reverse-glass theorem painting, oil on glass; New England, first half 19th century; $1,500–2,200. Theorems are hardly common, and they are rarely seen in reverse-glass technique.

Oil on stoneware urn, *Landscape;* another example of pottery painting from late-19th century Maine; $100–150.

Reverse-glass painting, *Statue of Liberty,* oil on glass; ca. 1890; $100–135. Victorian reverse-glass paintings remain underpriced.

Reverse-glass painting, *Landscape,* oil on glass; late 19th century; $65–90.

Oil on glass and under glass (reverse glass),▲ *Victorian House;* Upper New York State, ca. 1870; $2,000–3,500. A remarkable and outstanding example of reverse-glass painting.

Reverse-glass paintings, oil on glass; found in Maine, attributed to Prior-Hamblen school, first half 19th century; $450–625 each. *Top: George Washington. Bottom. Martha Washington.*

Fraktur-type watercolor, *Woman Holding a Flower;* Pennsylvania, first half 19th century; $1,200–3,000.

Watercolor, miniature portrait; late 18th-early 19th century; $900–1,600.

Watercolor, *Civil War Soldier;* ca. 1865; $750–1,200.

Watercolor, house; Maine, first half 19th century; $1,000–3,500.

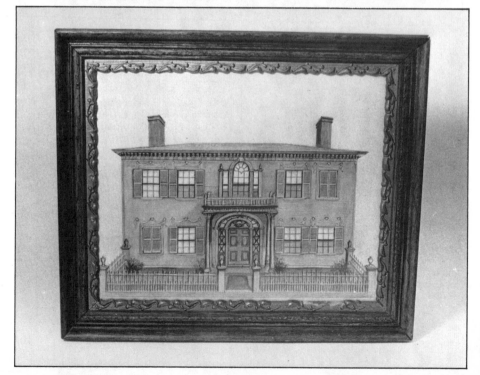

Rare watercolor, *Dancing for Eels, Catharine Market;* New York City, 1820; $2,000–3,750. An important documentary painting of old New York. Known location always increases value.

Trompe-l'oeil watercolor, *Feathers,* brilliant colors; signed "J. F. Bell," 19th century; $300–425.

Watercolor, family record; signed "William Murray, 1799"; $3,500–6,000. A fine example of a hand-lettered genealogical chart.

Fraktur painting, birth record; Pennsylvania, dated 1816; $1,700–3,200. The chip-carved original frame is a forerunner of 20th century tramp art.

Water color and printed family record; Maine, first quarter 19th century; $450–600.

Watercolor and printed marriage record; Lebanon County, Pa., 1831; $125–175. Hand-lettered fraktur are much more valuable than later printing-press editions such as this.

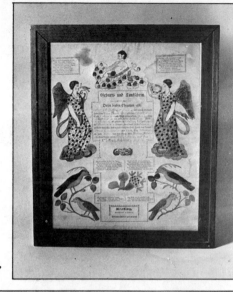

Watercolor memorial painting of the Smith family; ca. 1830; $1,000–3,000. Memorials of this sort were often done in needlework.

Theorem, oil on velvet; ca. 1820; $1,200–1,500. Theorems were essentially stencil pictures put together according to definite rules. Many were made in the 19th century, but current demand exceeds the supply. ▼

Theorem, oil on velvet; first half 19th century; $1,000–1,500.

Theorem, oil on paper; first half 19th century; $1,200–1,750.

Theorem, watercolor on paper; mid-19th century; $800–1,000. A fine bird enhances this piece, which shows the beginnings of Victorian influence.

Theorem, watercolor on paper; Maine, mid-19th century; $650–900. A very simple combination of white roses and green hummingbird.

Theorem, watercolor on paper; mid-19th century; $700–950. The hummingbird again, done with great charm.

Pencil sketch, *Young Child;* Maine, ca. 1880; $130–180.

Theorem, oil on velvet; ca. 1870; $75–100. A very late version.

Calligraphy and watercolor, *The Rescue;* second half 19th century; $1,200–1,650. An unusual and excellent example of calligraphy.

Calligraphy, *Spread-winged Eagle;* by Hosmer Godfrey, second half 19th century; $900–1,100. "Flourished" handwriting of this sort was very popular during the last century. Today, such pieces are becoming increasingly popular with collectors.

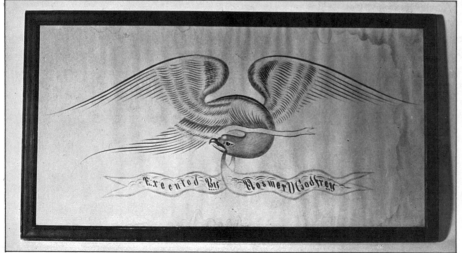

Ink on paper; 1849; $450–700. A colorful forerunner of the modern valentine.

Charcoal on sandpaper, *Landscape with Ruins;* Maine, ca. 1870; $150–275. The scene is highly suitable to the medium.

Tinsel painting, *Bird on Branch,* with well-decorated frame; East, late 19th century; $250–400. Tinsel paintings have been neglected and are still underpriced.

▲Charcoal on sandpaper, *River Landscape;* second half 19th century; $750–1,100. An unusual version featuring an Indian tepee.

Charcoal on sandpaper, *Monument with View of West Point, N.Y.;* mid-19th century; $900–1,600. An extremely important piece.

Tinsel painting in the manner of a theorem; mid-19th century; $350–700.

Silhouette of a man; mid-19th century; $150–225. Since silhouettes are easy to duplicate, collecting them requires careful study and expertise.

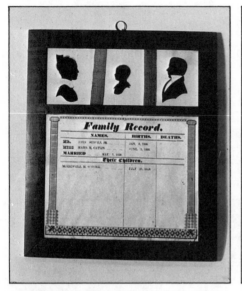

A most unusual family record with silhouettes of family members; New York, ca. 1830; $750–1,000.

Cut-paper picture; Pennsylvania, ca. 1835; $275–400. Decorative paper cutting is related to silhouette work but, unlike it, was usually done by women.

Elaborate cut-paper picture; Pennsylvania, mid-19th century; $600–850.

Left: Bird figures, pine; Pennsylvania, 19th century; $350–425. *Right:* Eagle, pine; 19th century; $150–275.

Eagle in flight, polychromed pine, carved on one side only; 1830–1860; $1,200–1,600.

Free-standing eagle, pine; mid-19th century; $2,500–4,000. Probably intended as a rooftop adornment.

Eagle on shield, polychromed pine; 1840–65; $3,500–5,500. A particularly strong example of primitive folk carving.

Wooden cigar-store Indian, detail; Michigan, ca. 1865; $12,000–20,000. Few tobacconist's figures were as sensitively portrayed as this one, which could almost be a portrait.

Eagle gatepost carved in the round, pine; 19th century; $2,000–3,250.

Ship's figurehead, polychromed pine; New England, ca. 1875; $20,000–35,000. Figurehead carving was an important craft during the 19th century.

Clothespin figure in pornographic pose, pine; 19th century; $200–275. Pornographic figurines of this nature were far more common in the supposedly austere Victorian era than one might at first suspect.

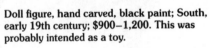

Half-modeled representation of a fish, pine; 19th century; $200–275.

Doll figure, hand carved, black paint; South, early 19th century; $900–1,200. This was probably intended as a toy.

Figure of Columbia, polychromed pine; Midwest, mid-19th century; $25,000–40,000. A rare large pilothouse figure.

Jigsaw-cut wall shelf, polychromed pine; $200–375. This was made as a souvenir of the Philadelphia Centennial.

Wall plaque with various patriotic and fraternal symbols; late 19th-early 20th century; $450–600.

Tradesman's symbols, polychromed pine; late 19th-early 20th century. *Top:* $75–100. *Bottom:* $200–325.

Whimsey, maple, inlaid with white wood; late 19th century; $250–325. Skilled carvers delighted in such tests of their skill. The decoration here is unusually lavish.

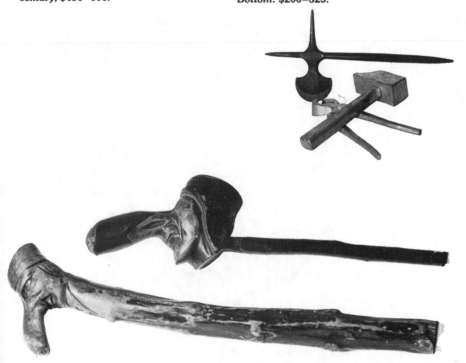

Half-modeled representation of a sailing vessel, wood; Maine, late 19th century; $350–500. Coastal communities produced many such shadow-box models.

Carved canes; New England, late 19th-early 20th century. *Top:* $150–275. *Bottom:* $175–300. Cane carving was a male pastime.

77

Giant carved pine shoes, probably an advertising device; Maine, 20th century; $95–110.

First Love, by John Rogers, plaster of Paris; 19th century; $400–525. While Rogers was an academic sculptor, his work was folk-oriented and was bought primarily by middle-class Victorians not far removed from the home farm.

Figure of a girl, plaster of Paris, or chalkware; Pennsylvania, 19th century; $225–350.

Plaque, polychrome plaster of Paris, or chalkware; 19th century; $750–1,000. An unusually large and detailed example of chalkware.

Figure of a bird, wrought-steel hollowware; early 20th century; $80–110.

Elaborate sailor's valentine, inlaid shells; 19th century; $450–600. Shellwork was a profitable tourist activity in many ports frequented by American sailors.

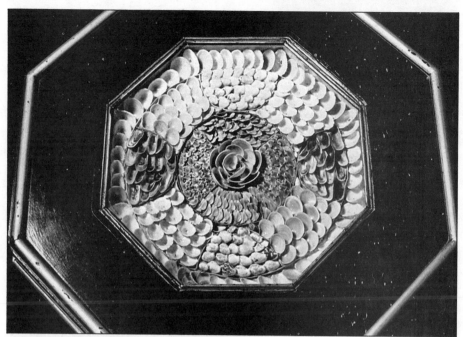

Scratch carving on fungus; late 19th-early 20th century; $30–45. This unusual art seems to have been practiced rather extensively in the Hudson Valley area of New York. So far it has had little appeal for collectors.

Sailor's valentine, box with inlaid shells, other materials, and motto "Remember Me"; $75–110. These pieces are just beginning to attract the attention of collectors.

Animal figures, wrought iron, probably produced as "end of day" pieces by a blacksmith. *Top:*$100–125.*Bottom:*$90–115.$

4.

GLASS

The collecting of early American glass, particularly glass bottles, ranks as one of our nation's major pastimes. Certainly, the present abundance of glass objects is one of the reasons for this phenomenon; yet, ironically, it was a great many years before the first settlers began to enjoy anything like an abundance of glass. The manufacture of glass is a difficult process that requires special materials and highly skilled workmen. The materials—sand for silica, potash as an alkali—could be found readily enough in the new land, but to mix and heat them properly required skills beyond those of most settlers. Several shops employing European glassblowers were opened in the seventeenth century, however—at Jamestown, New York, and Philadelphia. All failed. It was not until a German immigrant, Caspar Wistar, established a factory in Salem County, New Jersey, that a viable native industry could be said to have existed. That was in 1739! For a full century before, the colonists had had to depend on imported glass or go without.

Once the glass industry got started, however, it spread through the Northeast, along the Atlantic coast, and, after 1800, into the newly opened western states. The first products were bottles and window glass, and for decades these remained the major output of nearly every glass shop. Early bottles were crudely formed greenish-black ovals with long necks. They were blown by hand: the workman dipped a hollow iron pipe into a batch of hot glass, extracted a glob, and expanded it with his breath, much as a child blows a bubble through a straw. Black glass bottles are of interest to many collectors, but the native product is hard to distinguish from similar receptacles made in Europe and brought here in the eighteenth century or later.

The first bottles of distinctly American style were historical flasks, first produced around 1800. They are small vessels, usually no more than a pint or quart in capacity, that were blown in a mold. The mold, made of metal, wood, or pottery, was formed on the interior in the shape of the intended bottle. A glob of hot glass was inserted in the mold and expanded. The result was faster production of a group of vessels of more or less uniform appearance.

Historical flasks are embossed with a variety of motifs: important personages, such as Washington or Adams; patriotic slogans; flowers; trees; birds; and animals. There are hundreds of variations on these themes, and new ones are still being discovered. The flasks were filled with liquor, to be sold or given away at political rallies; but from the number that have survived, it is evident that many who drained the contents were equally interested in the container. Historical flasks have always been collected; and today they represent the highest priced and most active area of bottle collecting. The most common pieces go for thirty-five dollars, but a rare form was recently sold at auction for twenty-six thousand dollars. Many people keep their collections in vaults.

Fortunately for the collector, there are other less expensive types of bottles. Take medicine bottles. Until they were replaced by antibiotics in the second half of this century, proprietary medicines were the most common resort in time of illness. Many contained alcohol, and not a few relied for their healing qualities on such comforting agents as opium and morphine. Thus, whether for cure or comfort, it is not surprising that there are literally thousands of different types of medicine bottles. Many are plain blue or green vessels with nothing more than a manufacturer's name and address. A large minority, though, are embossed with interesting motifs or have unusual shapes. Bitters bottles, which contained a bitter but healing herb mixture (80 proof), may appear in the guise of cannons, human figures, log cabins, or even fish.

All figural medicine bottles and most bearing the word *bitters* are of value. But the great majority of common proprietaries sell for a dollar or two each. It's not that people don't collect them—thousands do—it's just that there are too many for them to command a higher price.

Much the same is true of canning jars. Prior to the invention of the Mason jar, in 1858, most food was preserved in salt or sugar and put by in wax-covered pottery crocks. The widespread acceptance of the vacuum jar around 1870 led to a proliferation of canning vessels. Most of these date from the period 1870 to 1930. Collectors

became interested in them about a decade ago, and for a while prices soared; even the most ordinary examples went for five dollars. But the jars kept coming out of the woodwork. It seemed as if there were millions! Back down went the market. Today, the rare forms, such as experimental types and bottles produced prior to 1860, command a fair price. Everything else has gone back to the dollar-a-bottle flea market.

Interest has now shifted to less common types of bottle, such as embossed beer and mineral-water bottles. Perfume and cologne bottles are of great interest for the figural shapes they frequently assume. Many of them were made in Europe, but they were sold here and collectors often are happy to overlook their foreign origin. Much the same is true of the colorful poison containers. Odd shapes and bright reds, greens, blues, and yellows predominate in this group, and their usually small size makes it possible to amass a sizable number without squeezing oneself out of the living room. Prices in all these areas are holding well and moving up.

As a general rule in bottles, one should look for the colorful and the unusual. In early methods of manufacture, the bottle was held with a rod called a pontil while the neck was being finished; the removal of this rod left a jagged scar on the base of the bottle. The introduction of the holding device known as the snap case, around 1850, put an end to this practice, so that at present, the so-called pontil-marked bottles command a premium. Watch for these. Color is another indication of age. The impurities in bottle glass result in an aqua or green color; decolorizing agents produce a white. Other colors are the result of the introduction into the batch of coloring agents. Since these were expensive in the early period, red, yellow, or blue glass was rare prior to 1850. A pontil-marked bottle in color has to be a good find—unless, of course, it comes from Mexico or Italy. Factories in both these countries have been manufacturing reproductions of American bottles since the end of the Second World War. Unlike the excellent facsimiles of historical flasks that were made in Europe in the 1930s, however, these bottles are not intended to deceive. They look new, are machine-made (except for the necks, which are frequently hand finished), and appear in strange artificial colors, the likes of which were unknown in the nineteenth century.

Even before 1800, a certain amount of household glass—plates, bowls, goblets, and the like—was being hand-blown and shaped. The process, though, was slow, and the product was expensive. A better means of manufacture was required. It appeared in 1825, when John P. Bakewell, of the Pittsburgh glasshouse of Bakewell and Page, patented a machine for making pressed-glass doorknobs. The process was quite simple. A glob of hot glass was introduced into a pressing device that incorporated a mold of the desired shape. Down came the press and out came the glassware. The patenting of various modifications during the next decade resulted in a complete revolution in the glassmaking industry. Within a few years, cheap pressed-glass bowls, goblets, pitchers, dishes, platters, cups, and other objects flooded the American market.

In the last hundred years, literally thousands of different pressed-glass patterns have been patented, many of them in complete table settings. Collectors have shown great interest in this field, and prices here are high, though stable. The early Victorian glass is considered most desirable, and colored pieces, in amber, blue, yellow, or red, are choice. Anyone entering the field is advised to obtain one of the many available pattern books and to collect by the pattern rather than the piece.

The importance of color in pattern glass reached its zenith just after 1900 with the emergence of what is now commonly called carnival glass, then known as taffeta lustre. In 1906, Frank Fenton established the Fenton Art Glass Company for the manufacture of colored pressed-glass with a fired-on iridescence. The gleaming metallic quality of this iridescence was what set the ware apart from all previous pressed glass. Several other glass manufacturers, including Northwood, Westmorland, Millerburg, and Imperial, soon entered the field, producing a wide variety of patterns and, especially, colors. Through use of various metallic salts, they were able to create previously unknown color variations, to which they gave equally unusual names, such as Helois green and clam broth. By 1910, hundreds of thousands of pieces were being marketed annually, with much of the product being exported to England and Australia.

By 1930, the interest in taffeta lustre was waning, and substantial quantities were sold wholesale to stores and carnival proprietors to be given away as premiums (from which the material obtained the name carnival glass). Interest revived again in the 1960s, and carnival is now one of the most popular glasswares among antiques collectors. Prices for rare specimens frequently run into hundreds of dollars. Moreover, several companies are once again manufacturing new carnival glass, including two of the original firms still in existence, Fenton and Imperial. For the most part the collector should have little trouble distinguishing between the new and the old: the new ware is in new patterns not previously used and is clearly marked with the manufacturer's name, something the original ware usually was not. The risk of confusion does exist, though, particularly since it is not difficult to grind off the new makers' marks. Collectors should become familiar with the early patterns and be suspicious of "rare" or unworn pieces.

All bottles and bottle prices listed in this chapter are courtesy of Jim Whetzel, Jim's Bottle Shop, Ardsley, New York.

Barrel-shaped amber whiskey bottle; Binninger and Co., New York, mid-19th century; $140–190.

Left: Green glass demijohn; early 19th century; $20–50. *Right:* Dark green porter bottle; 19th century; $45–75. Both, New England.

Pontil-marked dark green case gin bottle; East, 18th century; $75–125. Bottles of this sort were used for a variety of alcoholic beverages.

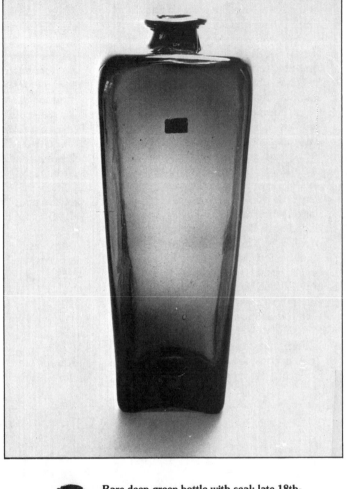

Very large yellow glass demijohn; New England, early 19th century; $150–175.

Rare deep-green bottle with seal; late 18th-early 19th century; $175–500. Bottles of this sort were made up with the initials of a particular customer.

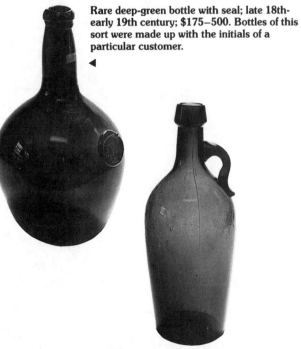

Amber whiskey bottle with handle; Macy and Jenkins, New York, 19th century; $25–50.

Square-bodied amber whiskeys; Louisville, Ky., 19th century. *Left:* Harris distilling Co.; $15–25. *Center:* Harris and Raleigh; $13–17. *Right:* N. Muri and Co.; $13–17.

Tall amber whiskey bottles; 19th century. *Left:* Hayner Distilling Co., Ohio; $17–22. *Center:* Jones and Banks, New York, with rare inside stopper thread; $75–85. *Right:* Charles and Co., New York; $12–15.

Paneled whiskeys; Goldberg Distilling Co., New York, late 19th century. *Left:* Amber; $27–35. *Right:* Less-common aqua; $50–60.

Left: Clear glass strap flask; Charles Rosso Co.; $5–10. *Center:* Amber whiskey flask with embossed eagle; $20–30. *Right:* Aqua whittled coffin flask; $5–15. All, New England, late 19th century.

Clear glass back bar bottles; 19th century. *Left:* Sunny Glen; $40–70. *Center:* Whiskey; $30–50. *Right:* Linquist; $35–55. Bottles of this sort were filled from barrels of whiskey for use in taverns and hotels.

Washington flasks; New England, first half 19th century. *Left:* G I-59,* aqua, Washington bust, sheaf of wheat on reverse; $125–150. *Right:* G I-34, Washington, bust of Jackson on reverse; $275–325.

Sunburst flasks; New England, 19th century. *Left:* G VIII-8, dark green; New Hampshire; $500–575. *Center:* G VIII-16, light green; $425–475. *Right:* G VIII-18, amber; $450–525.

* This number, and the similar ones on these pages, are from the McKearin system of numbers for historical glass. A complete explanation and listing of the numbers will be found in *American Glass*, by George S. and Helen McKearin (Crown Publishers, 1941).

Left: Railroad flask, G V-5, green; New England before 1850; $250–350. Right: Cornucopia, G III-13; Lancaster, N.Y., glassworks; $450–525.

Lafayette flasks; Coventry, Conn., before 1850. Left: Green amber, G I-80, Lafayette, bust of DeWitt Clinton on reverse; $950–1,100. Right: Amber, Lafayette, Liberty Cap on reverse; $700–850.

Masonic flasks; New England, early 19th century. Left: G IV-1, blue green, Justus Perry Masonic; $400–500. Right: G IV-24, amber half pint; $200–275.

Aqua pictorial flasks; ca. 1850. Left: Deer, G X-1, embossed "Good Game"; $300–375. Right: Sailing ship, G X-9; $175–225.

Left: Aqua flask; Louisville, Ky., glassworks; $150–200. Right: Ship flask, reverse bust of Franklin, aqua; Dyottville, Penn.; $275–350. Both first half 19th century.

Aqua Benjamin Franklin Masonic flask, G IV-36; New England, early 19th century; $1,000–1,300.

Left: Aqua flask with embossed anchor; Baltimore, Md., glassworks, Van Rensselaer,* Gp. 6   11; $100–150. *Right:* Aqua flask with embossed figure, marked "To Pikes Peak"; $60–120.

Calabashes, *Left:* Aqua, with figure of Jenny Lind, G I-103; $120–150. *Right:* Aqua, with figures of hunter and fisherman; $135–175. Both, Midwest.

Eagle flasks; New England, mid-19th century. *Left:* Amber, Van Rensselaer, Gp. 2, Div. 7; $90–110. *Right:* Amber double eagle, Van Rensselaer, Gp. 2, Div. 2,   4; $90–120.

Figural bitters bottles. *Left:* Dark amber Old Homestead; $200–250. *Center:* Aqua, barrel-shaped Hall's; $125–145. *Right:* Amber barrel-shaped Old Sachem; $150–190. All, Midwest.

* The Van Rensselaer numbering system, developed by Stephen Van Rensselaer in his book *Early American Bottles and Flasks* (1926), is supplementary to the McKearin numbering system.

Aqua bitters; East, late 19th century. *Left:* Mandrake Bitters; $10–15. *Center:* Lash's; $5–10. *Right:* Atwood's; $7–10.

Rare amber bitters, with original label; late 19th century. *Left:* Congress; $400–500. *Center:* Gordon's; $150–250. *Right:* Koehler Red Star Stomach Bitters; $300–350. All unlisted in texts on this type.

Labeled aqua proprietary medicines; East, late 19th century. *Left:* Dr. Fenner's Cough Honey; $10–15. *Center:* Dr. Bull's Cough Syrup; $10–15. *Right:* Hale's Honey; $12–18. Presence of an original label adds to value of a bottle.

Aqua sarsaparillas; East, late 19th century. *Left:* Hood's; $3–5. *Center:* Bell's; $12–18. *Right:* Dana's; $5–8.

Left: Amber Father John's Medicine; $3–5. *Center:* Willet's Bone Oil; $7–9. *Right:* Amber, Paine's Celery Compound; $5–10. All, East, 19th century.

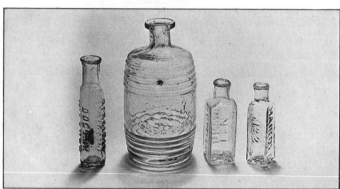

Pontil-marked aqua proprietary medicines; before 1850. *Left:* Hunt's Liniment; New York; $45–65. *Center:* Peter T. Wright and Co.; $25–40. *Right:* Jayne's Alternative; $30–45. Last two, Philadelphia.

Pontil-marked aqua bottles; before 1850. *Left:* Dr. McLaine's American Worm Specific; $25–40. *Center:* Golden Treasure ointment; $50–75. *Right:* Bottles 1 and 2 of Bachelor's Hair Dye; $25–35 each.

Left: Early tin-bound milk bottle, clear; $20–35. *Center:* Aqua floral pickle jar; $45–65. *Right:* Clear glass pickle jar; $25–35. All, East, late 19th century.

Pontiled household bottles; before 1850. *Top left:* True Cephalic snuff; $35–45. *Top right:* London snuff; $35–55. *Bottom:* Dark green glass eagle blacking with original label; $110–115.

File-top aqua canning jar, embossed name and bust of Lafayette. New Jersey, 19th century; $75–95.

Open-pontiled inkwells and ink bottles; New England, 1830–50. *Left:* Amber cone; $80–95. *Left center:* Dark green three-piece mold; $125–175. *Right center:* Amber umbrella; $90–110. *Right:* Dark green three-piece mold; $100–150.

Open-pontiled aqua cologne bottles; mid-19th century. *Left:* Dancing Indian; $90–130. *Center:* Lion of St. Marks; $110–150. *Right:* Monument; $80–115. It is doubtful that such colognes were made in the United States, but like barber bottles they have been adopted as "native."

Left: Light green pint master ink; $35–45. *Center:* Cardinal-colored turtle-back ink; $50–85. *Right:* Amber half-pint master ink; $30–40. All, New England, 19th century.

Cologne bottles; 19th century. *Left:* Green glass lantern with pewter top; $40–65. *Center:* Open-pontiled aqua shoe; $35–55. *Right:* Open-pontiled floral; $65–90.

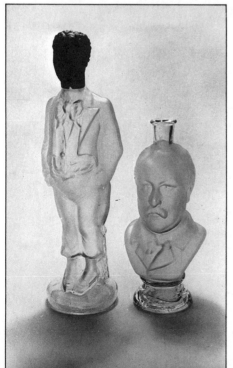

Clear glass colognes; 19th century. *Left:* 35–50. *Center:* Streetlamp; $35–50. *Right:* Shoe; $30–45.

Frosted glass figural bottles, probably used for liquors; 19th century. *Left:* Black waiter; $175–250. *Right:* President Cleveland; $90–150.

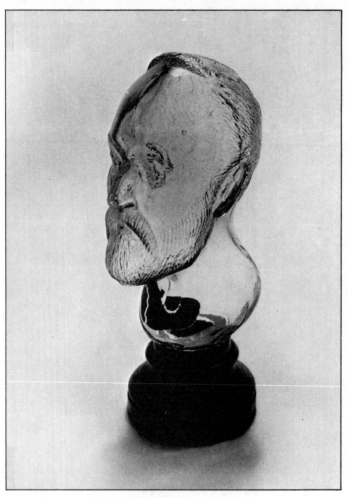

Rare clear glass figural bottle, President Garfield; late 19th century; $350–450. Probably a cologne.

Clear glass figural bottles; 19th century. *Left:* Jester, cologne; $60–75. *Center:* Bather on rocks, whiskey; $135–160. *Right:* Chinaman, cologne; $35–55.

Barber bottles; 19th century. *Left:* Green, decorated in white; $100–130. *Center:* Amethyst, multicolored decoration includes words "Bay Rum"; $90–120. *Right:* Blue, with flowers and oak leaves in blue; $75–100.

Barber bottles with hand-painted floral decoration in the Bohemian style; 19th century. *Left:* Light green; $65–90. *Center:* Amethyst; $85–120. *Right:* Green; $65–90.

Barber bottles; late 19th-early 20th century. *Left:* Reeded green and clear; $65–90. *Center:* Cranberry; $80–100. *Right:* Blue with hazel; $50–75.

Poison bottles; late 18th-early 19th century. *Left:* Sapphire diamond-pattern flask; $275–350. *Center:* Hobnail-pattern, straw-colored flask; $225–275. *Right:* Quarter-pint aqua diamond-pattern flask; $175–250. Early poisons of this period are rare and fairly expensive.

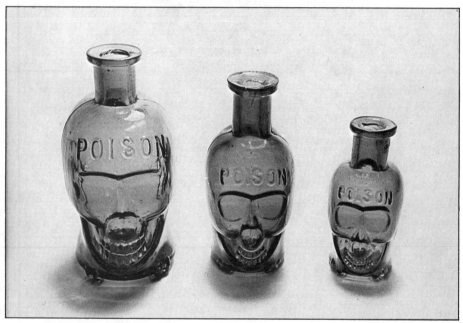

Cobalt poison bottles in shape of skull; 19th century. *Left to right:* $250–300; $300–375; $375–450. The smaller, the rarer.

Ribbed six-sided poison bottles; 19th century. *Left:* Peacock blue; $35–55. *Center:* Deep green; $40–60. *Right:* Cobalt blue; $35–55.

Coffin-shaped hobnail-embossed poison bottles; East, 19th century. *Left:* Amber; $65–95. *Center:* Amber; $40–60. *Right:* Cobalt; $90–130.

Candy container, ruby glass, gold trim; New Jersey, early 20th century; $40–65.

Mineral water bottles; East, last half 19th century. *Left:* Kissinger Water, green; $30–50. *Center:* Hathorn Springs, light amber; $35–55. *Right:* Hotchkiss, Congress and Empire "C"; $50–75.

Mineral water bottles; East, last half 19th century. *Left:* Dark bottle green, Clark and White; $50–65. *Center:* Hathorn Springs, green; $40–60. *Right:* Hotchkiss, Congress and Empire "E"; $35–50.

Machine-made candy containers; East, early 20th century. *Left:* Spark Plug, sun-colored violet; $60–90. *Center:* Rabbit; $40–65. *Top right:* Bulldog; $25–35. *Bottom right:* Hen on nest; $25–35.

Candy containers; East, early 20th century. *Left:* Wheelbarrow, wood and tin accessories; $35–45. *Center:* Windmill, tin blades and original candy; $50–75. *Right:* House; $70–100.

Candy containers; East, early 20th century. *Left:* Long hooded coupe; $55–75. *Center:* World War I tank; $50–65. *Right:* Locomotive; $45–75.

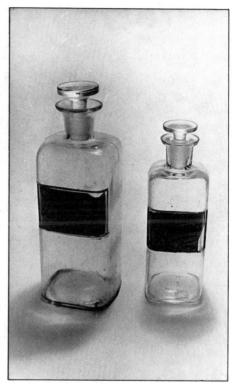

Cobalt blue druggist's bottles, with glass-covered labels; East, late 19th century. *Left:*40–65. *Right:* 35–55.

Clear glass druggist's bottles; Midwest, late 19th century. *Left:* 15–55. *Right:* 10–35.

Milk glass bottles. *Left:* Mustard jar in form of owl; $100–135. *Center:* Cologne in form of Napoleon statue; $600–750. *Right:* Reed's Apothecary; $35–55.

Clear glass whiskey samplers; 19th century. *Left:* Oyster shell; $45–55. *Center:* Dagger; $50–65. *Right:* Powder horn; $35–50.

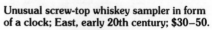

Clear glass nursing bottles; East, late 19th-early 20th century. *Left:* The Eagle; $60–85. *Center:* Bostonia; $5–10. *Right:* Baby's Delight; $40–55.

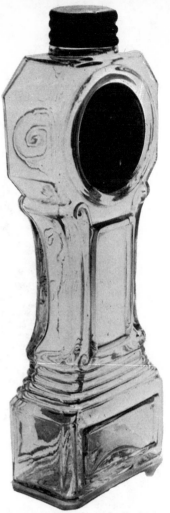

Blown three-mold decanter; New England, first half 19th century. *Left:* G III-5 quart; $160–220. *Center:* G II-18, pint decanter; $135–185. *Right:* G III-24, quart decanter; $130–175.

Three blown wine goblets; Midwest, 19th century; $40–60 each.

Pressed glass; Midwest, late 19th–early 20th century. *Left:* Covered candy jar; $25–35. *Center:* Diamond-pattern flask; $27–42. *Right:* Yellow glass butter dish in form of iron; $40–55.

Pressed glass; Midwest, 19th century. *Left:* Celery jar; $30–45. *Center:* Covered candy jar; $25–38. *Right:* Celery jar; $55–72.

Clear pressed glass, moon and star pattern; Midwest, late 19th century. *Left:* Fruit bowl; $30–48. *Right:* Celery jar; $42–58.

Very large pressed-glass punch bowl, daisy and button pattern; New England, mid-19th century; $215–285.

Clear pressed glass; Midwest, late 19th century. *Left:* Bowl; $15–25. *Top center:* Pitcher; $45–60. *Bottom center:* Sauce dish; $15–20. *Right:* Compote; $30–55.

Clear pressed glass; New England, late 19th century. *Left:* Egg cup in scroll with flowers pattern; $15–22. *Center:* Spoon jar in New England Pineapple pattern; $36–49. *Right:* Open sugar in scroll with flowers pattern; $40–55.

Pressed glass; Midwest, late 19th century. *Left:* Goblet in Norman Key pattern; $25–38. *Center:* Blue glass celery in Vernon Honey Comb pattern; $42–58. *Right:* Celery in Tandem Bicycle pattern; $30–42.

Clear pressed-glass pitcher in the double spear pattern; Midwest, late 19th century; $45–62.

Green pressed-glass pitcher, tray and two tumblers in feather-duster pattern; New England, late 19th century. Pitcher; $75–110. Tray; $45–65. Tumblers; $15–25 each.

Castor set in daisy and button pattern with pewter tops, blue, yellow, and amber bottles; New England, mid-19th century; $125–155 the set.

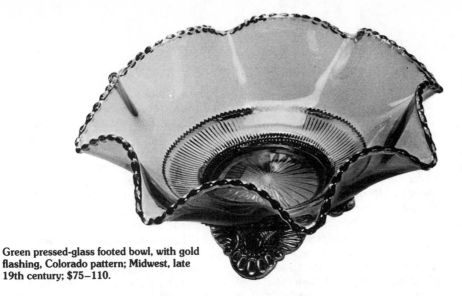

Green pressed-glass footed bowl, with gold flashing, Colorado pattern; Midwest, late 19th century; $75–110.

Flashed ruby glass decanter, block pattern; New England, late 19th century; $85–115.

Ruby pressed glass; New England, late 19th-early 20th century. *Left:* Flashed red low bowl in thumb-print pattern; $40–55. *Center:* Open sugar in ruby block; $30–40. *Right:* Spoon jar in button arches pattern, inscribed "Lucy B."; 1902; $25–40. Piece at right is typical of flashed glass sold or given away as souvenirs.

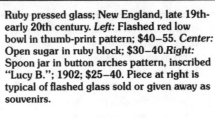

Gold flashed pitcher and two tumblers in moon and star pattern; Midwest, late 19th century. Pitcher; $125–155. Tumblers; $35–50 each.

Carnival glass, pitcher and three tumblers in the orange-tree pattern; Midwest, early 20th century. Pitcher; $140–175. Tumblers; $30–40 each.

5.

POTTERY

Redware

Redware, the oldest native-made American pottery, is a relatively low-fired, fragile ware that can be decorated in a variety of ways. Because of this decoration, it was the first American pottery to attract the interest of collectors. Even before 1900, they were acquiring examples of redware plates and bowls bearing marvelous designs painted or incised on their surfaces. Today, such pieces sell for thousands of dollars.

Fortunately, not all redware is so expensive. Pottery as a whole, in fact, is subject to an enormous diversity of pricing, greater than that in any other area of American antiques. A category such as redware, for instance, may be priced far above another, such as white earthenware. And within a given category some items may be extremely expensive—sgraffito-decorated redware—while others are quite cheap—unglazed redware. On the whole, however, redware prices have climbed steadily over the past half century and show no signs of softening. If you are looking for a bargain or a new and unexploited field, you won't find it here!

Nevertheless, some types of redware are still available to the average collector. All redware, since it is porous, must have at least one glazed surface. One may find a variety of simple pieces—jugs, bean pots, and jars, undecorated and glazed only on the interior—at moderate prices. These humble vessels reflect the potter's unwillingness to use more than a minimum of lead-based glaze, which was expensive. Equally common and not much more expensive are pots glazed with a clear lead on both inside and outside. Quite often, particularly in New England, the potter would add manganese to his glaze to produce a shiny black finish, which can be exceedingly attractive. Black-glaze redware has never really caught on with collectors and at present offers one of the better buys in the field.

Of course, many people cannot be satisfied with such simple ware and seek more elaborate examples. Because it is fired at such a low temperature, redware may be glazed in a variety of colors; reds, greens, yellows, browns, blacks, oranges, and whites—which would disintegrate at a higher heat—may be combined to produce dazzling compositions. In Pennsylvania, slip decoration was combined with sgraffito, in which a design was cut through one layer of clay into another of contrasting color. Elaborate pieces of this sort were never standard items but were specially made as gifts or for the potter's own use. They are, accordingly, quite uncommon and in great demand.

Beginning redware collectors are well advised to decide early on whether they wish to collect the choice pieces, in which case they must think in terms of hundreds or even thousands of dollars, or whether they will buy modestly but selectively. If the latter is the choice, then form should be a prime consideration. A wide variety of objects were made in brick red clay, including inkwells, sugar bowls, soap dishes, toys, platters, and dishware of all sorts. Seek out the less common examples. In color, too, it is still possible to find pots glazed in more than a single hue—the black-on-red pieces from the Connecticut River valley for example. It is better to pay a hundred dollars for a well-formed or unusual example than spend the same amount on a half dozen common bean and preserve pots.

Stoneware

In contrast to redware, stoneware has only recently come into its own. This pottery is fired from a dense white clay found in only a few areas of the country. The difficulty of obtaining raw material severely limited the development of stoneware production; and though there were eighteenth-century stoneware kilns in New York, New Jersey, and along the mid-Atlantic coast, the craft did not prosper until after 1825, when the opening of the canals allowed for the relatively inexpensive shipment of both clay and finished product.

Nevertheless, vast amounts of stoneware were produced all throughout the nineteenth century, and largely because of its great strength (stoneware is of the same hardness as steel), much has survived. However, with the exception of a limited number of astute collectors, this ware found little acceptance among antiques buffs up until the last decade. There are two reasons for this. First, because of the temperature at which it is fired, stoneware can be decorated only with cobalt (blue) and manganese (shades of brown or black). Second, partly because of its relatively late arrival on the ceramic scene and partly because it does not take kindly to molding, stoneware has been produced in only a limited number of forms. A few inkwells, flasks, and the like may be encountered, but for the most part one is faced with a broad array of crocks and jugs.

The tide turned for stoneware in the early 1970s. Spurred on by several informative books and the soaring of prices for redware, collectors started buying the heavier pottery. But today, the boom has passed. Prices for middle-line pieces have declined sharply, and far too many collectors are now sitting with acquisitions worth half what they were five years ago. On the other hand, good decorated examples are still commanding high prices, and there is no reason to believe this will change. As in all areas of antiques, fine quality pieces remain a good investment.

What characteristics should one look for in collecting stoneware? Just the same things that are found in all good folk art: appealing form and decoration. The earliest pots in this medium were sparsely decorated, but even in the eighteenth century, designs—such as ships, flowers, faces, and so on—were scratched into the wet clay, and these were often then filled with blue. Such primitive but charming folk forms are eagerly sought and highly priced. As the nineteenth century advanced, incised or stamped decoration gave way to freehand painted designs in blue, which made use of a wide panorama of figures greatly influenced by the then-popular Spencerian school of handwriting. While such design can and often does become trite and mechanical, the overall effect is pleasing and can be spectacular. Birds, flowers, houses, ships, even animals such as dogs, elephants, and tigers, parade across these pieces, which are an endless source of pleasure to their owners.

As mechanization overtook the stoneware industry during the late years of the nineteenth century, molded stoneware began to appear on the market. Potteries, particularly in Ohio and New Jersey, produced vast quantities of mixing bowls, pitchers, covered butter crocks, and chamber pots. These were usually glazed in white and blue, green, or yellow. A variation appears in solid chocolate brown. All pieces have various figures, floral and animal, molded into their surfaces. Though hardly old, such stoneware is in demand and prices have climbed steadily.

Yellowware

Certain clays, found primarily in New Jersey and Ohio, fire to an attractive yellow. As early as the 1820s, American potters were employing such earth in casting pitchers and bowls. In the late nineteenth century, yellowware mixing bowls became popular, and they are still being made. The most simple are undecorated, though they may be cast in a mold that provides a figured exterior. More popular are those examples that are banded, usually in some combination of brown or white; many collectors strive to obtain a matching set ranging in size from as little as three to as large as twenty-four inches in diameter.

Other forms in yellowware are less common. Rolling pins, molds, custard cups, spittoons, and pitchers are found, as are pie plates and serving dishes. None, however, may be said to be common.

Common yellowware represents one of the best buys for the collector with modest means. It is not hard to find and is exceedingly attractive and inexpensive. It remains one of the few "new horizons" in American ceramics.

But, of course, there are exceptions to all rules, and Rockingham—a form of yellowware glazed in mottled brown—is one. It is not and for many years has not been inexpensive. Partly because of the magic name of the Bennington Pottery at which so much Rockingham was made (and to which so much has been falsely attributed), it has long been a prime collector's item. There are few

sleepers here, and buyers should recognize that they will have to pay top dollar for any piece, even spittoons and bedpans.

White Earthenware

White earthenware is an exciting and relatively untouched area of American pottery. Collectors have for years concentrated on English and European earthenwares, most notably ironstone, and neglected the domestic product. This was a problem in the nineteenth century as well, so that American manufacturers sometimes resorted to faking English marks in order to market their ware among a populace unreasonably prejudiced in favor of the European product. There is a wide variety of American whiteware: some entirely plain, some bearing molded decoration, some decorated by transfer printing or hand painting. It is possible through diligent effort to acquire a complete and matching dinner service bearing the mark of one of our nineteenth-century potteries.

It may take time to acquire such pottery, but it will not take much money. American white earthenware remains greatly undervalued in nearly all parts of the country. Plates go for a dollar or two, covered serving dishes for as little as five dollars; less common types such as coffeepots, sugar bowls, and molds cost little more.

Spongeware

Some whiteware and stoneware was decorated by the application of blue, green, or brown, usually with a sponge or brush—hence the name spongeware. Such pottery tends to be heavy and monotonous in form, but these characteristics are largely overcome by the spectacular results achieved through the application of color. Spongeware is, today, extremely popular indeed; as a

result, prices for it are still on the rise.

Fakes and reproductions exist in the pottery field, though they are generally a problem only in the area of redware. In this century, several potters have established reputations by making copies of nineteenth-century sgraffito ware. They have never intended to deceive and have, indeed, often marked their pieces. Unfortunately, unknowledgeable dealers sometimes represent unmarked specimens as being older than they really are. Similarly, Mexican and southern European glazed redware appears from time to time on dealers' shelves, being offered, often in good faith, as native American pottery. It takes experience to distinguish such imports; generally, they tend to be lighter in both weight and clay color than American pieces and to have slightly "foreign" shapes—pitchers, for example, have an hourglass shape.

There have been rumors of stoneware fakes during the last decade, and some crude examples are known, generally involving the painting of a blue design onto an old but previously undecorated pot. Such work is so bad as to be capable of fooling only the most inexperienced amateur. In addition, a considerable amount of nineteenth-century decorated German stoneware has been imported. It often exceeds in quality our own output; but as long as it is offered as imported ware, it presents no problem for the collector.

Yellowware is not a sufficiently lucrative field to attract the faker, with the exception of Rockingham; and there the major occupation is attributing all unmarked specimens to Bennington, a chore that could take a lifetime! The same may be said for white earthenware, where it is most likely that faking would run the other way; that is, labeling as English pieces that were made right here in the United States.

Redware, glazed only on the interior; Pennsylvania, 19th century. *Left:* Bean pot; $20–35. *Center* Miniature jug; $10–17. *Right:* Sugar bowl; $25–40. These pieces are typical of inexpensive earthenware still available to collectors.

Redware finished in clear lead galze; New York-New Jersey area, mid-19th century. *Left:* Preserve jar; $35–45. *Center* Preserve or apple butter jar; $25–35. *Right:* Storage crock; $85–125. Matching top and fine shape put a premium on crock.

Redware; first half 19th century. *Left:* Water keg in clear glaze; Connecticut; $250–320. *Center* Miniature keg, or rundlet, in mustard glaze; $325–400. *Right:* Water keg in clear glaze; Ohio; $200–250. Fine glaze and condition of center piece and incised date "1846" on keg at right are highly desirable.

Redware in lead-base black glaze; New ▲ England, 19th century. *Left rear:* Preserve jar; $30–50. *Left front:* Rundlet; $100–135. *Right rear:* Preserve jar; $45–75. *Right front:* Spittoon; $35–50. Black-glaze redware is an excellent buy at present; small size of rundlet enhances its value.

◄

Redware. *Left:* Cake mold in clear glaze, black edging; New York, late 19th century; $65–80. *Center* Ovoid jug in black glaze, fine early form; Vermont, ca. 1820; $65–100. *Right:* Bowl in clear glaze, black touches; Connecticut, ca. 1850; $150–200.

Left rear: Large redware plate with white slip decoration on clear glaze; New England, mid-19th century; $250–325. *Left front:* Redware mold in brown glaze; New York, ca. 1860; $90–120. *Right:* Redware preserve jar decorated in brown with green streaks on olive glaze body; New York, ca. 1840; $240–310.

Three pieces of redware, clear glaze splashed with black; Connecticut, mid-19th century. *Left:* Crock; $145–190. *Center:* Dish; $215–270. *Right:* Milk pot; $160–195.

Connecticut redware. *Left:* Pie plate with yellow decoration; ca. 1850; $275–350. *Center:* Early creamer, clear glaze splashed with black; ca. 1830; $170–230. *Right:* Saucer with yellow slip decoration; ca. 1850; $125–175.

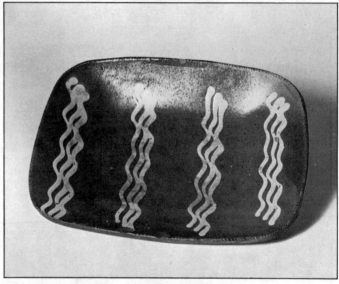

Redware loaf dish, yellow slip decoration on clear glaze; Connecticut, mid-19th century; $650–850.

Platter, yellow slip decoration; Maine, mid-19th century; $475–650. Fine form and good decoration.

Early Stoneware jugs; ca. 1800. *Left:* With mark of Clarkson Crolius, New York City; $400–525. Its open handles are characteristic of the period before 1815. *Right:* With blue-filled incised decoration; New York-New Jersey area; $450–750.

Left: Redware jug in white glaze; mark of Lorenzo Johnson, Newstead, N.Y., ca. 1870; $400–500. *Right:* Clear glaze redware jug; mark of Alvin Wilcox, West Bloomfield, N.Y., ca. 1840; $300–375. Marked redware is extremely rare; Johnson piece is one of less than a dozen examples known.

Fine examples of early and high-priced stoneware jugs; East. *Left:* In tan and umber salt glaze; Boston, Mass., ca. 1810; $400–475. *Center:* In dark brown glaze; New Jersey, ca. 1800; $225–300. *Right:* With blue decoration; by Clarkson Crolius, New York City, ca. 1840; $275–350.

Examples of early ovoid stoneware still available to collectors. *Left:* Cream jar; N. and A. Seymour, Rome, N.Y., ca. 1830; $95–135. *Center:* Jug; S. S. Perry, Troy, N.Y., ca. 1830; $75–95. *Right:* Cream jar; Warner and Humiston, South Amboy, N.J., ca. 1825; $60–85.

Mid-19th century stoneware from New England. *Left:* Salt-glazed flask; $50–75. *Center:* Inkwell; $55–75. *Right:* Mug with blue banding; $45–75.

Small stoneware. *Left:* Sander in brown glaze; New York, ca. 1830; $165–215. *Center:* Child's cup in salt glaze with blue banding; New Jersey, ca. 1880; $65–90. *Right:* Bank in brown glaze; Pennsylvania, ca. 1870; $45–75. Smaller pieces of stoneware are becoming hard to locate.

Stoneware milk pan in brown glaze; European, ca. 1880; $65–80. Brown glaze on this piece is frequently seen on pieces from second half of 19th century.

Left: Stoneware rundlet, blue lines; by Clarkson Crolius, New York City, ca. 1800; $800–950. *Center:* Stoneware water cooler, cobalt and umber decoration; J. A. & C. W. Underwood, Fort Edward, N.Y., 1865–67; $350–420. *Right:* Gray-glazed stoneware water keg; Ohio, mid-19th century; $135–185. Age and rarity put a premium on rundlet; presence of both blue and brown on water cooler is unusual.

Ash-glazed jug; Georgia, ca. 1880; $70–95. This glaze, sometimes called "tobacco spit," was favored by Southern potters.

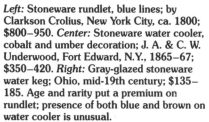

Metallic-finish stoneware. *Left:* Preserve jar in rich tan and black; Israel Seymour and Son, Troy, N.Y., 1850–52; $35–50. *Center:* Soap dish in orange brown; Ohio, mid-19th century; $70–95. *Right:* Jug in olive orange; Israel Seymour and Son, Troy, N.Y., ca. 1845; $50–75. Shiny and colorful metallic finishes can rival redware glaze in beauty. They are rare but unappreciated and undervalued.

Three stoneware preserve jars, salt glaze, blue decoration; Pennsylvania, ca. 1870. *Left to right:* $75–95; $90–125; $60–85. Jars of this sort were the forerunners of the Mason jar and the tin can.

Salt-glazed, blue-decorated preserve jars; New York City. *Left:* By Francis Laufersweiler, 1878–79; $125–165. *Center:* By Hudson River Pottery, 1850–55; $175–235. *Right:* By Louis Lehman, 1858–63; $145–215; An excellent demonstration of how regional preferences affect prices; to a New York collector these rather ordinary pieces of stoneware might be worth twice the quoted price.

Three dated cream jars in salt-glaze stoneware. *Left:* By Hudson, N.Y., Pottery; 1868 marks date the pottery opened; $200–275. *Center:* By N. Clark, Jr., Athens, N.Y.; $145–185. *Right:* By Clark and Fox, Athens, N.Y.; $215–265.

Blue-decorated stoneware. *Left:* Salt-glaze pitcher; by Bosworth, Hartford, Conn., ca. 1880; $175–350. *Center and right:* Two pieces by Farrington, Elmira, N.Y., ca. 1890. Batter jug; $235–325. Preserve jar; $90–115.

Salt-glazed storage crock with blue slip decoration; by Lamsen and Swasey, Portland, Maine, 1876; $235–290. The inscribed date marks this as a Centennial piece, one of a relatively small number known. Dated examples are not common, particularly those related to recognizable periods or events; this decoration greatly enhances value of an otherwise mundane pot.

Unusual patented stoneware water cooler, marked "The Gate City"; Ohio, ca. 1886; $135–170.

Stoneware crock, fine slip and brush blue
floral decoration; by Burger Brothers,
Rochester, N.Y., ca. 1870; $225–275.
Rochester produced some of the finest
decorated stoneware.

Salt-glazed stoneware crock; by J. and E.
Norton, Bennington, Vt., ca. 1855; $650–
800. Decorated in sophisticated style for
which Bennington is famous.

Two stoneware jugs with blue floral
decoration; typical of J. and E. Norton,
Bennington, Vt., ca. 1855. *Left:* $115–155.
Right: $90–135.

Stoneware jug with very fine parrot decoration in blue; by Whites, Utica, N.Y., ca. 1870; $325–450.

Blue-decorated stoneware churn; by W. J. Seymour, Troy, N.Y., 1870–80; $200–265. Stoneware churns are not common, and this one is enhanced by a fine bird.

Salt-glazed stoneware crock, with unusual bird in blue; by Whites, Utica, N.Y., ca. 1870; $400–575.

Stoneware crock with blue slip rabbit; by David Weston, Ellenville, N.Y., ca. 1870; $425–510. Stoneware was occasionally decorated with fanciful objects such as lions, elephants, fish, and even houses. Such pieces are uncommon but frequently overpriced in relation to their artistic merit.

Molded stoneware pitchers with blue decoration; late 19th-early 20th century. *Left:* $65–85. *Center:* With stencil decoration; $50–70. *Right:* $75–100. Typical factory-ware from the period.

Stoneware crock decorated with stamped, blue-filled cow; by Gardiner, Maine, Stoneware Company, ca. 1880; $145–215. Impressed as opposed to incised or freehand decoration is rare in stoneware.

Molded stoneware poodle, glazed in brown Albany slip; Ohio, ca. 1870; $125–180. This was probably cast in a mold intended for the making of Rockingham doorstops.

Molded stoneware in green and yellow, with white-glazed interiors; early 20th century. *Left:* Straight-sided pitcher; $35–50. *Left center:* Bulbous creamer; $30–40. *Right center:* Mixing bowl; $20–28. *Right:* Straight-sided pitcher; $45–60.

Mass-produced molded stoneware in blue and white; early 20th century. *Left:* Storage crock; $60–75 (with cover). *Right:* Straight-sided pitcher; $55–75.

Identical molded-stoneware pitchers slipped in brown, yellow, red, and green, early 20th century; $45–60. Pieces of this sort exist in rather large numbers, but a steady demand keeps prices relatively high.

Left: Molded-stoneware casserole in brown slip; $15–22. *Right:* Molded-stoneware creamer, brown glaze; $12–18. Both, ca. 1920. Common commercial ware that has attracted attention in recent years.

Blue spongeware; late 19th century. *Left:* Straight-sided pitcher; $175–225. *Center:* Low baking dish; $145–210. *Right:* Pitcher with blue bands; $185–240. A stylish and unusual piece.

Left: Blue spongeware spittoon; $70–95. *Right:* Banded-blue spongeware mixing bowl; $125–175. Both late 19th-early 20th century. Excellent examples of factory-molded pottery consisting of a stoneware or white earthenware body decorated in blue or other colors by use of sponges and brushes.

Blue spongeware water cooler; late 19th century; $220–275. A rare piece, hence the high price.

Banded-blue spongeware bowl and pitcher set; late 19th century; $300–375.

Three blue spongeware mixing bowls; 20th century. Smaller pieces were cast in a fluted mold. *Left to right:* $65–90; $50–70; $85–125.

Green and yellow spongeware; early 20th century. *Left:* Unusual small straight-sided pitcher; $55–75. *Center:* Deep bowl; $70–95. *Right:* Straight-sided pitcher with embossed flowers; $80–135.

Green and yellow spongeware; early 20th century. *Left:* Crock marked "Sugar"; $60–75. *Center:* Custard cup; $12–15. *Right:* Straight-sided pitcher; $90–140.

Three attractive banded-green spongeware mixing bowls; late 19th-early 20th century. *Left to right:* $70–85; $95–110; $80–100.

Multicolored spongeware, green and orange on yellow, early 20th century. *Left:* Covered sugar bowl; 75–110. *Right:* Deep dish; $90–115.

Multicolored spongeware; late 19th-early 20th century. *Left:* Bulbous pale blue pitcher; $70–85. *Center:* Very fine rust, green, and white serving bowl; $75–90. *Right:* Pitcher (damaged) in rust, green, and yellow; $125–175 if in good condition.

Yellow earthenware; Ohio, late 19th century. *Rear:* Pie plate; $35–50. Unusual in that it was pressed out in manner of early redware plates rather than being molded like other pieces. *Left front:* Pitcher; $45–65. *Center front:* Serving bowl; $50–75. *Right front:* Custard cup in Victorian Gothic pattern; $15–20.

Yellowware mixing bowls; Midwest, early 20th century. *Left:* $20–30. *Center:* White and dripped mocha banding; $55–70. *Right:* $15–25. Small or unusually decorated yellowware is a good investment.

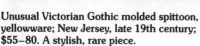

Unusual Victorian Gothic molded spittoon, yellowware; New Jersey, late 19th century; $55–80. A stylish, rare piece.

Yellowware from New Jersey, late 19th–early 20th century. *Left:* Crock with matching lid; $30–35. Rolling pin; $95–125. *Right:* Banded mixing bowl; $40–60. Brown and white banding distinguishes the hollowware. Rolling pins are uncommon and sought after in pottery; yellowware examples are most frequent.

Yellowware from New Jersey and Ohio; late 19th–early 20th century. *Rear:* Corn mold; $35–50. *Left center:* Miniature jug; $15–20. *Right center:* Blue-banded custard cup; $10–15. *Right:* Molded mug; $25–35. For commercial pottery, yellowware comes in a rather wide variety of forms.

Rare yellowware bowl with sponged blue "seaweed" decoration between brown bands; Pennsylvania, late 19th century; $185–235. Unusually lavish decoration for yellowware.

Late-19th century yellowware; Midwest. *Left:* White-banded mug; $65–80. *Center:* Pitcher with embossed drapery; $70–95. *Right:* Small swirl mold; $40–60.

Embossed yellowware mixing bowl with a pouring spout; New England, early 20th century; $45–75.

Banded yellowware; Midwest, early 20th century. *Left:* Mug; $75–95. *Center:* Miniature potty; $40–65. *Right:* Mug; $70–90.

Rare banded yellowware colander; Midwest, late 19th century; $175–250.

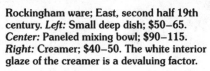

Rockingham serving dish; New England, mid-19th century; $75–90. Good strong color and fine shape distinguish this bowl.

Rockingham ware; East, second half 19th century. *Left:* Small deep dish; $50–65. *Center:* Paneled mixing bowl; $90–115. *Right:* Creamer; $40–50. The white interior glaze of the creamer is a devaluing factor.

Rockingham ware; New England, second half 19th century. *Left:* Deep dish; $65–85. *Center:* Custard cup; $20–30. *Right:* Large deep dish; $125–150.

Rockingham ware; mid-19th century. *Left:* Pitcher; Ohio; $200–265. *Center:* Paneled custard cup; $30–45. *Right:* Pie plate; $75–115. Both, New England.

Small objects in Rockingham ware; Midwest, second half 19th century. *Top:* Mug; $50–90. *Bottom, left and right:* Two soap dishes; $50–75; $35–50.

Three late Rockingham custard cups; Midwest, ca. 1890. *Left to right:* $12–15; $20–25; $20–25.

White ironstone; Midwest, 19th century. *Left:* Covered serving dish; $30–45. *Center:* Handleless cup and saucer; $15–20. *Right:* Covered butter dish; $35–50.

White ironstone plates lightly embossed; late 19th century. *Left to right:* $3–5; $6–8; $6–8. such embossing generally doubles the value of an ordinary plate.

White ironstone serving dishes; late 19th century. *Left to right:* $8–15; $15–22; $15–20. Like all ironstone, they have been mechanically molded and given a clear glaze.

Three examples of the common white ironstone pitcher; Midwest, late 19th century. *Left to right:* $15–20; 20–27; $25–38.

White ironstone platters; late 19th century. *Left to right:* $8–12; $15–20; $10–15. Light embossing on piece at left increases its value.

White ironstone platters; Midwest, late 19th century. *Rear:* $15–20. *Front:* 14" x 10"; $30–45. Larger pieces such as these are among more popular examples of American ironstone.

Pottery miniatures, 3" high or less. *Left:* Bean pot; New England, ca. 1910; $12–20. *Top center:* Stoneware jug; Midwest, early 19th century; $20–25. *Bottom center:* Yellow-glazed stoneware jug; Vermont, late 19th century; $15–20. *Right:* Redware porringer in clear glaze; Massachusetts, mid-19th century; $85–120. Miniatures are attracting attention and increasing in value.

Pottery miniatures. *Left rear:* Salt-glazed stoneware jug; New York, ca. 1870; $15–20. *Center rear:* Brown-glazed stoneware pitcher; $80–115. *Right rear:* Albany slip-glazed stoneware jug; Vermont, late 19th century; $25–45. *Front left:* Stoneware jug glazed in brown Albany slip; Norton and Co., Bennington, Vt., dated 1893; $175–250. Commemorative miniatures such as this, which marked the centennial of the old Norton Pottery at Bennington, are exceedingly rare. *Right front:* Redware jug; dated 1902; $30–45.

6.
SILVER AND PEWTER

Silver

The collecting of American silver poses both problems and opportunities for the enthusiast. The chief problem is that most eighteenth-century examples that are marked or otherwise clearly identifiable, with the exception of spoons and tablespoons, are unavailable to the collector of average means. The great bulk of them were long ago acquired by museums or wealthy individuals, and few are ever offered for public sale. On the other hand, eighteenth-century hand-wrought silver is only a small portion of the total produced in America in the past two hundred years. There is a vast quantity of fine sterling and plated ware still available. Most of it was manufactured between 1840 and 1930, in quantities sufficient to assure a reasonable opportunity for every silver lover to obtain a fair share.

The problems that exist in the collecting of silver are related to the nature of the metal itself. Silver is a precious and rare substance. Though much effort and wealth were invested in attempts to uncover local silver deposits, there were no major strikes in the continental United States until the great Nevada claims of the 1850s, by which time American silversmiths could well afford to import silver ingots. This was not the case in the eighteenth and early nineteenth centuries, though; experts believe that most early American silver was made by melting down coins or by recasting other silver objects that were either damaged or outdated. This alone may explain the dearth of eighteenth-century pieces today. Certainly, the shortage of silver was acute, so much so that some smiths even preserved, for later reuse, the tiniest silver filings produced in the course of finishing an object.

In discussing silver, it is perhaps best to begin by defining the terms. Silver in its pure state is too soft to utilize; it cannot hold a shape and would serve no purpose. The addition of a small quantity of copper, however, produces a lustrous, workable, and strong alloy, which has come to be known as sterling. It is .925 pure silver, or .925 "fine" in the parlance of the silversmith. The term *coin,* which was frequently stamped on silver from the period 1830 to 1860, refers to silver that is less than .900 pure silver. In England and other European countries, there were guilds of silversmiths that rigorously enforced adherence to proper weights, as well as assay offices run by the government that mandated the quantity of silver permissible in silver alloy. In the colonies, with the exception of a brief and unsuccessful venture in Baltimore, assay offices were never established; as a result, the use of the term *sterling* for an American piece does not always assure that it is of standard weight.

Despite the lack of legal safeguards, chemical analysis has shown that most early American sterling silver compares favorably in silver content with that produced at the same time in England and on the Continent. There are good reasons for this. Most silversmiths were the product of a five- to seven-year apprenticeship (either in America or abroad), during which one of the basic teachings was honesty. A worker who for years had dealt honestly with his master's wealth of silver was not likely to offer low-weight goods to his own customers. Moreover, if he did so, other smiths would be quick to call the public's attention to this fact. Also, the mechanics' societies that sprang up throughout the colonies following the War for Independence resembled the guilds in their enforcement of standards of honesty and workmanship.

The earliest American silver articles were made either by casting in molds or by raising—shaping by hand and tool from sheets of silver. Casting was for the most part confined to smaller articles such as porringers and to decorative elements that would later be soldered to the wrought vessel. Raising was a tedious process involving a variety of tools in order to transform the sheet of silver into a fully rounded piece—a coffeepot, say, or a bowl. A more rapid method was devised in the 1820s when the "spinning" of silver became popular. This procedure involved pressing a sheet of metal against a wooden form while the material was turned on a lathe. Under pressure, the metal assumed the shape of the form.

Spinning was greatly facilitated by the development of Sheffield plate. This was literally a metal sandwich, consisting of a sheet of copper pressed between two thinner sheets of silver. The resulting composition was harder than sterling and easier to work on a lathe. Since it was in large part copper, it was also much cheaper than sterling. Sheffield had been developed in the eighteenth century, but it did not reach full acceptance until the advent of more powerful rolling machines and the spinning process in the early nineteenth century.

In the 1840s, technology went a step farther with the discovery of electroplated silver, our modern silver plate; it was created by immersing a base metal, usually Britannia metal, in an electrolytic solution containing silver, which produced a chemical bond between the base metal and the silver. Both Sheffield and silver plate suffered from various defects, including the annoying fact that with time and use the silver would wear off. Nevertheless, both were relatively inexpensive, and they opened the silver market to a whole group of middle-class buyers, who up to that time had been unable to afford objects worked in such a precious medium. From 1840 on, vast quantities of silver plate were manufactured in American factories, and much of it is now readily available to the collector. Particularly desirable at present is sterling and plate in the Art Nouveau style so popular at the end of the last century. The rich, flowing lines of Nouveau pieces have a universal appeal, and they offer an excellent field for investment. Silver in the Art Deco style, a fad of the 1920s and 1930s, is just beginning to attract interest, and it too should find an eager public.

A maker's mark is an important element in the identification of American silver. In the colonies, the customs surrounding silver manufacture were greatly affected by the policies of the British government related to the making of objects in precious metals. In order to assure quality and uniformity, the British government required that all English silver bear a hallmark indicating the maker, the town in which the maker worked, and the year in which the object was made. These rules were never implemented in the colonies, and American smiths customarily marked their wares only with their initials, full name, or full name and city of origin. Some, particularly in the eighteenth century, did use false hallmarks in an attempt to create the impression that their goods were imported, but hallmarks were never required. Every serious student of American silver should own and use one of the standard books of American silvermakers' marks.

As one might suspect, silver, being valuable and in demand, has been faked. One of the most common techniques of deception is to remove the hallmark, and hence the proof of foreign origin, from a piece of English silver and pass it as an unmarked American piece. More sophisticated forgers actually impress a popular American mark in the altered piece; such famous manufacturers as Paul Revere, Myer Myers, and John Burt have thus had their ciphers placed on silver that never came within thousands of miles of their shops. Often, one can spot an altered mark by the fact that the wear normally covering the surface does not extend into the area of the mark. This too can be tampered with, though, so if in doubt, buy only from a reliable dealer who guarantees his wares.

Collectors of American silver can count on having a variety of forms from which to choose. In the 1600s, when few but the churches and the wealthy owned it, the metal was used primarily for shaping chalices, flagons, beakers, tankards, and the ever-popular porringer. In the eighteenth century, though, many other forms appeared, including coffee and tea sets, castor sets, trays, plates, bowls, pitchers, salts, boxes, candlesticks, and, of course, spoons in various sizes. As the nineteenth century progressed, these forms multiplied to provide the vast number available today.

Pewter

Though its popularity has declined considerably, pewter was for nearly two hundred years of major importance to the American household. Despite its softness and fragility, it was always preferred to wood and often to pottery. Accordingly, pewtersmiths were among the first metalworkers to appear in the colonies. Richard Graves is listed as working at Salem, Massachusetts, as early as 1635, and the oldest piece of marked American pewter bears the stamp of Joseph Copeland, active from 1675 to 1691 at Jamestown, Virginia.

These pioneer artisans worked under a major handicap. Pewter consists primarily of tin, to which a percentage of copper is added. But in those times, no tin deposits had been discovered in North America; all raw tin had to be imported from the vast mines at Cornwall, in England. The English at an early date put high duties on block tin while placing no duty at all on finished pewter. As a result, British pewter poured into the colonies, and for many decades local pewtersmiths were limited to repairing and reworking old pieces rather than making new ones.

What pewter local craftsmen did make was strongly influenced by European, particularly British, examples. Areas such as New York and Delaware, which had been settled by other national groups, showed traces of Continental styles, though these gradually disappeared as the English extended their control over these territories. In all cases, the colonial product differed from the Continental: it was of simpler construction, with clean and unpretentious lines—a direct consequence of the lack of material and the inability to afford costly bronze molds.

If the first American pewtermakers had problems, they also had advantages. The control of the European craft guilds did not extend to these shores, and our pewtersmiths were free to create and to develop without the rigid limitations that the guildhalls placed on workers. The "touch," or mark, of the colonial artisan was not controlled by law, and many of these people were highly individualistic. True, American workers tended to use variations of makers' marks found in their country of origin—for example, the rose and crown, the golden fleece, the lion, lamb, and dove of England—but in all cases they added unique elements of their own. The worker's initials, his hometown, or even some motto might appear on a piece. These early examples of marked American pewter are highly prized and expensive today.

After the Revolution, marks gradually became more standardized. At first there were patriotic motifs, particularly the eagle, which might be encircled with dots or stars representing the states, the number being increased with each new admission. Even these vanished, soon after 1812, to be replaced with simply the initials, full name, or name and locality of the pewtersmith. The vast majority of old pewter either is marked in this fashion or bears no mark at all. The absence of a mark, however, is no assurance that a given specimen was made in this country. While European pewter by law was required to be marked, not all of it was, and a substantial quantity of unmarked ware has entered this country over the years.

The fragile nature of pewter and the time required to manufacture ware that, although it sold for far less, had to be constructed basically in the same manner as silver—by casting or by handwork—put it at a disadvantage in competition with glass, tin, and pottery. Accordingly, manufacturers long sought a more practical medium. In the early years of the nineteenth century, the English found this in Britannia ware, first known as "hard metal," which consisted of an exceptionally durable and workable alloy of tin, antimony, and copper. Britannia could be cast or rolled into thin sheets without cracking and thus was accessible to metal spinning, an industrial process already used with brass and silver. Britannia was introduced on this continent in 1825, and within a few years pewter shops became small factories producing large quantities of standardized Britannia ware.

While perhaps less interesting to many collectors, Victorian factory-made pewter is a good investment. It is in general a good deal cheaper than earlier ware, and it comes in a wide variety of interesting forms.

Pewter forms tend to follow those of silver—it was not without reason that the former was known as "poor man's silver." The porringer, a small, handled, all-purpose vessel looking something like a cup, was the most common early type. It displays most of the decoration possible with pewter, primarily piercing or openwork, for the metal was simply too soft to bear the elaborate embossing and punching common on silver. Other early shapes are tankards; plates with a simple, smooth rim; bowls; large, round platters; and various teapots and coffeepots. At a later date, castor sets, pitchers, and a variety of lighting devices appeared on the market. In all cases, the forms, while clearly influenced by silver, show a much greater simplicity of design and decoration.

Coin silver spoons; first half 19th century. *Top:* Teaspoon marked "A. G. Stone," Massachusetts; $8–15. *Bottom:* Small serving spoon marked "Coin Silver"; $20–28.

Set of four large coin silver serving or tablespoons; East, ca. 1800; $225–275 for set of six matching spoons.

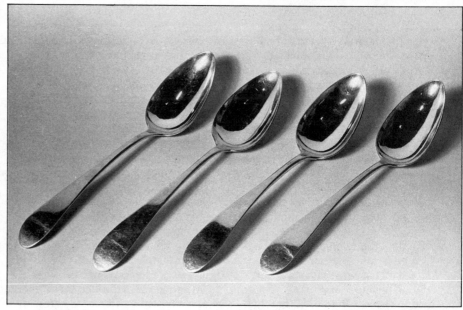

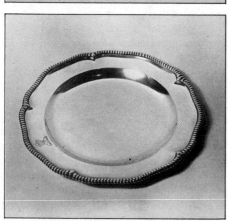

Coin silver serving dish with reeded rim; East, late 18th century; $225–275.

Left: Sterling silver and ivory tea strainer; $135–185. *Right:* Sterling silver grape scissors; $45–65. Both, East, mid-19th century.

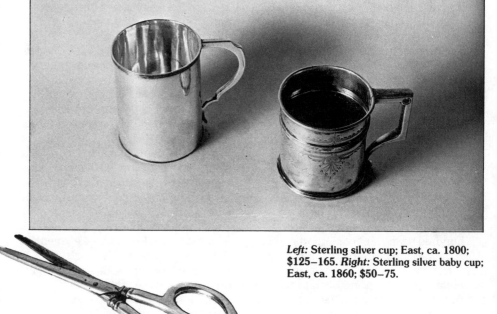

Left: Sterling silver cup; East, ca. 1800; $125–165. *Right:* Sterling silver baby cup; East, ca. 1860; $50–75.

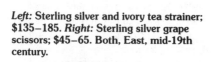

Sterling silver bud vase with a variety of decoration, including embossing, punchwork (hammered decoration), and incised work; East, ca. 1890; $75–105.

A group of sterling silver Victorian buttonhooks; East, mid- to late 19th century. *Top to bottom:* $30–33; $21–25; $17–20; $16–19.

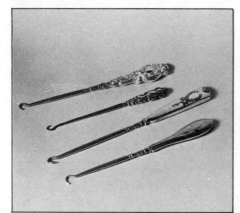

Sterling silver Art Nouveau pin dishes; late 19th century. *Left:* $75–90. *Right:* $60–70. Nouveau silver is still plentiful and inexpensive.

Art Nouveau sterling silver; ca. 1900. *Top:* Magnifying glass; $60–75. *Bottom:* Letter knife; $45–60.

Sterling silver Art Nouveau match safe; East, late 19th century; $90–130.

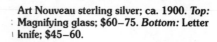

Unusual sterling silver Art Nouveau lorgnette; East, late 19th century; $135–185.

Silver-plate Art Nouveau brush and mirror; East, late 19th-early 20th century; $125–175. These sets are a good silver investment.

Strawberry spoon, sterling silver with gold wash; Tiffany and Company, New York City, early 20th century; $35–55. Any piece with the Tiffany mark is a wise purchase.

Top: Unusual sterling silver thermometer case; $40–55. *Bottom:* Two sterling silver pencils; $45–65 each. All, East, ca. 1910.

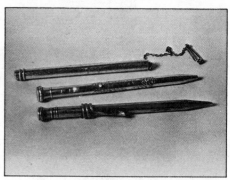

Sterling silver mesh evening purse; early 20th century; $75–110.

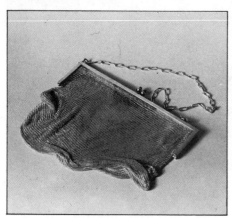

Napkin rings; early 20th century. Example at left is sterling; others are silver plate. *Left to right:* $35–48; $8–15; $12–16; $10–15.

Two sterling silver purses; East, early 20th century. *Left:* $75–125; *Right:* $100–145.

Commemorative spoons in silver plate. *Left:* $20–28. *Center:* $15–23. *Right:* Columbian Exposition, 1893; $35–50.

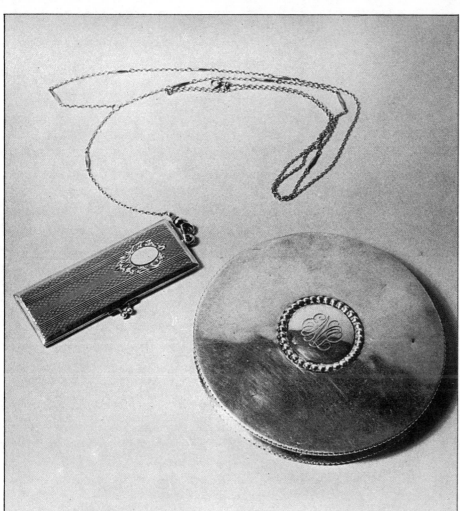

Sterling silver dressing table set; by Webster, ca. 1905; $225–300.

Left: Sterling silver hair locket; late 19th century; $125–165. *Right:* Sterling silver compact, early 20th century; $90–135.

Silver-plate creamer, sugar bowl, and tray; F. B. Rodgers; early 20th century; $50–75.

Art Deco table set, sterling silver and cut crystal; East, early 20th century; $275–375.

Pewter porringer; New York, 18th century; $250–350. Porringers with openwork handles like this one were widely made in the New York area.

Pewter teapot, marked Boardman, ▶ Connecticut, early 19th century; $275–325.

Pewter coffeepot; by Whitlack, Troy, N.Y., first half 19th century; $250–325. Marked pewter is always more valuable than unmarked. ▲

Pewter coffeepot; New England, mid-19th century; $190–245. ▼

Pewter coffeepots; mid-19th century. *Left:* ▲ Maine; $150–220. *Right:* Massachusetts; $135–195.

Pewter service pieces; 19th century. *Left:* Teapot; $125–155. *Center:* Coffeepot; $200–260. *Right:* Sugar bowl; $75–115. Handles of teapot and coffeepot are made of ebonized wood.

Fine pewter syrup pitcher, marked "Simpson and Benjamin," New York, ca. 1845; $350–425. Pieces of this shape were modeled on the famous Liverpool pottery jugs.

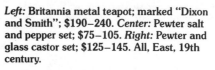

Left: Britannia metal teapot; marked "Dixon and Smith"; $190–240. *Center:* Pewter salt and pepper set; $75–105. *Right:* Pewter and glass castor set; $125–145. All, East, 19th century.

New England pewter; 19th century. *Left:* Porringer; $175–225. *Top center:* Cann, or mug; $85–115. *Bottom center:* Warming dish; $75–125. *Right:* Covered tankard; $200–260.

Pewter measuring cups; East, 19th century.
Left: $55–75. *Right:* $70–95.

19th-century New England mugs. *Left:*
Pewter; $115–145. *Right:* Britannia metal;
$65–95.

Bulbous pewter measuring cups; East, mid-
19th century. *Left:* $65–90. *Right:* $45–65.

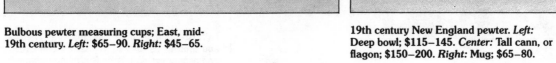

19th century New England pewter. *Left:*
Deep bowl; $115–145. *Center:* Tall cann, or
flagon; $150–200. *Right:* Mug; $65–80.

Above: Single-door paneled cupboard, pine and maple; New York, early 19th century; $1,500–1,850. *On cupboard:* Small painted dome-top chest; Pennsylvania, ca. 1860; $250–350. *Right:* Unusual fish sizer, wood; Great Lakes area, early 20th century; $600–850. Double-drawer blanket chest, red and yellow grain painting; Pennsylvania, mid-19th century; $2,500–3,500. A fine example of painted furniture. *Pages 130–131.* Rod-back kitchen chair, old green and red paint; East; early 20th century; $20–35. Coal and wood stove, "porcelain" over iron; East, early 20th century; $500–750. *On stove:* Banded yellowware bowl; Ohio, early 20th century; $40–60.

Opposite top: Victorian rocker, hickory and oak; Midwest, late 19th century; $135–185. Bed, brass and iron; East, late 19th century; $300–485. Sheraton-style candle table, pine and ash; New York, ca. 1835; $225–285. *Opposite bottom:* Four-slat ladder-back reclining chair, maple and pine; Pennsylvania; $195–285. Four-door pine cupboard; New England; $1,250–1,600. Both, mid-19th century; good country pieces. *Above: On wall:* High-quality hooked rug, wool on burlap, 19th century; $1,500–2,000. Table, walnut; New England, 18th century; $1,200–1,750. *On table:* Two pieces of Connecticut toleware; mid-19th century. Coffeepot; $900–1,300. Deed box; $600–750. *Above right:* Corner cupboard, pine and poplar; Pennsylvania, ca. 1840; $1,300–1,750.

Opposite: Left to right: Model of Amish buggy; Pennsylvania, 1910–20; $450–575. Weathervane; 1900–10; $600–750. Queen Anne corner chair; New England, 1760–70; $2,500–3,300. *Left:* Decoy; early 20th century; $240–275. Federal bench in original paint; New England, 1810–25; $1,800–2,300. *Above, on wall:* Geometric quilt; Pennsylvania, 1900–10; $850–1,000. Weathervane; New England, early 20th century; $600–750. *Below:* Harvest table, pine and maple, 12′ long; Pennsylvania, mid-19th century; $750–900. A variety of country chairs, pine and hardwood, some with splint seats; $50–110 each, depending on condition.

Page 136. Tin-paneled pie safe, old salmon paint; New Jersey-Pennsylvania mid-19th century; $650–800. *Above it:* A variety of wood and earthenware bowls; second half 19th century; $35–140.

Two pewter bowls; New York area, mid-19th century; $90–130 each.

Very large (16″ diameter) pewter charger, or serving plate; New York, first quarter 19th century; $250–330. ◄

Pewter bowls; New England, mid-19th century. *Left:* $100–135. *Right:* $75–95.

Pewter deep dish, 12″ in diameter; New York, mid-19th century; $135–160.

▲Pewter plates, 6″ and 8″ diameters; East, first half 19th century. *Left to right:* $75–110; $50–75; $60–75. Plate at left has simple rim characteristic of early American pewter.

Pewter plates ranging in size from 6″ to 10″ in diameter; East, 19th century. *Left to right:* $60–90; $40–65; $50–95.

Mid-19th century New England pewter. *Left:* Camphene lamp; $165–225. *Center:* Large (14″ diameter) charger; $200–245. *Right:* Handled cup; $60–85.

Pewter pieces from New York, 19th century. *Left:* Marrow knife; $75–115. *Center:* Porringer-shaped baby feeder; $65–95. *Right:* Matchbox; $60–90.

Left: Double-burner pewter camphene lamp; $180–230. *Right:* Pewter inkwell; $115–165. Both, New York mid-19th century.

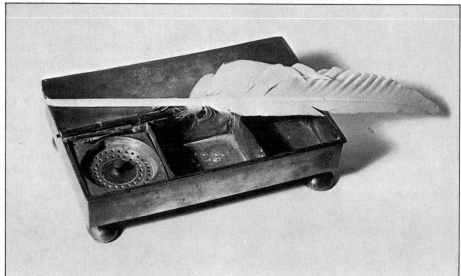

Footed pewter desk set; New York, early 19th century; $185–225.

Small pewter salt; New England, mid-19th century; $55–75.

Left: Pewter egg cup; $65–90. *Right:* Large pewter ladle; $100–140. Both, East, first half 19th century.

Child's pewter tea set; Massachusetts, late 19th century; $85–135.

Pewter foot or bed warmer, Pennsylvania, mid-19th century; $115–150.

Pair of fine early pewter candlesticks; East, first quarter 19th century; $300–350 the pair.

Pair of pewter candlesticks; first half 19th century; $150–200 the pair.

Tall pewter candlestick; New England, first half 19th century; $150–200.

Mid-19th century pewter candlesticks; East. *Left:* $75–95. *Right:* $110–145.

Tall pewter candlestick; New York, first quarter 19th century; $140–180.

Single-burner pewter camphene lamp; New England, mid-19th century; $165–200.

Pewter whale-oil lamp; New England, first half 19th century; $140–175.

Double-burner pewter camphene lamp; with mark of Sellow, active in Cincinnati, Ohio, mid-19th century; $250–325. Marked camphene lamps are uncommon.

Pewter fat lamp on pedestal, a so-called rabbi's lamp; East, first quarter 19th century; $210–260.

Pewter kerosene lamp with reflector; Pennsylvania, second half 19th century; $175–210.

Pressed or pattern glass whale-oil lamp, with pewter top; New England, first half 19th century; $180–220.

Pewter kerosene lamp on stand, a so-called student lamp; 1880–90; $300–375.

Double-burner camphene lamp, glass and pewter on marble base; East, mid-19th century; $220–260.

7

COPPER AND BRASS

Copper

No areas of American antiques present so many problems for the collector as do copper and brass. These metals have been known since prebiblical times, and advertisements make it clear that from the early eighteenth century American craftsmen were working in both mediums. But unlike silversmiths, these workers seldom chose to mark their products. Moreover, most native ware closely resembles its European counterpart. When one adds to this the enormous number of brass and copper objects that were imported into this country from southern Europe in the years after World War II, one can recognize the great potential for confusion that exists in assigning a date and place of manufacture to individual items. Nevertheless, the color and general attractiveness of both metals make them favorites among collectors.

Copper was used for weapons and utensils before the dawn of recorded history. It is a rather soft, malleable ore with an attractive reddish cast, and it takes a good polish. It does not form well in molds but can be wrought into many forms. Since it is a good conductor of heat, it was formed into warming pans, for instance, to warm the beds in the days before adequate heating of houses; in colonial times, a round or oblong copper pan, rather shallow in depth, would be filled with hot coals and passed between the bedclothes to take the chill off before the inhabitants climbed in. Warming pan covers were often decorated with punched or pierced designs; hung on a wall when not in use, the utensils provided a bit of beauty in the often somber colonial home.

Teakettles of copper are another favorite with collectors. Smiths in New York and Pennsylvania developed a flaring goosenecked form that is unique to these shores and though rarely marked can be recognized as distinctly native. Since raw copper imparts an unpleasant taste to food and may be harmful to health as well, copper cooking ware was lined with tin. A variety of such lined utensils is found, including open-hearth cooking kettles, oblong fish kettles and pans, saucepans, giant apple butter kettles, and a few field plates—copper dishes with an iron belt loop that were designed to be carried by workers for use at the mid-day meal.

Other and generally unlined copper ware includes measures of various sizes for both grain and liquids, funnels, components for liquor stills (always handy in those days before government control of distilling), lamp bases and filling vessels, skimmers, and flatirons.

The rust-resistant characteristic of copper also made it particularly suitable for the construction of objects that would be exposed to the weather. Weathervanes and trade signs come immediately to mind. Various garden accoutrements such as vases and gutters were also fashioned of the metal. Fishermen employed it both in ship's hardware and in the manufacture of various fishing lures.

Brass

Brass is an alloy, a combination of two parts copper and one part zinc. It too is of great antiquity, for the secret of smelting brass ingots by heating raw copper along with zinc-bearing compounds was discovered at the dawn of recorded history. The traditional process was a slow one, though, and a much better method for directly fusing copper and zinc was discovered, in 1781, by one James Emerson. Thereafter, more brass became available, though American producers suffered for many years from a lack of native zinc; the importation of the material forced them to price their goods higher than comparable foreign examples, which may be the reason that there has always been an abundance of non-American brass in this country.

Unlike copper, brass can be cast as well as stamped or wrought. As a result, there is a somewhat greater variety of brass objects available to the collector. The metal is also harder than copper, ductile, and highly malleable. It is easily joined and takes a high polish, resembling gold, for which it was often substituted.

The casting of brass household objects by founders skilled in the trade was an important area of early American metalcraft. First, a form or pattern in the shape of the desired object was carved of wood. It was then pressed into wet sand and enclosed within a boxlike container known as a flask. When the impression was satisfactory, the pattern was withdrawn and molten brass poured into the cavity. Once hardened, the final product was

polished and trimmed for use. Many objects were cast in brass, among the most important of which in the eighteenth and nineteenth centuries were furniture fittings: hinges, handles or pulls, and escutcheons to cover keyholes; all were collectively known as ormolu. Some are found with makers' marks, but none of these has so far been proved to be American.

Andirons were equally important products since fireplaces were the sole means of heating until the mid-nineteenth century. The many andirons produced were usually made either entirely of brass or of iron and brass combined. Styles varied, and andirons may be found with ball, urn, steeple, or lemon finials, and with ball, snake, or ball-and-claw feet. The leg was generally curved in the shape known to furniture experts as the cabriole. A good pair of andirons was expensive, even in the 1700s, and more than one brass master recognized this value by placing his name on his work, a thing he would not do with lesser objects made in the metal. Among the craftsmen who thus signed their work is Paul Revere. Prices for signed andirons start in the hundreds of dollars.

Numerous other items were cast in brass—the best buttons, for example, particularly those for military uniforms. Caspar Wistar, the famous Philadelphia glass manufacturer, was also one of our nation's first button makers. His button factory in Pennsylvania advertised for years in the Philadelphia newspapers, and the business was carried on for many decades by Wistar and his son. Important national figures such as George Washington wore initialed buttons, specimens of which bring high prices today. Other brass items commonly seen are doorknobs and knockers, candlesticks, irons, trivets, and heavy jelly kettles.

Cast brass is so heavy, though, that it is unsuitable for many purposes. Since the metal also can be wrought, hammered brass cooking utensils were standard ware in eighteenth- and nineteenth-century kitchens. In the 1850s, a more efficient method was developed when H. W. Hayden invented the process of spinning brass. In this method, a brass disk was rotated on a lathe between a die on the headstock and a rotating device on the tailstock. The worker pressed a tool against the turning disk, forcing the disk against the die until it conformed to the shape of the die. Spun-brass kettles and other similarly made vessels may be recognized by the multitude of concentric circles scarring their bottoms. Most spun ware was made in Connecticut, and much was marked with the name of its manufacturer—a rare occurrence with brass objects, as has been mentioned. Spun-brass kettles were light of weight and quite durable. They became an instant success and were sold throughout the East and Midwest by peddlers who piled great stacks of them upon their wagons or even carried them on their backs from town to town. Basins, measures, funnels, warming pans, dippers, and chocolate pots were also constructed in this manner.

As previously mentioned, the recent influx of European copper and brass (much of which is itself quite old) has presented serious problems for collectors. The chief objects that are imported seem to be dippers, warming pans, and kettles from Portugal and Spain and andirons and fireplace equipment, such as tongs and shovels, from England. Much more brass than copper is arriving. Among the former is a great deal of modern ware, but the careful collector should be able to recognize this since it is much lighter in weight than earlier pieces, shows no wear, and just doesn't look old. But the older pieces do present a serious threat to the market. Some collectors are already reluctant to buy anything other than marked pieces, such as spun kettles, or clearly identifiable American types, such as gooseneck copper teakettles. As in other areas, the most satisfactory solution is to buy from a reputable dealer.

Prices for both brass and copper are high and have been so for some years. Both are attractive accessories, and the pieces in greatest demand—marked andirons, kettles, and early buttons—command large sums. Warming pans and trivets are also expensive. For the collector of modest means, the accessible objects in these metals are the smaller utensils and the later spun-brass kettles.

Copper saucepans with brass handles; East or West. 19th century. *Top:* **$85–115.** *Bottom:* **$60–85.**

Copper cooking pot with wrought-iron bail handles; New England, 19th century; $55–75.

Crude copper saucepan; New York, mid-19th century; $30–45. This was probably used by a craftsman rather than in the home.

Very large, shallow-lipped copper cooking or baking pan; Pennsylvania, 19th century; $75–125.

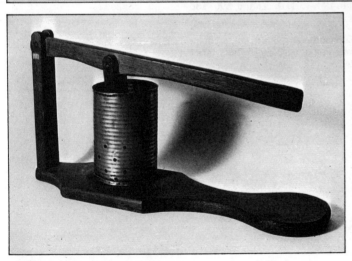

Left: Copper skillet, second half 19th century; $90–130. *Right:* Rare copper spinner's skein holder; early 19th century; $150–200.

Copper funnels; East, late 19th-early 20th century. *Left:* $20–35. *Right:* $30–40.

19th-century copper, East. *Left:* Funnel; $50–70. *Center:* Mug; $30–45. *Right:* Ovoid mug; $40–55.

Jelly press, hickory, pine, and copper; Pennsylvania, 19th century; $85–100.

Left: Copper field dish with iron belt loop; South, early 19th century; $75–110. *Center:* Copper kerosene lamp with brass fittings; New York, late 19th century; $65–90. *Right:* Unusual copper fishing lure; Maine, mid-19th century; $110–140.

Copper oilcan; Maine, late 19th century; $30–45.

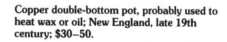

Fine engraved copper matchbox; New York, late 19th-early th century; $90–130.

Copper double-bottom pot, probably used to heat wax or oil; New England, late 19th century; $30–50.

Copper foot warmer, Pennsylvania, 19th century; $70–110.

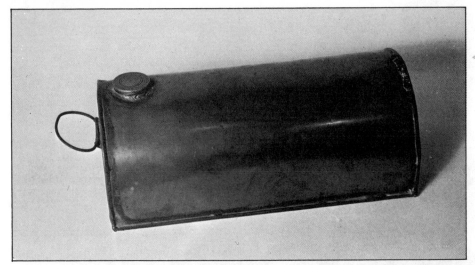

Copper rooftop ornament; Pennsylvania, ca. 1890; $150–225.

Copper spittoon; late 19th-early 20th century; $25–35. Hardly a common item, but of little interest to collectors.

Copper barber's hot-water reservoir; East, late 19th century; $85–135. This vessel was placed over a fire to maintain a supply of hot water.

Copper pipe for roof drainage system; East,
late 19th century; $125–175.▲

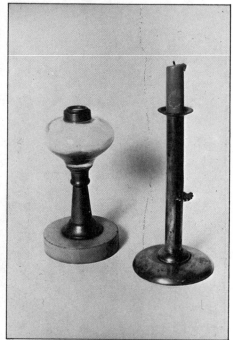

Left: Glass whale-oil lamp with brass base,
lacking burner, early 19th century; $75–100.
Right: Rare early copper-plated push-up
candlestick, late 18th century; $185–245.
Both, New England.▼

Left: Copper funnel; $35–50. *Right:* Rare
five-spout copper oil lamp; $120–145. Both,
mid-19th century.

Copper and glass kerosene lantern; East, late 19th century; $75–115.

Left: Very rare copper three-burner fat lamp with reservoir; New York, early 19th century; $150–210. *Right:* Pewter camphene lamp; mid-19th century; $150–200. ▼

Unusual copper standing or hanging fat lamp; East, late 18th-early 19th century; $165–225.

Large copper whale-oil lamp; New England, first half 19th century; $130–185.

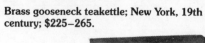

Brass gooseneck teakettle; New York, 19th century; $225–265.

Brass kettles with wrought-iron bail handles; New England, 19th century. *Left:* $95–125. *Right:* $60–95. Piece at left is older and shows good hammer work.

Punch-decorated brass bed warmers; Pennsylvania, 19th century. *Left:* $130–170. *Right:* $200–260.

Brass jelly kettle with wrought-iron bail handle; Connecticut, mid-19th century; $75–120. A good example of a spun-brass kettle.

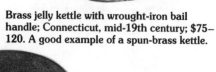

Top left: Brass cattle bell; $20–35. *Top right:* Brass chamber stick; $75–105. *Below:* Brass warming pan; $75–95. All, New England, mid-19th century.

Unusual brass hand-held skimmer; first half 19th century; $70–120.

Left: Copper pot with handles; $60–85.
Right: Brass coffeepot; $75–100. Both, East, mid-19th century.

Left: Brass spoon; $30–50. *Center:* Rare brass candle reflector in shape of miniature Queen-Anne-style tilt-top table; $185–225. *Right:* Brass spoon; $25–45. All, East, 19th century.

Brass skimmer with wrought-iron handle; Pennsylvania, mid-19th century; $65–95. Pieces similar to this are being imported from Europe.

Top: Hammered brass dipper or ladle with wrought-iron handle; New Jersey, ca. 1850; $70–110. *Bottom:* Small stirring spoon, cast brass with cutout handle; Pennsylvania, mid-19th century; $60–85.

151

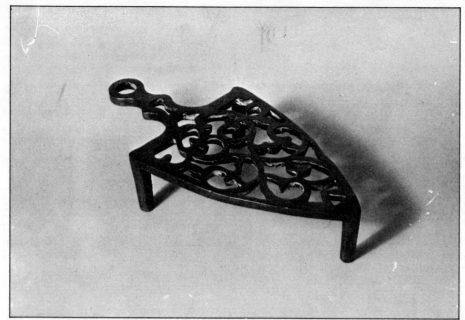

Cast-brass trivet; late 19th-early 20th century; $70–110.

Set of brass animal bells; late 19th-early 20th century; $90–120.

Pair of brass and iron penny-foot andirons; New York, ca. 1800; $250–350.

Pair of brass and iron andirons; East, first half 19th century; $150–185.

Brass folding telescope; New England, mid-19th century; $160–230.

Brass and iron fireplace tongs; New York, ca. 1800; $175–225.

Brass and iron goffering iron for use in pressing clothing; East, first half 19th century; $150–200.

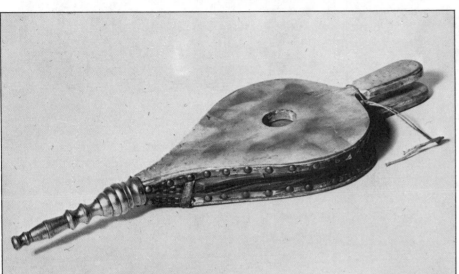

Brass, leather, and wood fireplace bellows; New England, mid-19th century; $75–125.

Fine-quality brass merchant's scale; Delaware, mid-19th century; $175–245.

Small brass scale of the sort often used by jewelers; Connecticut, 19th century; $65–90.

Craftsman's brass door marker or advertising sign; 19th century; $165–225. A quite uncommon piece.

Left: Brass and bone snuffbox; $50–80. *Center:* Brass and horn powder horn; $75–115. *Right:* Brass pie crimper; $60–85. All, New England, 19th century.

Upper left: Brass and glass candleholder; $100–140. *Upper right:* Rare brass carpenter's scribe; $55–85. *Bottom:* Brass snuffer tray; $30–45. All, 19th century.

Left: Brass school bell; New England, late 19th-early 20th century; $35–45. *Right:* Sheet brass candlestick; New York, 19th century; $45–60.

Extremely tall brass wedding ring push-up candlestick of hog scraper variety; Connecticut, mid-19th century; $300–450. Possibly unique.

Left: Brass candleholder designed to be fitted with wooden handle; East, early 19th century; $175–245. *Right:* Miniature cast-brass candleholder with snuffer; late 19th century; $90–135.

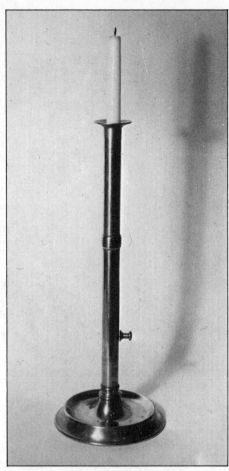

Tall spun-brass candleholder; East, late 19th century; $200–270. Possibly an altarpiece.

Grouping of cast-brass candlesticks, Maine and Massachusetts, first half 19th century. *Left to right:* $75–115; $165–245; $85–135; $200–240.

155

Left: Brass scoop; $30–45. *Right:* Very rare brass pump lamp; $200–265. Both, East, mid-19th century.

Rare miniature brass candle lantern; New York, early 19th century; $140–175.

Brass lantern with slide door and isinglass shield; New York, mid-19th century; $150–200.

Brass and pressed-glass lamps; mid-19th century. *Left:* Camphene lamp; $140–180. *Right:* Whale-oil lamp; New England; $110–140.

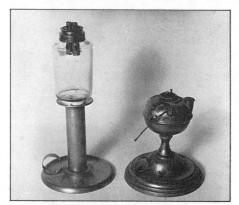

Left: Brass whale-oil lamp; New England, first quarter 19th century; $90–120. *Right:* Brass fat lamp; early 19th century; $135–200.

Brass kerosene hand lamp; East, late 19th century; $145–185. An interesting early kerosene lamp.

Small brass kerosene lamp; East, late 19th century; $80–125.

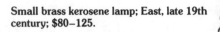

Triangular kerosene lantern with a brass fount and tin top; New England, ca. 1880; $75–105.

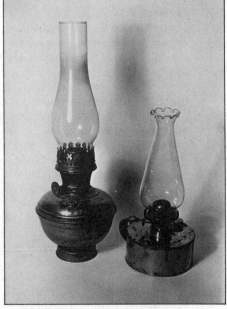

Two brass kerosene lamps; New England, early 20th century. *Left:* $90–120. *Right:* $40–60.

Left: Brass kerosene lamp designed for wall bracket; $65–95. *Right:* Brass kerosene hand lamp; $50–70. Both, New England, early 20th century.

8.
IRON AND TIN

Ironware

Objects of iron and tin are closely related, and both have been on the American scene for many years. Wrought iron, which is hammered into shape at a forge, was being made at Jamestown, Virginia, in 1607, and by 1685 there was an iron furnace at Saugus, Massachusetts, where the rich supplies of native iron ore were converted into bar iron for domestic use as well as for export to England.

The few pieces of identifiable seventeenth-century American iron are practically indistinguishable from their European cousins, but by the early eighteenth century, a distinct native style began to emerge. It was characterized by simplicity, lack of noticeable ornamentation, and a direct relationship between form and function. These qualities have remained the hallmarks of good American ironware.

Some of our earliest wrought iron was intended for the kitchen hearth, and such cooking utensils as pots, grills, roasting skewers, and trivets are among the most popular objects sought by collectors. Wrought door hinges, tools, and weapons are also of great interest.

Most iron cooking pots were not wrought but rather cast, by pouring molten metal into sand forms. Cast iron contains a substantial amount of carbon and is consequently hard and brittle; it cannot be worked at a forge. Since it does not withstand shock well, it saw limited use in the earliest period; but by the early 1800s, it was used to fashion many types of objects—stoves, flatirons, machinery, and household utensils. Today, much of our collectible iron is cast iron.

Wrought iron may be distinguished from cast iron by its grainy appearance in the rusted state, whereas cast and milled iron (a mid-nineteenth-century form of industrial iron) rust to an even, orange-peel-like surface showing no discernible grain. In addition, a series of coarse ridges may often be seen running through wrought pieces in the direction in which they were "drawn," or shaped by the smith.

There are several varieties of collectible wrought- and cast-iron objects, including fireplace and kitchen equipment; builders' hardware, such as nails, door hinges, and latches; cabinet hardware; locks; and iron used on horse-drawn vehicles.

Most examples are plain and undecorated. Only rarely do names or dates appear, and when they do, they greatly increase the value of a specimen. A few metalsmiths, such as the well-known Peter Derr of Pennsylvania, signed their work, and such items bring a premium. Except for such rare examples, however, prices in this field are quite reasonable. Old iron comes up often at yard sales, flea markets, and country auctions, and a nice collection can be made without any great expenditure.

For many years, collectors could buy native iron without concern for reproductions or importations. Alas, such is no longer the case. Since the Second World War, a substantial quantity of wrought and cast iron has been imported, primarily from southern Europe. Many of these forks, spatulas, and spoons are practically indistinguishable from American-made products. True, some are more elaborate; and any ornamental piece must be regarded with suspicion, for with the exception of some Pennsylvania hardware, little American iron was highly decorated. But much of the imported ware is plain—and old. For a few dollars, a chance may be taken on a doubtful piece, but better-quality iron should be purchased only from a reputable dealer who guarantees the authenticity of his wares.

Tinware

Tinware is made predominantly of iron. A lighter-weight metal, it is formed by running sheet iron through rollers to produce an extremely thin body; this is then dipped in molten tin, which covers the sheet iron with a shiny and rust-resistant surface. Many items that could be manufactured in iron—pots, kettles, and so forth—could also be made in tin; and the lighter weight of the tin made it particularly attractive to itinerant peddlers who traveled the back roads of this country in the nineteenth century bringing much-needed utensils to isolated families and communities.

Perhaps 90 percent of all old tinware found today is undecorated. For some tinsmiths, such as those of the Shaker communities, this was a matter of principle. They were producing an honest, functional product, and decoration would have been contrary to both their religious principles and their

esthetic judgment. Among the bulk of the tin manufacturers, more practical considerations governed. Decoration took time, and time was money. New tin had an appealing gleam; in fact, along with pewter it was often referred to as "poor man's silver." But since it was fragile and aged quickly, neither producer nor consumer was much interested in fancy frills.

Certain pieces, on the other hand, customarily were decorated. Teapots and coffeepots, bread trays, and various storage containers were normally seen in the dining room as well as the scullery, and for these there had to be some adornment. In many instances, the metal alone might be worked. Elaborate designs could be produced by punching, scalloping, crimping, or piercing the surface of the tin, by hand or machine.

Pennsylvania-made tinware, in particular, is often decorated by piercing or punching. The former technique, which created a pattern by cutting holes completely through the metal, was employed on foot warmers, cheese molds, colanders, and the tin panels of pie safes. Punching, on the other hand, resulted in a raised design of individual dots. It was favored for teapots and coffeepots. A variation was wriggling, in which a pattern was incised on the vessel by striking it with a sharp implement that was moved slightly at each stroke. Neither punching nor wriggling broke the surface of the metal. Both techniques might be combined in the same piece, such as a candle shade or barn lantern.

Painting on tin, or japanning, was also extremely popular. As early as the eighteenth century, tin was gilded with gold leaf; in the nineteenth century, a major industry concerned itself with "flowering," or painting, tin. The decorators—who were often women—first coated the metal with japan, a soft, lustrous, tar-base black paint. They then decorated it in oils, freehand or with the aid of stencils. Though few such pieces were ever signed, experts can frequently determine their place of origin through the decorator's use of distinctive motifs and patterns.

In Pennsylvania and New Jersey, painted decoration was often combined with crystallization, generally on the bottom of a bread or bundt tray, produced by applying acid to the surface of the tin. The sparkling texture gave added charm to showpieces, which were frequently displayed to visitors and carefully preserved for generations.

Painted tin, or toleware, has long been collected. It is extremely popular and also expensive. Most pieces show wear and may have lost a portion of their decoration, yet all but the meanest examples sell for sums in excess of a hundred dollars. Such a seller's market has, naturally enough, led to reproduction, some innocent, some not quite so. Painting on tin, often old tin, is a recognized craft, and some of the modern compositions are taken directly from old examples. They may be very well done, and if artificially aged, they can present a problem for the unwary. In seeking to determine the age of a given specimen, first check to see whether there are scratches and signs of wear in the japanning. It is softer than the oil decoration and on old pieces will have abraded. The oil paint itself will be "alligatored," or covered with a pattern of hairline age cracks, and there will also be wear on the unpainted bottom. Finally, the piece should not be "too perfect." Old-time decorators worked fast and made mistakes—they smudged the surface, painted off center, and didn't balance their compositions. Modern imitators are likely to be more exacting.

Graniteware

In the late nineteenth century, factories began to produce large quantities of granite- or agateware—sheet iron coated with a porcelainlike substance. Graniteware was largely intended for the kitchen and the bath; thus, cups, bowls, dippers, soap dishes, coffeepots, platters, pans, and pie plates are the most common objects in this medium. Unlike the older ironware and tinware, graniteware forms are rather prosaic; but the charming and fanciful surface is most appealing. The background color is generally white, with which any number of other hues—gray, blue, green, red, yellow, or brown—may be mixed in a swirled design.

The making of tinware was centered in the Northeast, generally along waterways, where there was ready access to raw material, which was mostly imported. Such centers as Berlin, Connecticut; Stevens Plains, Maine; and Dedham, Massachusetts, became famous for their production. There were in addition extensive manufactories elsewhere. New England tinsmiths often spent the winter working in the South; Pennsylvania, Ohio, and Virginia were major sources; and there were even floating tin shops on the Mississippi River! As a result, tin, particularly of the undecorated variety, may be found almost anywhere in the United States.

With the exception of tole, tinware is moderately priced and offers an interesting field for collectors. It has much variety, and attractive examples are common, particularly in the area of graniteware, where whole sets of a particular color combination may be acquired.

A variety of tin scoops; New England, late 19th-early 20th century; $5–18, depending on size and form. Scoops were used in both home and shop and are quite common.

Teakettle, cast iron; Hutton Foundry, Troy, N.Y., ca. 1860; $185–245. A fine example of the gooseneck teakettle.

Footed drip pan, cast iron; New England, late 19th century; $20–35.

Left: Unusual griddle, cast and wrought iron; New England, early 19th century; $135–160. Combination of feet and hanging loop on a griddle is rare. *Center:* Wafer iron, wrought iron; Maine, ca. 1860; $90–140. *Right:* Fireplace toaster, wrought iron; Maine, mid-19th century; $160–230.

Left: Warming pan, sheet metal and brass; 20th century; $14–21. *Center:* Pot with handle, cast iron; ca. 1850; $45–55. *Right:* Small pot with handle and hook, cast iron; ca. 1850; $35–40. All from Maine.

Left: Gooseneck teakettle, cast iron, with unique hanging fixture; ca. 1830; $135–195. *Center:* Fine grill, wrought iron; $80–150. *Right:* Footed frying pan, cast iron; $60–90. Both grill and frying pan are mid-19th century. All pieces, New England.

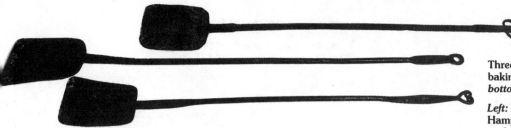

Three wrought-iron oven peels for use in baking; Maine, mid-19th century. *Top to bottom:* $80–110; $60–85; $125–165.

Left: Hanging griddle, cast iron; New Hampshire, ca. 1860; $85–135. *Right:* Oven peel, wrought iron; Massachusetts, ca. 1870; $60–85.

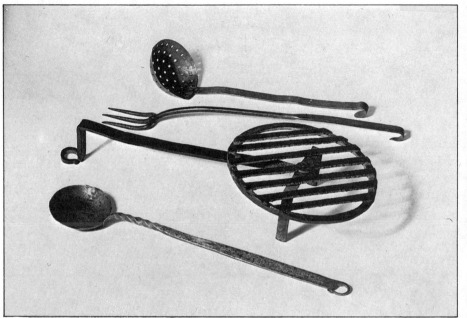

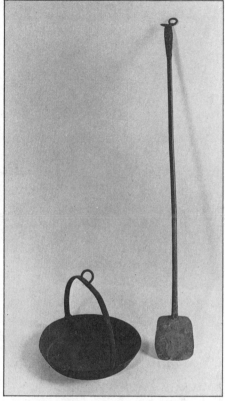

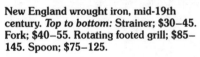

New England wrought iron, mid-19th century. *Top to bottom:* Strainer; $30–45. Fork; $40–55. Rotating footed grill; $85–145. Spoon; $75–125.

Top: Well-decorated fork, wrought iron; Pennsylvania, ca. 1830; $135–175. *Bottom:* Punch-decorated spatula, wrought iron; New Jersey, ca. 1850; $75–110.

Swivel-base toaster, wrought iron; Maine, ca. 1850; $190–270.

161

Skewer rack and skewers, wrought iron; New England, mid-19th century; $150–225.

Three New England trivets; 19th century. *Left:* Sheet iron and wood; $45–60. *Center:* Triangular wrought iron; $40–65. *Right:* Wrought iron with good finial; $75–125.

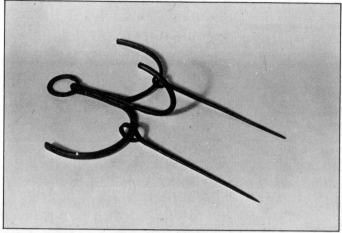

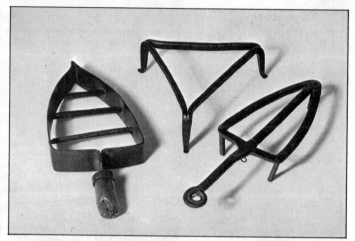

Left: Eggbeater, steel and cast iron; Midwest, ca, 1900; $15–20. *Center:* Long-handled chopper, wood and wrought iron; New York, ca. 1860; $35–50. *Right:* Bread knife, steel and cast iron; Ohio, early 20th century; $10–15.

Muffin pan, cast iron; Midwest, early 20th century; $65–90.

Three elaborate choppers, hardwood and steel; Pennsylvania, mid-19th century. *Left to right:* $45–70; $50–85; $35–55.

Candy mold in shape of a lamb, cast iron;
East, early 19th century; $75–100.

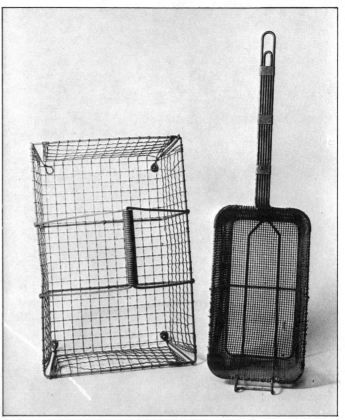

Iron wireware; 20th century. *Left:* Fruit or
vegetable carrier; $22–28. *Right:* Deep fryer;
$15–18.

Fruit-shaped molds, cast iron; Midwest, early
20th century. *Left:* $45–65. *Right:* $35–50.

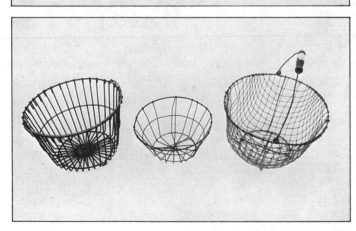

Egg and produce baskets, iron wire; 20th
century. *Left to right:* $35–55; $10–20; $25–
35.

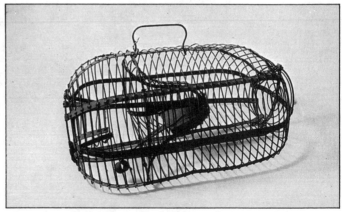

Rattrap, iron wire and sheet steel; New
England, late 19th century; $45–70.

Charcoal-heated cast flatiron; New England, 19th century; $30–45.

Clockwise from left: Sadiron cast; $20–30. Flatiron, sheet and cast iron; Midwest, mid-19th century; $50–65. Sadiron, cast, with wrought handle; $30–45.

Sewing bird, cast iron; New England, 19th century; $125–150. An extremely attractive specimen of a popular collector's item.

Front to rear: Elaborate bootjack, cast iron; New England, late 19th century; $35–50. Bootjack, wrought iron; New York, ca. 1850; $30–50. Sadiron, cast, with wrought handle; late 19th century; $35–60.

Tobacco cutter, cast iron; Connecticut, late 19th century; $25–35.

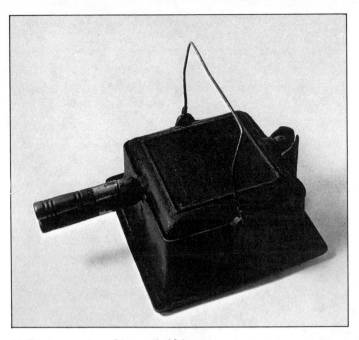

Waffle iron, cast iron; Ohio, early 20th century; $30–45.

Coffee mill, cast iron and wood, red and gold paint; manufactured by Charles Parker, Meriden, Conn., late 19th century; $350–425.

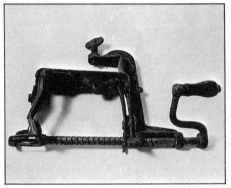

Patented cherry pitter, steel and cast iron; New Hampshire, 19th century; $35–55.

Bread-dough mixer, sheet and cast iron; Midwest, late 19th century; $25–35.

Scale, cast iron and steel; Midwest, 19th century; $75–105.

Tole-decorated scale, iron and tin; East, 20th century; $50–75.

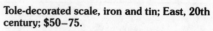
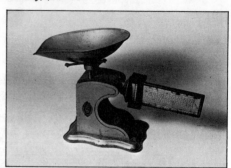

Parlor stove, cast iron; Atlanta Stove Works, Georgia, late 19th century; $250–375.

Teapot, tin and wood; Maine, early 19th century; $60–85. A remarkable example of the reproduction in tin of a silver form. Pot is modeled on a silver teapot of the late 18th century.

Coffeepot, tin and brass; New England, mid-19th century; $50–75. Fine style, interesting construction.

Field coffeepot, tin and iron; New England,
late 19th century; $40–65. A good piece
typical of those widely used in shops and
factories.

Large roasting pan, sheet tin; New York, late
19th-early 20th century; $20–30.

Connecticut tinware; 19th century. *Left:*
Dipper; $15–30. *Center:* Shallow bowl; $20–
28. *Right:* Funnel; $5–12. Good specimens
of readily available tin.

Brown-bread molds, tin; New England, late 19th century. *Left to right:* $15–25; $10–15; $15–25; $10–15. Reeded pieces are more desirable.

Hinged bread-baking mold, tin; Maine, late 19th century; $20–30. An attractive form.

Massachusetts tinware; 19th century. *Top left:* Brown-bread mold; $12–17. *Top right:* Barrel, old green paint; $33–40. *Bottom left:* Storage box; $9–13. *Bottom right:* Storage box, old black paint; $10–15. Unusually small pieces.

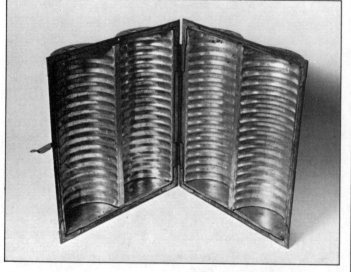

Candy molds, tin; New England, early 20th century. *Left to right:* $5–10; $5–10; $10–15. The more ornate the form the higher the price.

Shaker dipper, tin and iron wire; New York, mid-19th century; $135–185. Good workmanship and simplicity of design typical of Shaker pieces.

Left: Funnel, tin; $5–10. *Center:* Crimped mold, tin; $25–35. *Right:* Food grater, tin and wood; $45–70. All, New England, 19th century.

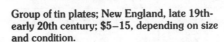

Group of tin plates; New England, late 19th-early 20th century; $5–15, depending on size and condition.

◄ Tinware. *Left:* Scoop; $5–10. *Center left:* Drinking cup; $3–6. *Center right:* Canning funnel; $3–6. *Right:* Open-handled drinking cup; $7–12. All, early 20th century.

Left: Child's cup, stamped tin; Pennsylvania, late 19th century; $25–40. *Right:* "ABC" plate, stamped tin; Massachusetts, late 19th-early 20th century; $40–55 ►

169

Top left: Eggbeater, tin; $15–22. *Top right:* Flour sifter, tin; $7–15. *Bottom:* Potato ricer, tin; $12–20. All, 20th century.

Egg poacher, tin; marked "Kreamer," 20th century; $10–15.

Group of tin measures; New England, 20th century. *Left to right:* $3–5; $4–8; $8–15.

Group of sifters, tin and iron wire; late 19th-early 20th century. *Left to right:* $20–30; $25–40; $20–35; $15–25. Handle and small size add value to example in right foreground.

Tin lunch boxes, Connecticut, early 20th century. *Left:* With inner compartments for hot foods; $25–40. *Right:* In old black paint; $25–35.

Left to right: Tin sander, oil pot, and gum pot; Maine, 19th century. *Left to right:* $20–30; $25–35; $4–6.

Double-lid lunch box, tin with pierced decoration; Connecticut, mid-19th century; $85–145.

Tinware; New York, late 19th century. *Left:* Scraper; $3–6. *Center:* Shaker; $5–10. *Right:* Covered canister; $15–25.

Map case, tin, old green paint; New York, late 19th century; $65–95.

Extremely elaborate pierced colander; Pennsylvania, mid-19th century; $240–310. An example of fine decoration on tin.

Left: Coffeepot with offset spout, tole; Connecticut, ca. 1860; $275–375. Rather sparse decoration in red and yellow on black somewhat limits the value of ths piece. *Center:* Coffeepot, undecorated tin; $25–35. *Right:* Syrup pot, undecorated tin; $10–17. Both, New England.

Left: Tin matchbox, black and gold stencil; $15–22. *Center:* Set of tin spice cans in holder, black paint; $35–55. *Right:* Unpainted tin milk can; $15–23. All, Connecticut, late 19th century.

Painted tinware; Maine, 19th century. *Left:* Hanging matchbox, old blue paint; $20–35. *Center:* Deep dish, tole, red and yellow on black; $175–250. *Right:* Hand-painted drinking cup; $12–22.

Box with lift top and brass handle, tin, decorated with stencil designs in red, yellow, and gold; Pennsylvania, mid-19th century; $175–225.

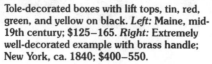

Tole-decorated boxes with lift tops, tin, red, green, and yellow on black. *Left:* Maine, mid-19th century; $125–165. *Right:* Extremely well-decorated example with brass handle; New York, ca. 1840; $400–550.

Serving tray, tin, stencil decorated; New England, mid-19th century; $175–265.

Stencil-decorated oblong serving trays; New York, late 19th century. *Left:* Gold and silver stencil on black ground; $80–130. *Right:* Red and silver stencil on black ground; $125–155.

Stencil-decorated covered roasting pans, gold and silver on black; Pennsylvania, 19th century. *Left:* $185–215. *Right:* $165–190. Covered pans of this sort are quite uncommon.

Left: Oval serving tray decorated in green and silver stencil; $45–75. *Right:* Stenciled, red on black scalloped serving tray; $60–90. Both, Connecticut, late 19th century.

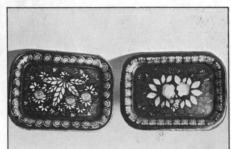

Covered pitcher, tin, white with hand-painted green and yellow decoration; New York, late 19th century; $75–110. Vessels of this sort are often mistaken for watering cans, but this piece is part of a set that includes a similarly decorated washbowl. The set was used with Victorian cottage furniture.

Wall mirror and accessory box, stamped tin
and glass; Massachusetts, late 19th century;
$20–35. Stamped mirrors and boxes of this
sort were particularly common in the late
Victorian period.

Stove-top bake oven, tin and iron; marked
"The Ideal–New York," early 20th century;
$35–65.

Fireplace bake oven, tin and iron; Maine, ca.
1825; $250–350. An extremely early and fine
tin accessory.

Birdcage, tin, recent black paint; Maine, late
19th century; $160–220. A spectacular
form.

174

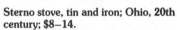

Sterno stove, tin and iron; Ohio, 20th century; $8–14.

Baby bath, tin and iron wire, old white paint; Maine, late 19th century; $45–75. Interesting form and color, but something that hasn't caught on.

New England tinware, late 19th century. *Left:* Gardener's insect sprayer; $7–15. *Right:* Maple syrup vat whistle; $25–40. When the sugar reached a boil the whistle would alert the workers; a rare piece.

Foot warmer, pierced tin and pine; Rhode Island, ca. 1850; $90–135.

Watering can, tin; East, early 20th century; $10–22.

Rare wriggle-decorated dustpan; Pennsylvania, ca. 1870; $135–185. A most unusual piece.

Churn, undecorated tin; New York, late 19th ▲ century; $30–55. A rather uncommon use for tin.

Washbowl, graniteware, blue on white; New York, early 20th century; $20–35.

20th-century graniteware; New England.
Left: Coffeepot, violet on white; $45–60.
Right: Colander, white on blue; $20–33.

Blue on white graniteware; Midwest, 20th century. *Left:* Pie plate; $5–10. *Right:* Cooking pot with spout and bail handle; $10–15.

Green and white graniteware; New York, 20th century. *Left:* Washbowl; $2–4. *Right:* Pie plate; $5–9. While the overall green of the bowl is common, the flowed green on white, as seen in the pie plate, is not frequently encountered.

Graniteware; New York, 20th century. *Left:* Bowl, mottled red and orange; $2–4. *Center:* Pie plate, speckled white on blue; $3–6. *Right:* Serving bowl, white with blue banding; $2–4.

Common gray graniteware; Midwest, 20th century. *Left and right:* Pie plates; $3–6. *Center:* Very large (14″ diameter) tray; $6–11.

Gray graniteware; Midwest, 20th century. *Left:* Funnel; $5–8. *Right:* Slop jar; $7–15.

177

9.
TEXTILES

Before the era of factory-made goods, most textiles for the home were made at home: blankets, sheets, clothing, and even in some cases carpets. In the rugged early years of colonial life, these articles were primarily utilitarian. With the enormous burden of chores, and few resources, women had all they could do to keep the family warmly clothed; they had little time to think about decoration. But by the early eighteenth century, especially in the cities and on southern plantations, wealth had created leisure and a taste for luxury. Beyond merely providing for the family, women could now turn their attention to embellishing their homes and the clothing they wore.

Embroidery

The chief decorative technique at their disposal was needlework, specifically, embroidery. Even in the seventeenth century, personal inventories had frequently mentioned "wrought" or "needleworked" cushions, carpets, and cloths. About the same time, the sampler came into existence, both as an educational device—to train a girl in the various embroidery stitches—and as a showpiece—to display her talents. The earliest samplers, such as the one created in 1653 by Lora Standish, daughter of Captain Myles Standish, were long narrow panels on which the needlework was set out in horizontal bands. By the late eighteenth century, the form had become square or slightly oblong, with the addition of a border to frame the text. Nearly all samplers are dominated by an alphabet or a pious inscription. Better specimens include embroidered figures, houses, animals, ships, and flowers, as well as the maker's name and date—all often executed in a variety of stitches.

By 1850, the stitching of samplers had mostly been discontinued; there are few interesting examples from a later period. Samplers have been collected for many years, and large numbers of very similar English examples are on the market. Names and dates are of little help in distinguishing them, so the wise buyer looks for specimens that are not merely signed but also incorporate a recognizable American place name.

Women's academies, which were established in large numbers in the late eighteenth and early nineteenth centuries, included "fancy work"—elegant sewing—as an important part of their curriculums. In addition to samplers, made mostly by the younger girls, needlework pictures were popular—carefully stitched representations of houses, landscapes, ships, flowers, and historical and biblical scenes. The most common form was the mourning picture, a standardized composition containing a large urn-shaped memorial (which often bore the name of a deceased relative), several weeping willow trees, and the figures of mourning survivors.

Like samplers, mourning pictures were also made in England, but most were made in the United States, and their source can often be identified by the names they bear or the localities they illustrate.

Quilts

Few American antiques are more popular, here or abroad, than patchwork quilts, remarkable works of art that are also practical and truly native. Though patchwork quilts were made in England, the craft was developed to its finest form on these shores—by women with little formal education and certainly no artistic training.

Actually, what is popularly known as the quilt should more correctly be called the stitched coverlet, since the term *quilt,* as popularly used, covers several different techniques: patchwork, or piecing, is the sewing together of small, colored patches of cloth so as to form a particular design; quilting is the taking of tiny running stitches to bind together several layers of cloth (normally, two or three layers); appliqué is stitching colored cloth design elements on top of a solid piece of cloth. Later "quilts" often are not quilted at all but are tied—stitched together with a single tufted stitch at regularly separated intervals. Likewise, the earliest American quilts, from the eighteenth century, contain no patchwork; rather, they are made of solid pieces of cloth—cotton or linsey-woolsey—fastened together with quilting that is sometimes remarkably elaborate.

Nineteenth-century quilts—pieced or appliquéd—are quilted too, more often in geometric patterns than in the floral patterns common in the preceding century. In any case, the earlier the quilt, the finer the stitching.

The design elements of appliqué quilts are usually figurative—garlands, flowers, and occasionally birds and animals. Pieced quilts, with much smaller individual pieces, are most often geometric; their designs are remarkably intricate and spectacularly beautiful. They carry equally fascinating names, which either describe an image that the pattern resembles—Crown and Thorns, Flying Geese—or commemorate an event—Lincoln's Platform—or are purely poetic—Delectable Mountains.

Eighteenth-century quilts are hard to find on the market these days. More common are pieced and appliquéd quilts, which first appeared in the late eighteenth century and have continued to be made right up to our own day (though with noticeable changes in design and type of cloth). Pieced and appliquéd quilts are usually made of cotton, occasionally of wool; a notable exception is the Victorian crazy quilt, made of scraps of silk, satin, and velvet seamed together and bound over with elaborate embroidery stitches. At this point the original purpose of the quilt, to provide a bed covering, disappears. Crazy quilts, too fragile for beds, served only as decorative throws for furniture or pianos.

Quilts vary in desirability dependent on several factors. Earlier pieces are sought not only for their age but for the fact that their designs are frequently unique, whereas at a later date many patterns became standardized. Signed quilts are important, particularly the friendship quilts, in which each block was sewed by a different person; the whole was intended as a gift for a new bride or a minister's wife. Dated examples are, of course, also most desirable. Quilt prices are, in general, quite high, even for the common types. Any quilt in good condition will sell for at least fifty dollars, and sought-after variations such as early free-form quilts, Amish, and crib quilts may go for as much as a thousand dollars. It is hardly surprising then that quilts are being made, repaired, and cut down, in the interest of providing for this active market. At a bare minimum, quilt collectors should learn to distinguish between the tight, even flow of the machine stitch (common in quilts made after 1900) and the freer hand stitch. It is helpful to know something of the materials used at different periods and the approximate age of more popular patterns. The presence of seeds in the cotton stuffing is another indicator of age (they may be felt with the fingers or seen if the quilt is held up to the light). Quilts made before 1880 are likely to contain them, since only by that date did the mechanical seed picker become universal.

Coverlets

While every woman was a quilt maker—and some men were too—the highly patterned woven coverlets popular today were produced by a limited number of people. Some housewives had their own looms; others relied on the itinerant weavers, who carried their looms in a wagon. After the middle of the nineteenth century, factories took over the chore entirely.

The American coverlet is based on English and European designs, though it varies sufficiently that there is no danger of its being confused with the foreign product. American coverlets are woven in two or more strips, each about two and a half to three yards long, and seamed together. Colors vary and in earlier examples were produced by use of natural dyes.

The least complex type is the overshot weave, which has a linen or cotton warp and a woolen weft. Its geometric patterns appear in three tones, dark, light, and a half tone. It is the first type of native woven coverlet, and some of the oldest of existing examples are traceable to the eighteenth century.

In New York and Pennsylvania, a variation, the Summer–Winter coverlet, was popular in the early nineteenth century. This is two-toned—traditionally, blue and white; dark on the side where the colored woolen pattern dominates, lighter on the reverse where the linen warp is found. Again, geometric patterns predominate, though they are more complex than in the overshot.

Block, or double-woven, geometrics are more complex, produced by interweaving a natural-colored cotton fabric with a colored woolen one; they are completely reversible.

Latest and most spectacular are the Jacquard, or fancy floral coverlets, which were made in one piece on a larger loom (often in a factory). The pattern is dominated by a central floral medallion surrounded by elaborate borders, often containing flowers, birds (including the eagle), trees, buildings, and human figures. Unlike earlier coverlets, Jacquards were frequently signed and dated by their makers and also may bear the names of their original owners.

Coverlets are extremely attractive and desirable antiques. Prices are generally much more reasonable than for quilts; good specimens sell for seventy-five to one hundred dollars and really top pieces go for no more than three hundred dollars. Names, dates, and inscriptions add greatly to value.

Hooked Rugs

Hooked rugs are the youngest group of American textiles. There are few specimens that can be reliably traced to the first half of the nineteenth century; the first written mention of the craft appears in 1838. This is odd, particularly in light of the fact that rug hooking is not difficult. The materials required—old rags, a hook or bent nail, and, perhaps, a wooden frame—are easily obtainable. The process is hardly complex. A design is drawn in charcoal or crayon on a piece of burlap or other coarsely woven material. The worker then attaches short pieces of rolled cloth to the hook and draws them through the backing, using a variety of colors to produce the pattern.

The most desirable hooked rugs are those that were done from a design created by the worker. These are often spontaneous and truly artistic. After the Civil War, most rug makers copied standardized commercial patterns, which were stamped onto burlap backing. These are considerably less inspired.

Of the three types of hooked rugs—pictorial, geometric, and floral—collectors are at present most interested in pictorials. These are least common but still abundant; the designs depict everything from cats, dogs, and

other animals to houses, human figures, and complete pastoral scenes. Those that commemorate an event such as a wedding or Fourth of July celebration are much sought after.

Geometric rugs are, superficially at least, the simplest of all since the design consists of a repeated basic form, such as a circle or a square. In fact, some makers supposedly laid out their designs using tea cups or bricks, the outlines of which they would trace on the backing. Nevertheless, the color and line variations in geometric hooked rugs can be as subtle as those found in a modern painting. They are particularly suitable for use with modern furniture, and they are very popular today.

There are many different floral rug patterns. Some, such as those made in Canada and the Waldoboro, Maine, area, have raised, or "hove up," portions and are extremely attractive. Most, though, are rather ordinary examples of Victorian excess. Hooked rugs attracted collector attention for the first time in the late 1920s and early 1930s. At this time florals were all the rage, and vast numbers were made. The new interest in these floor coverings, which may be traced to a ground-breaking exhibition at New York's Museum of American Folk Art in 1975, has concentrated more on pictorials and geometrics. Prices remain favorable to the buyer at present. Good rugs can still be found in country shops for ten or fifteen dollars, while standard prices range from thirty to eighty dollars. A truly unique rug may go for a thousand dollars, but those are few and far between.

Mention should also be made of rag, or braided, rugs, which were made throughout the late nineteenth and much of the twentieth centuries. Homemade examples are constructed simply by coiling and binding together strands of rolled rag. The same material was also woven into larger rugs on special looms. Both types are seen frequently at country auctions and house sales, and prices are still very low. These attractive and inexpensive rugs represent an exciting and relatively unexplored area of folk craft.

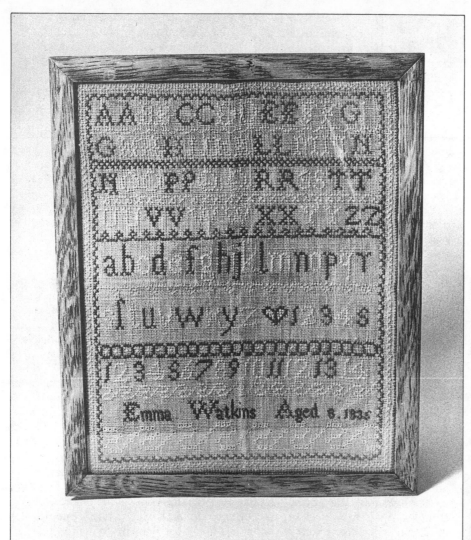

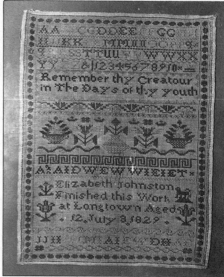

Sampler; by Emma Watkins, Maine, 1838; $130–175.

Sampler; by Elizabeth Johnson, Longtown, N. J. (?), 1829; $400–500. Good needlework and interesting details in a fine early sampler.

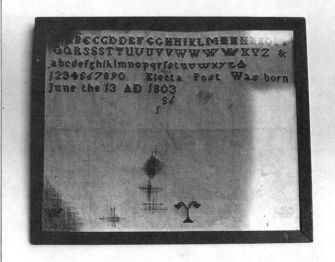

Sampler, probably unfinished; by Electa Post, first quarter 19th century; $90–130.

Sampler; New England, 1841; $350–450. Excellent pictorial detail makes this a very desirable sampler.

Needlework picture (crewelwork); by Mary Martim, 1823; $375–500. In composition this piece is similar to a theorem.

Needlework mourning picture; early 19th century; $850–1,000. One of the many memorials dedicated to Washington in the decades following his death.

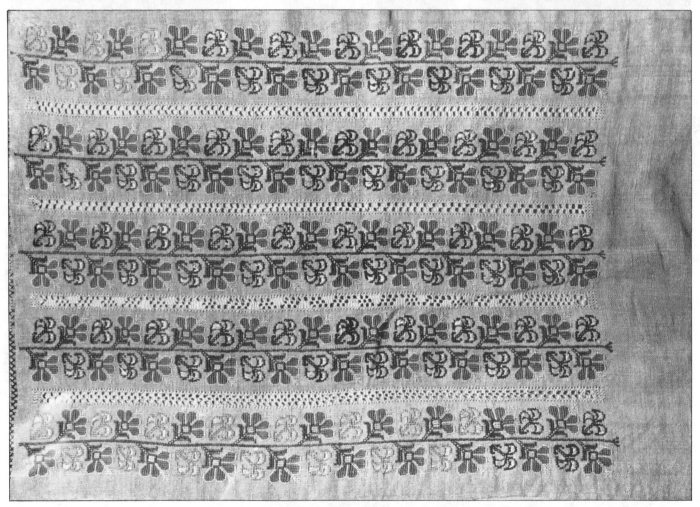

Section of embroidered cloth; New England, mid-19th century; $85–125.

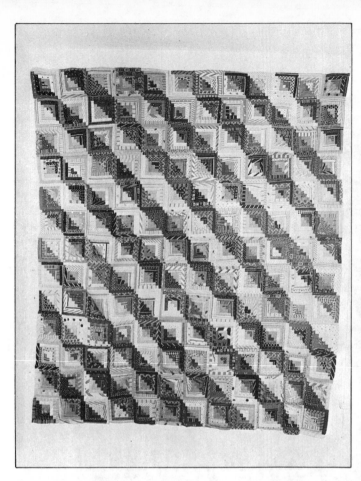

Log Cabin quilt, Straight Furrows variation, cotton, predominantly browns; New York, late 19th century; $350–500.

Light and dark Log Cabin quilt in the unusual medium of wool, predominantly lavender and brown; Pennsylvania, 19th century; $375–525.

Log Cabin quilt, Courthouse Steps variation, cotton, brown and aqua; Pennsylvania, late 19th century; $250–325.

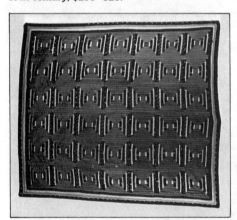

Log Cabin quilt, Plowed Furrows variation, cotton, predominantly orange and brown; Massachusetts, ca. 1900; $225–300.

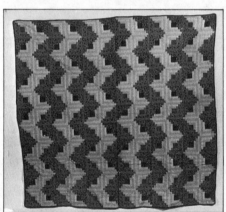

Detail of light and dark Log Cabin quilt shown above. ▲

Light and dark Log Cabin quilt, cotton, predominantly blue; Indiana, early 20th century; $400–550. This is a single-bed size.

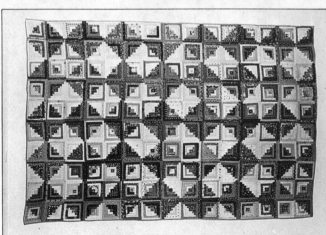

Double-T quilt, cotton, in unusually bold colors, yellow and rust; Pennsylvania, late 19th century; $300–400.

Zigzag quilt, cotton, predominantly browns; New York, late 19th century; $185–265.

Spectacular Star of Bethlehem quilt, cotton, multicolored; Pennsylvania, late 19th century; $700–875.

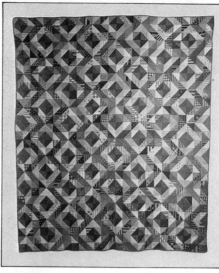

Cross and Crown quilt, cotton, multicolored; Pennsylvania, late 19th century; $175–235

Geese in flight quilt, cotton, brown on white; Rhode Island, second half 19th century; $350–500. A well-done and attractive quilt.

Star quilt, cotton, black and gray on white; Pennsylvania, late 19th century; $250–300.

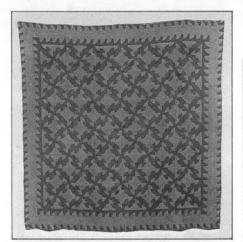

Drunkard's Path quilt, cotton, red and green; Pennsylvania, 19th century; $425–500.

Courthouse Square quilt, cotton, red and white; New York, late 19th century; $185–265.

Blazing Star quilt with Oak Leaf appliqué border, cotton, red and white; New Jersey, 19th century; $550–675.

Stars quilt, cotton, multicolored; East, late 19th century; $170–230.

Postage Stamp quilt, cotton, multicolored; New York, early 20th century; $365–445.

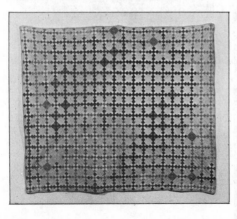

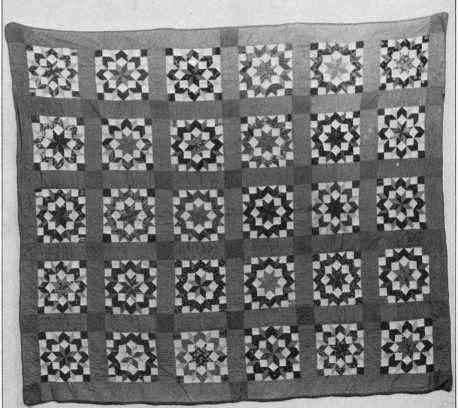

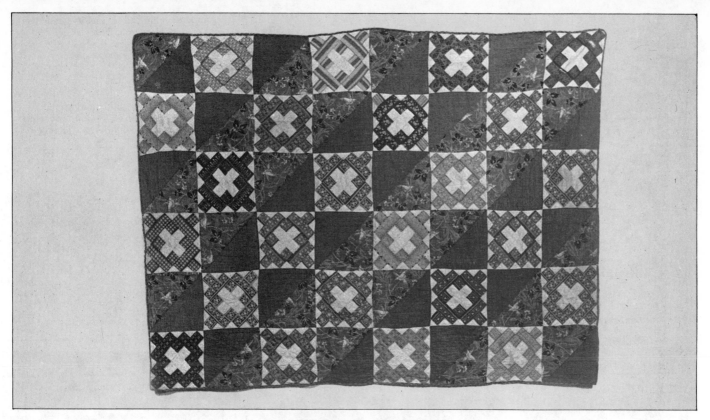

Courthouse Square quilt, predominantly red and green; New York, early 20th century; $100–140.

Diamond quilt, cotton, blue, red, black, and white; New York, 20th century; $360–420. A good example of the geometric quilts popular in the early part of this century.

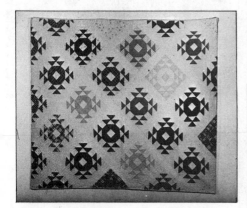

Crown and Thorns quilt, cotton, multicolored; New York, 20th century; $125–175.

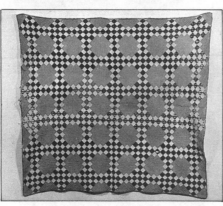

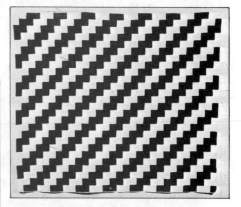

Lightning quilt, cotton, blue and white; New York, 20th century; $600–750.

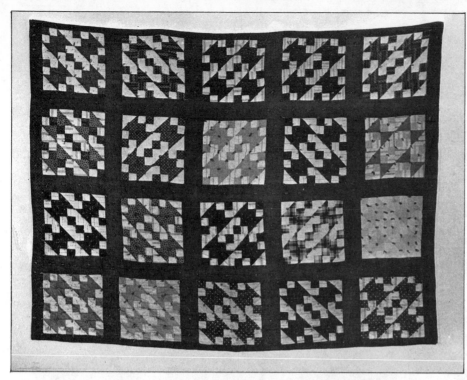

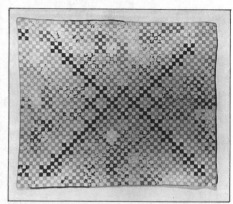

Geometric quilt, cotton, multicolored, tied not quilted; New York, 20th century; $90–120. Tied quilts are less desirable and less expensive than quilted examples.

Postage Stamp crib quilt, multicolored; New Jersey, 20th century; $275–350. Crib quilts are now attracting long-overdue attention.

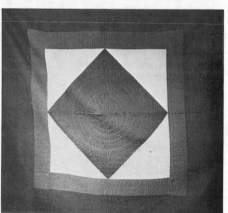

Rare and finely done Amish quilt, wine, green, and dark blue; Pennsylvania, 19th century; $2,500–3,500. Amish quilts are enormously popular with collectors.

High-quality Friendship Crazy quilt, silk with a variety of embroidery stitches; Massachusetts, late 19th century; $375–450. The squares represent many of the states.

Crazy quilt, silk and velvet with a variety of unusual embroidery stitches; New York, late 19th century; $450–600.

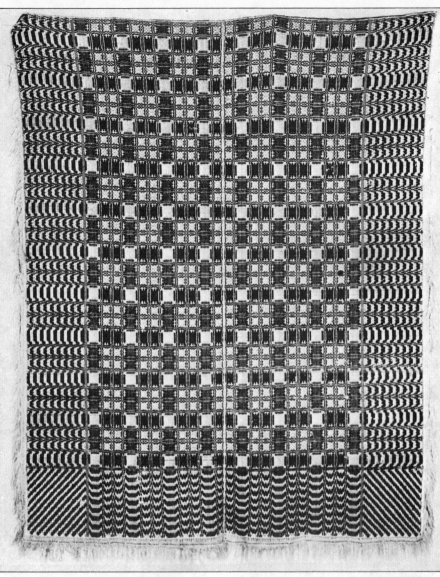

Overshot-weave coverlet, wool and cotton, blue and white; Pennsylvania, mid-19th century; $200–275.

Very fine fringed overshot-weave coverlet, cotton and wool, red and white; Pennsylvania, mid-19th century; $250–350.

Overshot-weave coverlet, wool and cotton, red, green, and black; Ohio, 19th century; $200–250.

Overshot-weave coverlet, cotton and wool, blue, light blue, and white; New York, mid-19th century; $175–225.

Summer-Winter coverlet, cotton and wool, blue and white; New Jersey, mid-19th century; $150–200.

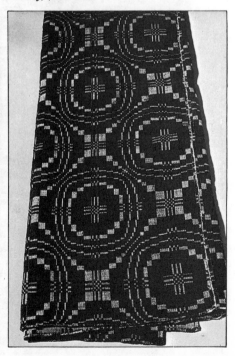

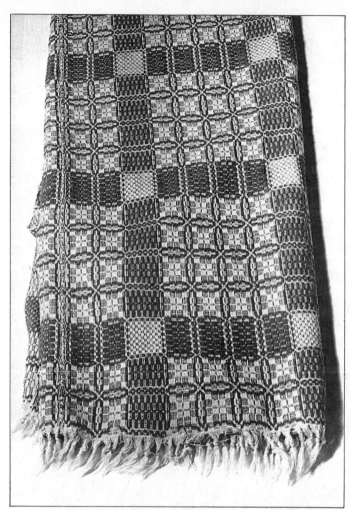

Unusual fringed overshot-weave coverlet, cotton and wool, red and white with an interesting pattern; New York, mid-19th century; $250–350.

Jacquard coverlet, cotton and wool, blue and white; by M. Coleman, dated 1825; $600–750. Fine eagle and state-house border.

Jacquard coverlet, cotton and wool, blue and white; by Archibald Davidson, Ithaca, N.Y., dated 1838; $900–1,200. A reversible coverlet with a superb border of running deer, trees, eagle and statehouse.

Fine fringed overshot-weave coverlet, cotton and wool, blue and white; Pennsylvania, 19th century; $200–300.

Jacquard coverlet, cotton and wool, blue and white with eagle and statehouse border; dated 1829; $550–700.

Jacquard coverlet, cotton and wool, multicolored; by J. Packer, Brownsville, Pa., dated 1839; $350–450. A good example of the floral coverlet.

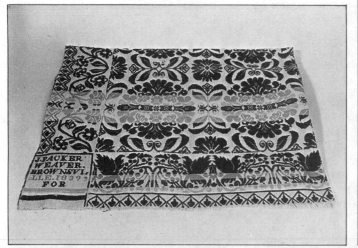

Strong Jacquard coverlet, cotton and wool, red and white; by J. Van Ness, Palmyra, N.Y., dated 1849; $1,000–1,300. The large eagles at corners are unusual.

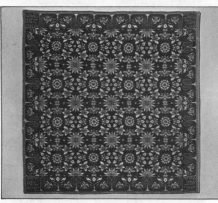

Jacquard coverlet, cotton and wool, blue and white, with eagle and weeping willow border; made for Margaret S. Parker, Orleans County, N.Y., dated 1839; $525–600.

Two woven table covers, with motifs of eagle and mounted George Washington; by J. Cunningham, North Hartford, N.Y. *Top:* Blue on white; dated 1841; $400–500. *Bottom:* Red on white; 1841; $450–600.

Geometric hooked rug, rag on burlap, red, black, and gray; Pennsylvania, late 19th century; $75–100.

Remarkable hooked rug, wool on burlap; mid-19th century; $1,500–2,000. A real piece of folk art and an outstanding example of a hooked rug.

Hooked rug with Maltese cross, wool on burlap, multicolored; New England, late 19th century; $80–130.

Geometric hooked rug, wool and rag on burlap; New England, late 19th century; $100–150. An attractive rug of the sort that goes well with modern furnishings.

Floral hooked rug, rag and wool on burlap; Massachusetts, 20th century; $40–60. Simple pattern-made rugs of this sort are readily available today.

Floral hooked rug, rag on burlap; New York, 20th century; $70–105.

"Ric-rac" hooked rug, rag on burlap, multicolored; Connecticut, early 20th century; $55–80. An attractive and inexpensive geometric rug.

Floral geometric hooked rug, rag on burlap; New York, late 19th century; $65–95. Good detail and interesting colors make this a desirable piece.

Pictorial hooked rug, wool on burlap; Pennsylvania, second half 19th century; $125–165. Stenciled pattern on burlap base of this rug is dated 1867.

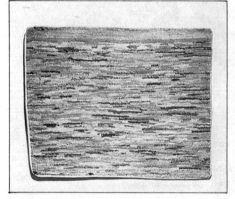

Pictorial hooked rug, wool on burlap; New England, 20th century; $250–350. A nautical rug of the sort often made along the coasts of Maine and New Hampshire.

Pictorial hooked rug, rag and wool on burlap; Maine, 20th century; $140–200.

191

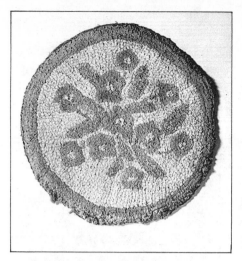

Hooked floral chair cover, rag on burlap; Connecticut, 20th century; $15–25. Small hooked pieces of this sort are low priced and make attractive wallcoverings. Pictorial examples will bring $30–40.

Pictorial entrance rug, rag on burlap; New York, 20th century; $75–125. A desirable figure, but late date of rug reduces its value.

Hooked entrance rug, wool on burlap, black and gold; Pennsylvania, early 20th century; $175–245. An interesting rug in attractive colors.

Hooked floral seat cover; rag on burlap; New York, 20th century; $45–65.

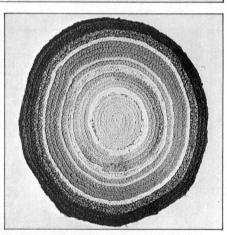

Round braided rug, multicolored; New York, 20th century; $45–75. Rugs of this type were usually made at home from remnants of rags.

Oval braided r g, multicolored; New England, 20th century; $35–60. Good color and low price make these rugs an excellent buy.

192

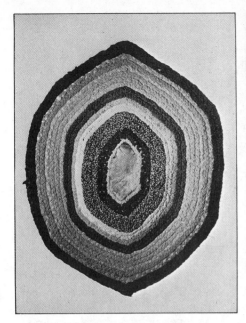

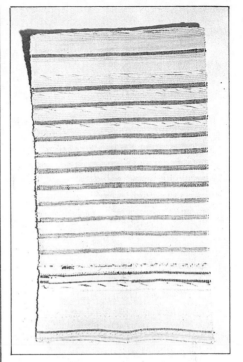

Hexagonal braided rug, rag and leather, multicolored; New York, 20th century; $60–85. Leather center and six-sided shape make this an unusual example.

Woven rag rug, multicolored; Vermont, late 19th century; $30–55. Such rugs were woven on looms in sizes as large as 10′ by 12′.

Woven rug, blue and white; Maine, 20th century; $15–25.

Berlin work picture, wool with beadwork; Maine, ca. 1860; $75–110.

Needlework motto; Maine, early 20th century; $35–55. Mottoes of this sort were often worked to be hung in homes or churches.

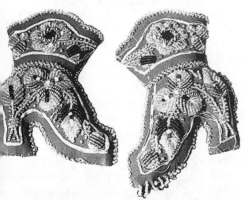

Beadwork pincushions in form of high shoes; New York, late 19th century; $85–125, the pair. Highly detailed beadwork of this sort was often done by Indians on reservations for sale to tourists.

Beadwork pincushions; New York, late 19th-early 20th century. *Left to right:* $35–55; $30–45; $35–45. these pieces are now becoming popular.

10.
WOODENWARE

Particularly for the new collector, or one of modest means, woodenware provides a vast field for exploration and purchase. Since nearly every utilitarian object has at one time or another been made of wood—or treen, as it is often called—the variety of forms available is far greater than in any other field of antiques. Even the most casual lover of antiques is aware that plates, bowls, and spoons were often made of wood instead of the pottery or metal common today. It is less often recognized that other objects common today in many mediums were once manufactured exclusively from treen. Coffee grinders, ink bottles, washing machines, flour sifters, and meat grinders are just a few examples. We know the purpose of these implements; but every day there come to light other, strange wooden utensils to which we can assign neither name nor function. The need for which they were fashioned has long since vanished; and so they exist, like objects from an Egyptian tomb, as mysterious and fascinating artifacts.

Partly because of its abundance, and partly because of a certain snobbish prejudice against such simple, handworked things, old treen has remained at a reasonable price level while other antiques have risen steadily in value. True, unusually attractive or signed or decorated pieces have always been sought after, but average woodenware is still one of the best buys available. For a few dollars, one can often obtain the nucleus of a good collection.

Making Treen

At the time of the colonization of this country, there existed in Europe guilds of coopers, men whose craft concerned the working of wood. Many of them came to this country, including the well-known John Alden of Plymouth Bay. Those whose labors are of greatest interest to us are the "white coopers," or dish turners, the men who made utilitarian housewares. Some of their production—spoons, plates, and shallow bowls; the so-called flatware—was cut out and shaped by hand. A tree would be felled, hewed to an appropriate size, and then roughed out with an ax and a cooper's adz (a curved iron blade with a short handle). When necessary, as in the making of bowls, the interior might be burned out

to facilitate gouging. Such simple methods were similar to those employed by the American Indians, and early colonial treen is often difficult to distinguish from that shaped by the Indians.

Advanced collectors are always on the lookout for hand-finished flatware. They watch for odd shapes that reflect the natural form of the material used; they run their hands along the outsides and insides to detect the rough marks of the maker's tools. It is an exciting game—but an uncertain one. Wooden flatware can be of great age, but it can also be very recent. Settlers moving west made it to replace broken dishes and lost spoons. Poor people in the Ozarks and other isolated areas whittled out useful items throughout the nineteenth and early twentieth centuries. They are, in fact, still doing it! Given some rough wear, stain, and a few years' weathering, such pieces sometimes can scarcely be distinguished from their seventeenth-century cousins. Moreover, in the past decades there has grown up a thriving import business devoted to the sale in this country of European treen, primarily Spanish and Portuguese. These specimens are for the most part quite old, hand carved, and in form not unlike similar objects produced on this continent. It takes experience to distinguish American from foreign woodenware. There are no hard and fast rules. Generally, one should be aware that the imported pieces are of unfamiliar woods rather than our own pine, maple, or ash and are usually more elaborately decorated. If on top of this the form looks slightly unfamiliar, the piece is probably an immigrant.

From the very first, American coopers worked with a lathe as well as freehand. The basic purpose of the lathe is to produce a circular movement so that an object fixed on the machine can be shaped as it rotates by chisellike tools pressed against it. A great variety of hollowware—goblets, deep bowls, tankards, sugar and salt containers—can be made on a lathe. The earliest of these devices, the spring-pole lathe, could cut only half a revolution, so that anything made on it had to be turned and worked in two stages. Specimens cut on such a lathe often can be distinguished by the fact that the tool marks on the two sides are slightly out of line.

By the seventeenth century, the fully turning mandrel lathe had been developed, and it is on some variation of this machine that most old American hollowware has been cut. Early pieces turned on a mandrel lathe can be recognized by the wide, deep concentric lines cut into their outer surfaces. As machine-powered lathes were developed in the nineteenth century, the cooper's hand was replaced by a locking device that held the cutting tools. As a result, later work shows a pattern of tightly drawn and very even concentric circles, a consistency that can be achieved only with mechanization.

Various wooden storage containers, particularly boxes, are of great importance to collectors. At one time, the making of such containers was a highly specialized craft. "Wet," or "tight," coopers made kegs and casks for liquids. "Dry," or "slack," coopers produced barrels for bulk commodities such as flour or sugar. There were even "butt" coopers to make whiskey barrels and hogsheads and "rundlet" coopers to turn out small kegs and water flasks. There were also those artisans who manufactured boxes. Because their technique consisted of several rather simple stages, it was the first area of the craft to be handled in something akin to modern production-line methods. A box top was cut, usually from pine, by use of a pattern, or template. Sides were formed from a single, thin, flexible strip of wood, known today as veneer, butted up against the edges of the top; the ends of the piece were then usually overlapped, cut off straight up and down, and nailed into place. Common round cheeseboxes of the type still manufactured are good examples of this method. Earlier specimens might be joined to top and bottom with tiny wooden pegs, and the side fastenings would also be pegs or copper brads; factory-made boxes of the late nineteenth and early twentieth centuries will be fastened only with tiny wire nails or glue. By 1850, vast numbers of boxes were being made, often by women, in small shops throughout the land. The operators worked by the piece, usually being paid three to seven cents per hundred.

Though made in basically the same way, there is a second type of box that varies from the type just described: instead of being cut off vertically at the veneer joint, one end of the thin panel is cut into triangular "fingers"; these in turn are either inserted into holes previously cut in the veneer or tacked into place. Such containers often are extremely well made and have for many years been spoken of as "Shaker boxes." There is no doubt that Shaker craftsmen did make such boxes, since their labeled specimens are known, and they may well have developed or at least refined the technique. On the other hand, old advertisements make it clear that many non-Shaker coopers were quite capable of producing high-quality fingered boxes. As with "Shaker baskets," it is advisable to buy as Shaker only marked examples or those with a reliable history of origin in a Shaker community.

Age Signs
Since so much woodenware is of relatively recent origin, it is important to be able to judge the age of a given specimen. Fortunately, the characteristics of wood itself assist us in this process. As wood ages, it shrinks across the grain. In bowls this effect is especially noticeable, and old examples will often be oval rather than round. In boxes, the shrinking tops and bottoms draw away from the veneer sides. Barrel staves separate; knots in wood drop out, leaving holes in the surface. Aging wood also grows lighter and with handling takes on a velvet smooth quality hard to duplicate by other means. Look also for wooden pegs and crude wrought or cut nails—all long ago ceased to be employed in the manufacture of woodenware. Repairs can also be important clues to age. Wooden objects were once so important that when damaged they were restored rather than thrown out. The presence of a wrought-iron butterfly hinge to repair a cracked bowl or a piece of copper at the foot of a candleholder goes a long way to assure age and authenticity.

Boxes, barrels, and bowls in particular may bear internal clues to age and former use. Spice boxes still smell of their long-gone contents; grease bowls show a dark oil stain; milk containers are bleached white; butter bowls have a distinct fat line; and any vessel once used for chopping will bear across its interior a network of fine lines, indicating the relentless attack of the iron food chopper. Paint, where present, should be hard and spidery with age and worn away at points of contact, such as handles, bottoms, and lips. Of course, some of these marks of authenticity can be faked, but not all, and the presence of several in the same piece is a strong indication that you have found a fine, old piece of woodenware.

Certain items indicate their antiquity by form alone. Few salts, inkwells, noggins, or tankards were produced in wood after 1850, so for these and other archaic items there exists a certain built-in guarantee of age.

Burl
Certain trees, particularly ash, elm, and maple, produce large protuberances on their trunk and limbs when attacked by insect pests. The grain in such growths, instead of running in straight lines, becomes convoluted. Since fracture in wood occurs along the grain, the twisted interior of a burly piece makes it extremely durable. It also takes a high polish and shows an attractive grain. Both Indians and the early settlers were drawn to such wood. They burned and gouged out the interiors of burl blocks to make massive mixing and eating bowls and laboriously whittled smaller pieces into cups, scoops, and plates. Since burl growth was never common and is, moreover, extremely hard to work, pieces were never abundant and are rare today. This factor coupled with the beauty of highly polished burl has led to great collector enthusiasm. Few good specimens of American burl sell for less than a hundred dollars. There is a problem, however. The Europeans also worked in this wood, and some of their burl is now entering this country. Aside from the characteristics previously mentioned for distinguishing foreign treen, it should be noted that most of the nondomestic ware is of oak, a wood whose burly form was rarely if ever employed here.

Decoration and Marking
As in other areas of antiques, decoration enhances the value of treen. Most wooden objects were left in the natural state or, at most, varnished or shellacked. Mortars, barrels, boxes, and the like were frequently given a solid coat of paint on the exterior. Red, gray, brown, green, and blue are the most common colors. Such examples are considered more desirable; and the addition of decorative motifs—bands or floral patterns of a contrasting color—further enhances the quality of a piece.

Early specimens, particularly those from Pennsylvania and New England, may show carved or incised names and dates and chip-carved ornamental devices, such as stars, hex signs, and rosettes. Generally, such work indicates that the piece was made for presentation; as such it is unique. Names, where present, generally prove to be those of owners rather than makers; for the most part, it was not common for woodenware manufacturers to mark their wares. An exception is the box industry, in which mass producers during the second half of the last century often stenciled their names on their products. This was also frequently true of the makers of patent churns, washing machines, and similar household gadgets.

Decoration can be faked and pieces repainted. Fortunately, most such specimens are crudely done. New paint looks new. It does not show wear at contact points, and it does not have age cracks. Those who repaint also frequently touch up areas that would rarely have been painted originally, such as the interiors of bowls and scoops. Also, the new decoration may be of a type wholly unsuited to the piece or the area from which it comes.

Butter molds. *Left:* Maple, with leaf pattern, Maine, ca. 1900; $35–45. *Right:* Pine and maple, initial; New England, 19th century; $65–85. Butter prints and molds are among the most popular of all woodenware; those with an initial are rare. Piece at right probably bears initial of its owner.

Left: Butter mold, maple, with sheaf of wheat pattern; New Hampshire, early 20th century; $30–45. *Center:* Butter print pine; with pinecone and leaf pattern; Maine, 19th century; $50–65. *Right:* Butter mold, birch, with sheaf of wheat pattern; Massachusetts, early 20th century; $35–45.

Cake mold, pine, with eagle pattern; Pennsylvania, mid-19th century; $250–300. A well-designed piece of folk art.

Back row: Two boxed butter molds, pine; Massachusetts late 19th century. *Left:* $45–60. *Right:* $35–50. *Front row:* Butter prints. *Left:* Pine, with floral pattern; New York, 20th century; $25–35. *Center:* Maple, with pineapple pattern; Pennsylvania, mid-19th century; $100–150. Piece is highly valuable because of its uncommonly large size. *Right:* Pine, with pineapple pattern; Maine, late 19th century; $40–55.

196

Top: Sugar cutter, wrought iron and pine; New England, ca. 1850; $50–75. Sugar cutters were common until the introduction of granular sugar in the years following the Civil War. *Bottom:* Maple-sugar mold, pine; Massachusetts, early 19th century; $40–55.

Juice press, walnut, with wrought-iron accessories; Maine, 18th century; $175–225. An extremely early example of a common household item.

Maple-sugar molds. *Left:* Hinged, pine, with cow shape; Maine, ca. 1850; $70–85. *Center:* Pine, with heart shape; New Hampshire, ca. 1880; $50–75. *Right:* Pine, with fish shape; Maine, ca. 1850; $75–95. Molds such as the fish and cow are true folk art and should increase in value.

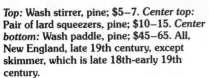

Top: Wash stirrer, pine; $5–7. *Center top:* Pair of lard squeezers, pine; $10–15. *Center bottom:* Wash paddle, pine; $45–65. All, New England, late 19th century, except skimmer, which is late 18th-early 19th century.

Cigar mold, pine; Connecticut, early 20th century; $15–25. A common and popular collector's object.

Sailor's wooden accessories. *Top left:* Weighted mallet, maple; $40–55. *Top right:* Needle box, pine and bamboo; $40–60. *Bottom left:* Fid, mahogany; $65–90. *Bottom right:* Box, turned pine, with scratch-carved decoration; $85–115. All, mid-19th century. Scratch decoration considerably enhances the value of any woodenware.

Top: Well-carved wash stirrer, pine; Ohio, late 19th century; $45–65. *Center:* Button-ended rolling pin, maple; Connecticut, 19th century; $30–45. *Bottom:* Hand-carved scoop, pine; New York, early 19th century; $25–35.

Left: Scraper, maple; New York, ca. 1920; $6–10. *Center:* Maul, pine and oak; New York, ca. 1910; $5–7. *Right:* Pestle, or masher, maple; New York, ca. 1920; $3–5. Good specimens of well-aged but not very old woodenware.

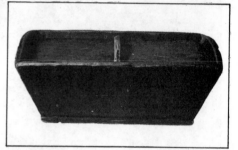

Dough box, pine, with old green paint and original cover, East, mid-19th century; $175–235.

Factory-made sander, turned and line-decorated pine; Maine, ca. 1875; $45–60. Wooden sanders are relatively rare.

Double lift-top box, pine; Pennsylvania, late 19th century; $45–75. Possibly used as a scouting box or carpenter's line-and-chalk holder. Good carving on handle enhances its value.

Stack of four grain measures, oak and pine; Daniel Cragin, active in Wilton, N.H., in the 1880s; $200–275 the set. Extremely large and small sizes are most valuable. Since the maker of grain measures was normally required by law to stamp his name on his products, it is possible to acquire complete marked sets.

Bottom left: Shaker box, pine and maple, salmon paint and black latticework decoration on cover; Ohio, mid-19th century; $300–450. Top center: Cheesebox, green paint; Maine, ca. 1910; $35–50. Top right: Cheesebox, gray paint; Maine, ca. 1890; $40–65. Both of pine and birch. Bottom right: Cheesebox, pine and hickory, old red paint; New York, ca. 1870; $75–100. Authenticated Shaker boxes such as the one illustrated command a premium among collectors.

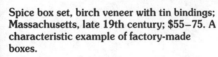

Spice box set, birch veneer with tin bindings; Massachusetts, late 19th century; $55–75. A characteristic example of factory-made boxes.

Left: Barber's box, pine; Pennsylvania, 19th century; $50–70. Right: Utility box, pine and horn; mid-19th century; $75–135. This box evidences extremely fine craftsmanship.

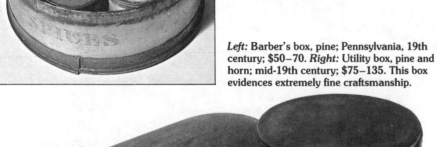

Left: Scoop, burl ash; New York, ca. 1840; $120–160. Center: Bride's box, pine and maple; Midwest, mid-19th century; $175–225. Right: Funnel, pine; New York, mid-19th century; $55–85.

199

Examples of common boxes readily available today. *Top:* Hinged wall box, old white paint; Maine, early 20th century; $25–35. *Center:* Slide-top candle box, oak; Massachusetts, late 19th century; $40–65. *Bottom:* Ballot box, pine in old red paint; Maine, late 19th century; $30–50.

Box in shape of a book, pine, old black and white paint; New York; $175–250. A mid-19th century whimsey, and quite rare.

Box, pine inlaid with white wood, natural finish, brass handle and latch and unusual molding; New York, ca. 1880; $125–170.

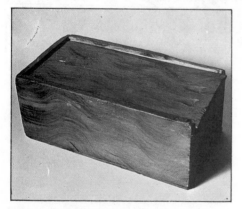

Slide-top candle box, pine, with smoked decoration on yellow; Maine, 19th century; $150–220. Painted boxes are in great demand today, and the more elaborate the decoration the higher the price.

Box, pine inlaid with birch, old black paint, diamond inlay in gold; Connecticut, ca. 1860; $135–200.

Lift-top box, pine, with burned decoration; New England, 20th century; $20–35. This decorative technique, known as pyrography, was a popular hobby during the period 1890–1920. Specimens are common but increasing in value. A coming area for collectors.

Cranberry rake, pine; Maine, late 19th century; $35–50. Tools of this sort are at present of little interest to most collectors and so may be obtained easily.

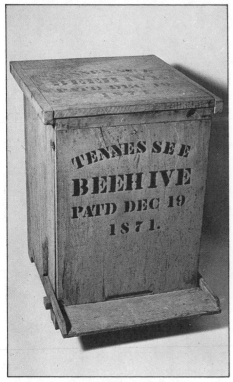

Patented beehive, pine, blue paint; Tennessee, ca. 1871; $75–110. A piece of this sort may vary greatly in value. It would have a substantially greater worth in Tennessee or vicinity than in other areas of the country.

Left: Grain shovel, pine; Massachusetts, ca. 1850; $100–145. *Center:* Line winder, pine and maple; Maine, ca. 1850; $70–95. Used by fishermen to dry line. *Right:* Early pestle, pine; Maine, ca. 1830; $40–60. Used in a crude samp mortar in an area where no grain mill was available.

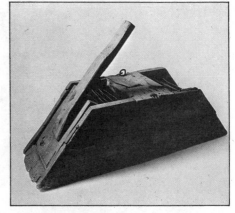

Rattrap, pine and iron; New England, late 19th century; $40–55.

Coffee mill, pine, with brass and iron fittings; New England, late 19th century; $50–75. Dovetails and brass make this a desirable example of a common item.

Bean-sorting rack, pine; Pennsylvania, late 19th-early 20th century; $30–55.

Meat grinder, pine and iron; New York, mid-19th century; $145–215.

Folding wash wringer, pine and cast iron; patented by the Larkin Company, New York, late 19th century; $75–105.

Churn, pine bound in iron, old gray paint over blue; Maine, ca. 1860; $165–225. Churns are popular collector's items.

Footed churn, pine; New England, late 19th century; $65–80. A homemade version of a popular factory-made churn.

Churn, pine in yellow paint; New England, late 19th century; $75–110. A good example of a commercially manufactured patented churn.

Cheese press, pine and oak; Pennsylvania, ca. 1850; $150–200. Dovetails and pegs indicate the handmade nature of this early press.

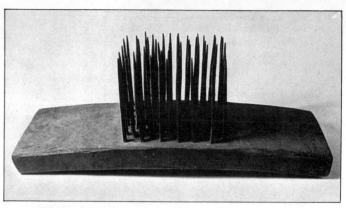

Flax hatchel, oak with wrought-iron spikes; Maine, early 19th century; $65–90. An unusual example; good body shape and fragments of flax still caught in the teeth.

Flax hatchel, maple with cut nails; New England, mid-19th century; $40–55. This piece has an unusual cant to the body.

Flax wheel, pine and maple, unpainted; Maine, ca. 1850; $180–235. A good example in working order.

Spinning wheel, pine and maple; New England, late 19th century; $250–320. Graceful lines and good condition in a popular object.

Flax wheel, pine, ash, and birch, blue with red and white trim; Iowa, dated 1863; $275–375. Signed and dated spinning and flax wheels are the top of the line in this field.

Swift, birch and maple; Maine, late 19th century; $90–125. Few pieces of woodenware can boast of the sculptural quality possessed by the swift, a simple device for holding and measuring yarn. Decorated specimens often sell for several hundred dollars, but a simple piece such as this goes for considerably less.

Yarn winder, oak and pine; New Hampshire, ca. 1830; $50–70. Serving the same purpose as a swift but lacking its adjustability, the yarn winder was a crude but often attractive device.

Clock reel, pine and maple; New York, ca. 1850; $85–145. Another spinner's measuring device of attractive shape. Any decoration would enhance its value.

Amish sewing box, pine, old red and brown paint; mid-19th century; $205–265. A simple Pennsylvania form.

Left: Shaker-made spool rack, birch; $125–165. Holes in rack once contained pegs to hold spools. *Right:* Tiny mirror, turned birch; $75–105. Both, New England, mid-19th century.

Left: Tape loom, pine and oak; Massachusetts, ca. 1830; $75–115. Small hand looms of this sort were used to make suspenders or decorative braid. *Right:* Bucket for carrying water or milk, pine and hickory; 19th century; $60–85.

Left: Canteen, hickory and pine; ca. 1850; $90–115. Canteens are generally early since they were soon replaced by tin or glass containers. *Right:* Flour or sugar storage bucket, pine and maple; ca. 1900; $30–45. Storage buckets of this sort are frequently refinished and used for storing magazines. Both, Maine.

Well bucket, pine bound with iron; New Hampshire, late 19th century; $75–100.

Storage buckets; New England, late 19th century. *Left:* Old yellow paint; $50–70. *Right:* Old red paint; $45–60. Original color adds value to pieces such as these.

Shaker-made firkin, or cask, in pine, hickory, and birch; Massachusetts, late 19th century; $265–355. A fine example of Shaker craftsmanship.

Left: Knife box, pine, old blue paint; Massachusetts, ca. 1870; $35–50. *Center:* Water barrel or keg, oak, old green paint; New Hampshire, ca. 1860; $55–70. *Right:* Mortar and pestle, pine; Maine, early 19th century; $45–65.

Grease bucket, staved pine bound in iron, old blue paint; Vermont, ca. 1850; $135–200.

Storage bucket, pine bound in iron, old blue-green paint; New York, ca. 1860; $75–110.

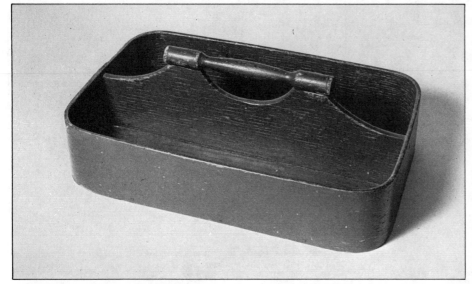

Shaker knife box, pine and birch, old red paint; Maine, late 19th century; $75–100. Boxes of this sort were made and sold commercially by the Shakers at the end of the 19th century. They are not uncommon, but like all Shaker items, they are costly.

Knife box, pine, dovetailed, with cut-out heart and old yellow paint; Pennsylvania, ca. 1850; $240–310. A top-quality piece.

207

Turned wooden plate, pine; New England, ca. 1830; $100–145. Treen plates are getting harder and harder to find.

Unusually large pie peel, pine; New England, ca. 1870; $75–95.

Left: Single-handled rolling pin, maple; New York, ca. 1880; $15–25. *Top right:* Breadboard, pine; New York, ca. 1900; $10–20. *Bottom right:* Mixing bowl, bird's-eye maple; early 20th century; $45–70. Attractive wood like bird's-eye maple adds to the value of otherwise routine items.

Left: Mortar and pestle, lignum vitae; Maine, ca. 1860; $60–85. *Right:* Unusually large mixing bowl (30″ diameter), pine; Maine, ca. 1880; $95–145. Large size or odd shape is a plus in bowls.

Unusual oval chopping bowl, pine; New Hampshire, ca. 1860; $125–165. Butter paddle, maple; $8–15.

Checkerboard, pine; New York, late 19th-early 20th century; $75–100. An example of playing boards often made by hand.

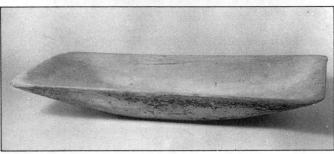

Very large chopping bowl (32″ x 17″), pine, old green paint on exterior; $185–225. A very fine shape.

Watch box, walnut and pine; New England, ca. 1800; $450–600. A Federal style piece dating from the days when the master of the house often owned the only timepiece and it might be used as a clock when not on his person. A very rare specimen.

Two crude bootjacks, pine; New York, late 19th-early 20th century. *Top:* $20–35. *Bottom:* $15–25. Example at top has been carved to take advantage of natural form of root.

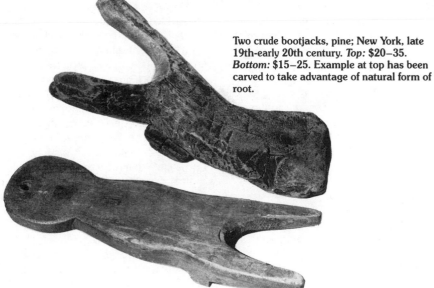

II.
BASKETRY

It has sometimes mistakenly been assumed that the colonists learned basketmaking from the American Indians, but such is clearly not the case. Basketmakers were common in Europe and the Far East long before Columbus, and old records indicate that they were among the earliest arrivals on these shores. Of course, since both settlers and natives knew the art of basket weaving, there was a certain interchange of technique and style between them. Today, many professional basketmakers in the United States are of Indian descent.

At present, the most common woven basketry form is some variation of the basket itself; but surviving examples indicate that at one time the technique was used to produce a greater variety of forms—such as fish traps, funnels, and cribs.

As recently as five years ago, baskets, except for the very unusual ones, were a glut on the antiques market. Today, all that has changed, and the market continues to rise. However, the field is still open, and good pieces can be found at country auctions, yard sales, and in shops. Prices vary greatly, but it is still possible to spend no more than a few dollars for a good specimen.

The serious collector of baskets must view his avocation in a historical perspective rather different from that of other antiques. Few baskets are really old. Both material and construction make for a fragile container, one that was often put to hard use; consequently, many were long ago left bottomless in field or shed. Moreover, baskets are still being made. Great numbers were produced in Appalachia during the 1920s and 1930s. Baskets are still made there as well as in New Hampshire, Maine, and New Brunswick, where basketmakers, often of Indian extraction, turn out examples indistinguishable in style from those their ancestors made a century ago. Since few baskets are signed or dated, it is extremely difficult to determine just how old they are. But there are certain signs that do indicate age: abrasive wear on the bottom; natural darkening in color; holes, indicating brittle ends or sections that have snapped off over the years; and in baskets decorated with paint or dye, a mellowing or fading of color.

Baskets are basically homely, simple objects, and the wise collector will look not so much for great age, signatures, or dates, as for originality of style, excellence of technique, and a love of the craft manifested in a beautiful and useful form.

Splint Basketry
More than 50 percent of all old baskets on the market are made, at least in part, of splint—long, flat strips of oak, ash, or hickory. For many years, splint was produced by the laborious process of soaking logs, splitting them, and shaving them to size. Though some modern basketmakers still employ this method, most now use commercial splint, which is machine-cut into extremely thin pieces. The hand-cut variety may be recognized by its relative thickness (at least an eighth of an inch), the lack of uniformity—few strips are of the same width—and its rough texture, since the froe or drawknife used by the craftsman lacks the planing effect of the machine. The presence of hand-cut splint is some indication of age in a basket, since machined material was not widely available until the 1880s. If solid wood parts such as handle, ears, or rim show marks of a knife and handwork, one may assume a nineteenth- or early twentieth-century origin.

Most splint basketry is made in the crosshatch technique, in which the strips of splint are woven across each other at right angles, creating a checkerboard surface. Less common and therefore in a sense more desirable are items made in the hexagonal, or openwork, weave, in which the bands of splint cross each other at a forty-five-degree angle, creating six-sided openings in the surface. The hexagonal weave was used for baskets that required considerable drainage, such as fish, clam, or oyster carriers or cheese-drying baskets. Since there was relatively little need for this type, hexagonal baskets are comparatively rare.

Most splint baskets are unmarked. A few bear a name or signature, which is usually that of the owner rather than the maker—except for those made at the northeastern Shaker settlements in the nineteenth century, which were stamped with ciphers such as "Sabbathday Lake" or "Shaker." Unfortunately, the general interest in all things Shaker has led some people to label as Shaker any well-made basket that at all resembles known marked examples. A word to the wary here: there were many excellent non-Shaker basketmakers—indeed, hundreds—and their ware is frequently indistinguishable from that made at Shaker shops. Don't pay high prices for a "Shaker" basket unless it has a good mark or an authenticated history linking it to one of the sect's settlements.

By 1880, the invention of splint-cutting machines and wire staples had sparked the development of a thriving commercial basket manufactory. The bulk of the containers produced were for berries or vegetables; they are readily distinguished from handmade specimens by their wide, thin, machined splints and their wire staples, tacks, and handles. The earliest types may bear a stamped trademark.

Decoration of any sort, being relatively uncommon, especially in old pieces, adds interest to all kinds of baskets; it is most frequently seen on splint containers. The earliest decorative technique used was overall painting or staining in a solid color such as red, brown, blue, or green; a good coat of old, well-faded paint should double the price of any basket. Also much sought after is the so-called Indian decoration—colored circles, squares, stars, and the like applied to the natural surface by a stamp. In addition, commercial splint was frequently stained red, green, blue, or gold. Basketmakers might use stained splint in combination with the unstained to create a variety of color patterns.

Willow Basketry
The long slim shoots of the willow tree make an ideal basketry material. They are supple and over time more durable than splint. Willow containers are mentioned in eighteenth-century inventories, so there is no doubt that they have long been popular. Their greatest period of use, though, was in the late years of the last century. In the 1870s and 1880s, farmers in places such as the Finger Lakes region of western New York State began to cultivate purple and Caspian willow for sale to manufacturers, who ran the shoots through machines to produce a standard size and shape. The commercial willow was sold primarily to city basket weavers who used it in a variety of decorative ware, from

jardinieres and planters to hanging baskets, sconces, and bottle covers. Though a few unusual types, such as cradles, bonnets, and chicken-nesting boxes exist, willow has always been used chiefly for baskets and trays.

Some variation of the crosshatch weave is most common in willow baskets, but a number of other weaves were also used, and sometimes in the same piece. Current interest in willow basketry is not noticeably great. This is partly because so much of it is not old at all, perhaps thirty years at most. In addition, the forms are limited, and the baskets are difficult to distinguish from the willow or cut-reed baskets (a close relative) that are regularly imported from Asia.

Willow basketry is nevertheless a valid craft that has produced some attractive specimens. Look for the older pieces, which will show bottom wear and cracked strands and may appear in the natural brown wood, now weathered, rather than the dark brown stain and shellac so common in recent work. Heavy field baskets and old covered hampers are the most interesting forms. Occasional examples may be painted in a solid color; but since the material is not flat, they will rarely carry stamped or stenciled decoration. There are, however, some interesting small, handled baskets that bear floral designs carefully painted on by hand. These are of some age and though not uncommon are not yet much appreciated. They may well be the best buy in willow.

Willow, along with reed, splint, and rattan, was employed in the construction of the well-known Nantucket baskets. These are round or oval containers, generally with handles, that have been made on and near Nantucket Island, Massachusetts, since the time of the Civil War. They have several characteristics that appeal strongly to collectors: they are often marked with a maker's name and the date and place of manufacture. They are very well made and of a distinctive

type. Their tightly woven willow body rising from a block of wood at the center bottom is unique and assists in the identification of unmarked examples. So does the fact that the handles are set into metal rather than the usual wooden ears.

Nantucket baskets in good condition may sell for hundreds of dollars apiece, even though many of the most attractive ones were made only a few decades ago. Moreover, they are still being made for sale today. The danger of confusing the new with the old, and the serious possibility that the present craze—and inflated prices—for them will not continue much longer, mean that the collector of these baskets should proceed with great caution.

Straw Basketry

Straw—generally rye—was used in basketmaking by the German settlers of Virginia, Pennsylvania, Delaware, New Jersey, and Maryland. It was not woven but rather sewed in long strips and then coiled. Each successive round of straw was bound to the developing vessel by pieces of grass, thread, or string. The technique limited the product to round or oval shapes; and, as a result, the forms of straw baskets are rather restricted. Most common are small bread-raising baskets, covered hampers, and egg baskets. Less often seen are conical beehives known as skeps, grain sower's baskets, and winnowing trays.

Because of the nature of the material, decoration is limited. A few pieces are painted, but most are found in the natural color. Handles, hardware, or fastenings of any sort (other than the twine that binds the vessel together) are uncommon.

Pricing of straw baskets varies greatly. Their production was confined to a small section of the country, and in that area the supply is ample and prices moderate. In other locations where the supply is smaller, the demand for examples may drive prices up well above the average.

Miscellaneous Basket Types

Aside from the three major types of basketry, collectors may hope to encounter vessels made from materials found only in certain areas of the country. From the South come trays and baskets made from the needles of the Florida, or longleaf, pine. They are constructed in much the same manner as rye straw baskets and generally date from the present century. A typical type consists of a glass-covered tray about which the pine needles are woven, the tray itself containing seashells and a salutation such as "Greetings from Ft. Lauderdale."

In the Appalachian Mountains, honeysuckle vines, carefully cut and trimmed, have served in the construction of sturdy sewing and storage hampers. Porcupine quills were also employed in that region to make attractive baskets, which were offered to tourists and have, as a result, been dispersed throughout the country.

Throughout the Northeast and along the Great Lakes, several types of long-leafed swamp grass have been used to make the so-called sweet grass baskets. The grass is braided and coiled, often quite intricately, resulting in an extremely sophisticated basket type. Most such baskets were made by women, and most were small, no more than a couple of inches high. Miniature baskets, which were sometimes made also in willow or splint, are now among the most popular items in the antiques field; a tiny basket will often sell for several times the price of its brother of normal size.

In the Midwest, corn shucks have served as basketmaking material. Loosely woven, they may form a bread plate or fruit-drying tray, or they may be coiled into an airy storage hamper. In Indiana, they were even made into horse collars. Unfortunately, most such items were not highly prized and were discarded as soon as they had to be replaced. As a result, only a limited amount of corn-shuck basketry is to be found today.

Swing handle splint market basket; Massachusetts, ca. 1880; $125–175. A classic example of the well-formed, completely handmade vessel so popular with collectors. Note the hand-carved ears and handle.

Splint market basket; Maine, ca. 1900; $50–70. A completely hand-finished basket in a common form.

Splint market or school basket; New Hampshire, ca. 1910; $75–95. A later basket of machine-cut splint in a form most popular with collectors, many of whom use them for handbags.

Splint field baskets. *Left:* Round; Maine, ca. 1900; $45–60. *Right:* Square; New Hampshire, ca. 1900; $50–70. Baskets of this sort are very common. They served both to carry produce from the field and to transport it to market.

Splint egg baskets; New Hampshire, ca. 1900; $70–95. A good basket made from machine-cut splint.

Small kidney-shaped basket with handles; East, 20th century. *Left:* Splint; $70–100. *Right:* $50–65. Sweet grass and splint.

Splint baskets with handles; late 19th century. *Left:* Nantucket style; New England; $115–165. *Center:* Swing handle; New England; $135–185. *Right:* Kidney shape; Southeast; $75–110.

Splint and iron-wire oyster or clam basket; Pennsylvania, ca. 1880; $100–130. The wire bottom is unusual.

Splint field basket; New Hampshire, ca. 1890; $80–115. A particularly strong example of a common type widely used on eastern farms.

Early splint field basket; New England, ca. 1870; $75–105. An extremely well-formed basket similar to those made in the Shaker shops.

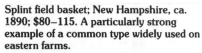

Splint wool basket; Southeast, late 19th century; $210–270. Footed baskets of this sort were often used to dry dyed wool.

Large splint wool-storage basket; New York, early 20th century; $65–85. The variation in form from top to bottom is skillfully done.

Splint drying baskets; Connecticut, ca. 1880. *Top:* 13″ x 22″; $80–120. *Bottom:* 4″ x 12″; $60–85. Baskets of this nature were used to dry sliced apples and other fruit. They are fragile and seldom found, particularly in the larger sizes.

Small, rough splint berry basket, 4″ x 4″; New England, late 19th century; $50–70. The forerunner of the machine-made berry basket.

Covered splint goose-feather basket; Maine, ca. 1920; $135–185. Unusual form and good size make this a most desirable item.

Extremely large splint storage basket with cover, 40″ high; Maine, ca. 1920; $150–190. Large baskets are always choice. The use of red, green, and yellow dyed splint in this piece enhances its already substantial value.

Splint sifter, possibly used in shelling beans or peas; Pennsylvania, late 19th century; $65–80.

Rare splint nose basket used for feeding livestock; New York, late 19th century; $175–235. Among the hardest to find of all basket forms.

Splint fish or eel trap; New England, 19th century; $200–250. Another extremely uncommon piece of basketry.

Very early handmade splint creel; East, ca. 1870; $75–115.

Uncommon splint pigeon basket; New Jersey, 19th century; $90–130. Pigeons were released from such baskets at pigeon shooting contests.

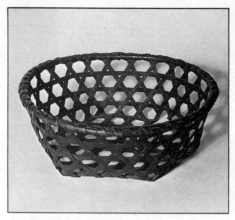

Splint cheese or field basket, hexagonal weave; East, late 19th–early 20th century; $175–250.

Fine splint table baskets, hexagonal weave; Connecticut, 20th century. *Top:* 140–190. *Bottom:* $75–105. Late but interesting and well-woven pieces.

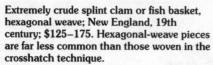

Extremely crude splint clam or fish basket, hexagonal weave; New England, 19th century; $125–175. Hexagonal-weave pieces are far less common than those woven in the crosshatch technique.

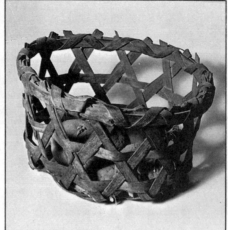

Splint cheese basket, hexagonal weave; New England, late 19th century; $250–300.

Early factory-made splint field basket; Ohio, late 19th century; $55–70. An interesting version.

Painted splint baskets. *Left:* Loom basket, old white paint; Maine, ca. 1910; $45–60. Loom baskets were used to hold a weaver's thread bobbins. In the 20th century, the form was modified to serve as a brush and comb holder. *Right:* Field basket, orange paint; New York, ca. 1880; $65–95.

Factory-made splint field basket with handle; 20th century; $35–55. A type not yet of much interest to collectors, though it has good form.

Commercially cut splint baskets with red and green banding; New England, early 20th century. *Left:* Table basket; $30–40. *Right:* Market basket, with fine carved handles; $65–95.

Machine-cut splint storage baskets with interwoven red and blue bands; New England, early 20th century. *Left:* $45–60. *Right:* $65–85.

Left: Cut splint work basket with handles and Indian decoration in red; $90–130. Indian decoration, applied with sponge or corncob, adds to value of any basket. *Right:* Small splint knickknack basket; $20–35. Both, New England, early 20th century.

Well-made commercially cut splint work basket; early 20th century; $75–100. The sweet-grass rim indicates a New England origin.

Factory-cut splint table or work basket with Indian decoration in red; New York, ca. 1910; $75–100.

Left: Elaborate splint sewing basket, red and blue stain; Maine, ca. 1930; $30–45. The twisted splint decoration is typical of Maine Indian work. *Right:* Splint market basket, New Hampshire, ca. 1920; $15–25.

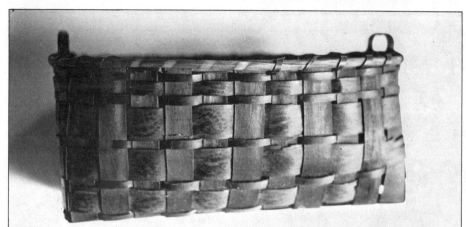

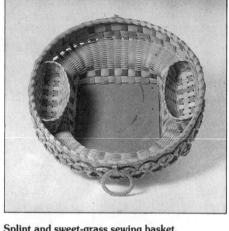

Splint and sweet-grass sewing basket, decorated with red-stained splint; Maine, ca. 1930; $65–90. Interior compartments are unusual in basketry. A choice item.

Splint storage baskets; Maine, ca. 1920. *Left:* With stained splint decoration; $25–45. *Right:* $20–35. Late, factory-made baskets of machine-cut splint; both probably once had lids.

Splint and sweet-grass basketry; Maine, 20th century. *Rear:* Unusual tray, 4″ x 8″; $45–65. *Left:* Covered box, 3″ x 4″; $25–35. *Center:* Basket with handle, 2″ diameter with pink-stained splint; $20–30. *Right:* Basket with handle, 3″ diameter; $30–50.

Splint and sweet-grass basketry; Maine, 20th century. *Left:* Covered sewing basket, 8″ diameter, 4″ high; $25–40. *Center:* Table basket, 7″ diameter, 8″ high; $15–25. *Right:* Covered pin box, 3″ diameter; $30–45. The combination of braided sweet grass and machine-cut splint is typical of 20th-century Indian baskets from Maine and New Brunswick.

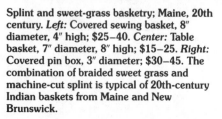

218

Splint and sweet-grass basketry; Maine, 20th century. *Left:* Miniature urn with handles, 4″ high; $15–20. *Back right:* Urn with handles, 9″ high; $25–40. *Front right:* Basket with handles, 3″ diameter, red and blue stain; $20–30.

Willow and sweet-grass box with cover and feet; New Hampshire, late 19th century; $45–70. An unusual example of a Victorian sewing or whatnot box.

Splint and sweet-grass basketry; Maine, 20th century. *Rear:* Barrel-shaped storage basket, 16″ high; $40–55. *Left:* Covered box; $20–35. *Right front:* Tapered, covered sewing basket; $25–40.

Splint and sweet-grass basketry; Maine. *Left:* Covered box; $17–23. *Center:* Hat-shaped box with pink splint ribbon; $25–32. *Right:* Basket-shaped pincushion; $13–18. 20th-century basketry whimsies are common.

Splint and sweet-grass basketry; Maine, 20th century. *Left:* Handled basket showing unusual skill in weaving of grass; $25–40. *Center:* Large tray with handle, 10″ in height and diameter; $30–45. *Right:* Fan; $20–30.

Splint and sweet-grass basketry; Maine, 20th century. *Back left:* Covered basket, banded in pink, 4″ high; $25–40. *Front left:* Fancy basket with handle, 1½″ high; $15–22. *Back right:* Covered box, 3″ high; $25–37. *Front right:* Urn, red, 3″ high; $15–25. Miniatures are becoming increasingly popular with collectors. Smaller items such as these are an excellent investment.

Willow field basket; New York, 20th century; $15–30. A form still made, of small interest to collectors.

Willow clothes or field basket; Midwest, 20th century; $10–20. A utilitarian piece in a style still seen. Handles are constructed as an integral part of basket.

Willow market basket with cover; New Hampshire, early 20th century; $60–85. A particularly well-shaped example in this medium.

Willow market or field basket with handle; Midwest, late 19th century; $40–65. Good weaving and old red paint make this a desirable example.

Covered willow sewing basket; New York, late 19th century; $50–75. An example of good willow basketry.

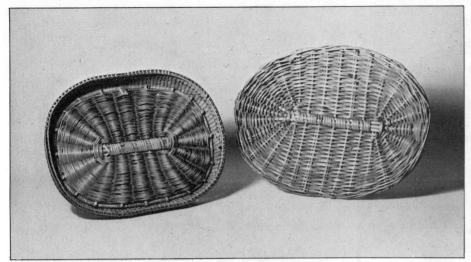

Willow basketry; New York, 20th century.
Left: Serving tray; $10–17. *Right:* Basket
cover; $3–7.

Willow storage basket; Southeast, late 19th-
early 20th century; $10–20. An unusual form
in crude weave.

Willow openwork serving or table basket;
20th century; $20–35. The sort of willow
basketry practiced in children's camps.

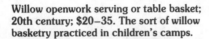

Willow and iron animal carrier; early 20th
century; $85–115. The forerunner of the
modern cat and dog carriers.

Willow backpack or Indian basket;
Pennsylvania, late 19th-early 20th century;
$75–105. Such baskets are still often made
by hand.

221

Extremely large willow traveling case, 3' x 3'
New York, late 19th century; $90–140. Very
few of these old suitcases have survived.

Painted willow; Pennsylvania, 20th century.
Left: Silent butler, pink; $7–10. *Right:*
Openwork flower basket, red; $30–40.

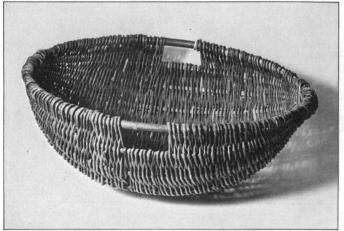

Split willow open-handled field basket;
Southeast, late 19th-early 20th century;
$110–140.

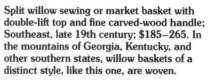

Split willow sewing or market basket with
double-lift top and fine carved-wood handle;
Southeast, late 19th century; $185–265. In
the mountains of Georgia, Kentucky, and
other southern states, willow baskets of a
distinct style, like this one, are woven.

Split willow market basket, wood handle;
Southeast, late 19th-early 20th century;
$95–120.

Willow and wood fruit-drying tray; New York, late 19th century; $75–110.

Rye-straw bread-raising basket; New Jersey, late 19th century; $30–45. Rye-straw basketry was practiced primarily in Pennsylvania, New Jersey, and Virginia.

Rye-straw field basket; Pennsylvania, late 19th century; $175–250. Extremely well made and rare.

Large rye-straw beehive or skep; Pennsylvania, 19th century; $125–185.

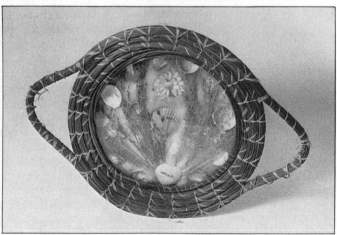

Rye-straw and wood beehive or skep; Pennsylvania, late 19th century; $90–120.

Pine-needle tray decorated with shells and dried vegetation; Florida, 20th century; $20–35. Souvenir pieces like this were made mostly in Florida, though they were often stamped with the names of towns in other states.

223

12

LIGHTING DEVICES

In frontier settlements, from the earliest days until well into the nineteenth century, firelight was often the only artificial light that was available. Though farm people did most of their work between the hours of dawn and dusk—a practice that continues into our own time—daylight hours seldom allowed enough time to complete the daily chores. Houses were poorly lit by their few small windows, but wood was plentiful, and often a fire was kept burning at all hours—winter and summer—to cook the meals and warm the water for washing, as well as to provide light and heat.

In new settlements in heavily forested areas, firelight was supplemented by the burning of pitch-pine knots, slivers of wood that gave off a bright though brief flame. As early as 1642, the author of *New England's Prospect* noted that

> Out of the pine is gotten the candle wood that is much spoke of, which may serve as a shift among poore folks, but I cannot commend it for singular good because it drippeth a pitchy kind of substance where it stands.

Pine knots—or light wood, as it was called in the southern colonies—were burned on the hearth or in fire pans, wrought-iron basins that were set in a corner of the fireplace. For outdoor work or for fishing, open-work iron baskets called cressets were filled with blazing knots. They made a bright light but a dangerous one and could not be used indoors.

Though pitch pine was used for lighting as late as the mid-eighteenth century, the devices used in firing it were so few and so crude that associated antiques either are uncommon or have gone unnoticed. A few fire pans are in museum collections, but they are seldom seen elsewhere. Much the same may be said of cressets.

The common cattail, or swamp rush, which grows in damp areas, was another crude early device used to provide interior light. It was prepared by stripping part of the outer bark from the rush; the pithy heart thus exposed would then be soaked in tallow or grease and, once dry, burned in a wrought-iron cliplike holder. The rushlight holder was usually mounted on an iron tripod or a wooden block. Because the light generated in this manner was both uncertain and smoky, pine knots were generally preferred in

this country, though rushlight was widely used in Europe. Rush holders are frequently seen at antiques shows and museums, but it is likely that most have been brought over from the Continent; none are known to bear the mark of an American smith.

Candleholders

Both knot and rush were regarded by the settlers as little more than temporary expedients to light their homes. Almost from the beginning, the Massachusetts Bay Colony imported English candles, and as soon as enough tallow became available from wild or domestic animals, the domestic manufacture of candles began. In every home and until well into the nineteenth century, fall was the traditional period for candlemaking—as it was for slaughtering of livestock, whose fat provided the necessary tallow. To make the candles, the tallow was mixed with water in great iron pots, boiled, and then skimmed until of a suitable consistency. Candlewicks were prepared by attaching loosely spun hemp, tow, or milkweed cotton (known as silk down) to short sticks. The wicks, hanging downward, were then dipped repeatedly into kettles of hot tallow and after each dipping were allowed to dry, so that layers of fat built up successively until the desired thickness was achieved. The process was not as lengthy as it might sound, and a rapid worker might turn out two hundred candles in a day.

Candle molds were also employed, both by the homemaker and by itinerant candlemakers. These molds, of tin, pewter, or pottery, were set in a frame accommodating any number from a single stick to eight dozen. Wicks were inserted into the individual tubes, and boiling tallow was poured in; when it cooled, the finished candles were removed. There was a commercial candle manufactory in Massachusetts as early as the 1750s, and gradually the chores of candlemaking were taken over by other such factories. The candle sellers who once traveled from farm to farm with their tin molds now carried only the finished product.

Candles were made of substances other than tallow. Beeswax was employed to a limited extent, particularly for church lighting; and in New England the pale green, sweet-smelling bayberry candle was always a favorite. It was a chore to pick

the tiny berries, but their wax could be dipped or molded into candles that were harder than tallow and would not melt during the hot summer months; nor did they smoke. Even better candles could be made from spermaceti, a waxy substance obtained from the head of the sperm whale. It was not common, though, and candles so manufactured were too expensive for the average citizen.

Candle-associated antiques are of great interest to collectors. Molds come in a variety of shapes and tube quantities. The most common were made of tin and sell today for about six dollars per tube. Pewter and earthenware molds are much more expensive, especially the marked pottery ones, such as those made by the potter Alvin Wilcox, of Westmoreland, New York. Cylindrical tin candle boxes with lift tops, made to hang on a wall, are popular, particularly if tole-decorated. There are also numbers of wooden slide-top boxes, which were intended for shipment or storage of larger quantities of candles. These vary greatly in price depending upon age and decoration: late factory-made dovetailed examples may be purchased for a few dollars, while a fine old grain-painted piece may go for several hundred.

Tin tinderboxes were essential to the lighting of fires and candles, and these flat, round containers are still occasionally seen. If complete, they will contain flint, steel, and a piece of tinder (usually scorched linen). They are seldom decorated, and their identity often goes unrecognized.

The most popular of all candle antiques is the candlestick or candleholder. It comes in many shapes and may be made of wood, pottery, iron, tin, pewter, brass, silver, or gold. As one might suspect, given the flammable nature of the candle, metal is the preferred material.

The first device made to hold candles was a pointed piece of iron onto which the base of the candle was stuck. It was soon replaced by a hollow tube—the candlestick—and the only significant modification since has been the development of the ejector, a device for elevating the candle as it burns down in order to ensure complete use. Probably the most familiar type of candlestick is the so-called hog scraper, a tin or iron tube holder with a sliding ejector on the side and a wide, round base that was supposedly used for removing the bristles from freshly killed hogs. Hog scrapers have attracted a lot of attention lately. Many are signed by their makers, and these go for thirty-five to forty-five dollars each. The addition of a decorative brass band around the middle of the stick—called a wedding ring—ensures an even higher price.

Tube-type candlesticks vary in height from three to sixteen inches. Some were fitted with floor stands; these metal or wood candlestands, some of which could be adjusted in height, seem to have been quite popular during the eighteenth and early nineteenth centuries. Chandeliers were introduced in the mid-seventeenth century and were made in some number; they were used most often in churches, taverns, and public halls. A good, early wood and tin or iron chandelier with original paint commands a high price in today's market. Unfortunately, though, the demand exceeds the supply, and reproductions are common. Most are advertised as such by their manufacturers, but once a replica has changed hands a few times, its origin may become obscured. This is particularly the case with those pieces that are copied directly from known colonial examples.

Old iron candleholders and stands have also been imported from southern Europe. Though some of them are too ornate to pass for native fabrications, most are simple enough in form to look uncomfortably like something that might have been made in Massachusetts or Pennsylvania. Let the buyer beware.

Lamps

The concept of the oil lamp, a hollow receptacle in which an inflammable fluid is burned, is very old. Though they varied considerably in design, all ancient lamps consisted of a fluid-holder, usually round or oval, and a wick of cloth or tow. One end of the wick was usually supported on a raised shelf on the nose of the vessel to keep it free of the fuel. Both hanging and standing lamps are found, some with elaborate decoration. The most common are the oddly named Betty lamp and its more complex sister, the crusie, a Scottish variation that incorporated a second lamp and wick below the first; unburned oil dripped from the upper into the lower reservoir and was there consumed rather than being wasted.

Both types of lamp were popularized here by German and Swiss settlers, who brought the first ones with them and were soon manufacturing their own, generally of wrought iron or steel. Makers, particularly in Pennsylvania, tended to mark their lamps, and such names as Hurxthal, Derr, and Eby are prized among collectors. Lamps of this sort were also made in red earthenware, though they are far less commonly found in that medium than in metal.

As is true of candleholders, metal Betty and crusie lamps have been imported in quantity. Since the imports closely resemble native examples, unmarked lamps must be regarded with suspicion. Again, a reliable dealer is the best protection.

Though widely used for hundreds of years, the various open lamps shared common defects. They did not give off a strong light, and they wasted fuel. This problem demanded an answer; and in 1787, England's John Miles supplied one with the whale-oil, or agitable, lamp. This consisted of a sealed reservoir with a tightly fitting burner, which had two or more metal tubes to hold the wicks. The new lamp burned whale oil, which was then becoming available in quantity. The lamp was cheap, clean, and attractive. Early specimens were made of tin, brass, or pewter, but with the introduction of mechanical pressing in the 1820s, pressed glass became the favorite material. Such important American manufacturers as the New England Glass Company and the Sandwich Glass Company produced vast quantities of whale-oil lamps in a variety of patterns, all of which are known and avidly collected at present.

Actually, the whale-oil lamp was a derivation of the Argand lamp, patented in 1783 by the Swiss Amie Argand. This controlled-air-draft lamp had a vertical tubular burner containing a single tubular wick that was hollow in the center. The heat of the flame created a draft in the center of the wick, which increased combustion and, consequently, the amount of available light. Argand lamps also used whale oil.

By the middle of the nineteenth century, whales were becoming scarcer and the cost of whale oil was mounting. One Isaiah Jennings had invented a "burning fluid," which consisted of alcohol and turpentine, later modified to eliminate the alcohol; the final product, known as camphene, was widely used in the 1840s and 1850s. The results were sometimes disastrous. Camphene was extremely volatile, and fire and

explosion were visited upon its users. Modifications in the design of camphene lamps decreased the risks somewhat, but the problem was not resolved until the introduction of refined petroleum, or kerosene, in 1854.

The kerosene lamp made obsolete all that had come before. The basic principle, an air draft, was not unlike that of the Argand lamp, but the safety and low cost of fuel (particularly after the opening of the western Pennsylvania oil fields in the late 1850s) made it attractive to everyone. Kerosene lamps are still manufactured today, and in principle they have changed little. They have been made of several metals as well as of glass. Most popular with modern collectors are the "gone-with-the-wind" and Aladdin lamps, both of which have brass or white metal bases; the former boasts one or two large, round, hand-painted ball-shaped shades. These lamps are popular enough to have been reproduced, but many original examples are also available. Gone-with-the-wind lamps may sell for over a hundred dollars apiece, while Aladdin lamps are less expensive. They may be found both in the original nickel finish and in brass from which the nickel has been stripped.

Pressed-glass kerosene lamps are by far the most common. They arrived on the scene after most of the great pressed-glass manufactories had closed their doors, but enough are found in attractive patterns to keep enthusiasts busy. Prices are generally reasonable, averaging eight to twelve dollars for all but the choicest pieces.

Lanterns evolved in basically the same manner as lamps. Early specimens burned candles; then whale oil, camphene, and kerosene had their turn. The first panes were of thin, shaved horn, followed by isinglass and, finally, glass. The so-called Paul Revere lantern, a cone-shaped device of tin with pierced decoration, is popular—and often reproduced—as are the very large early ship's and tower lamps. Among oil lanterns, the most interesting are the many different railroad lanterns manufactured by Dietz and other producers. These are increasing in value, since they are sought by two groups, lighting collectors and railroad buffs.

Note: Other illustrations of lighting devices may be found in Chapter 6, "Silver and Pewter," and Chapter 7, "Copper and Brass."

Adjustable candlestand, wood and iron; New York, early 19th century; $600–750.

Left: Pricker-type candlestick, wrought iron; New York, late 18th century; $75–100.
Right: Standing or hanging candleholder, wrought iron; Pennsylvania, 18th century; $200–275.

Candle and rushlight holder, wrought iron; probably New England, late 18th-early 19th century; $260–340. These pieces are difficult to distinguish from European examples.

Very fine double candleholder with weighted base, tin and iron; New York, ca. 1820; $850–1,200. Pieces of this sort are rare and choice. *Hanging from center:* Candle snuffer, pewter; New England, 19th century; $60–90.

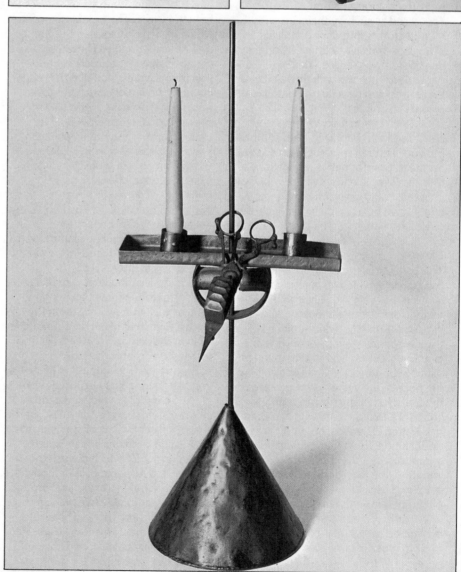

Candelabra, wrought iron; East, 19th century; $250–350. Pieces similar to this are being made today in southern Europe.

Pair of candelabra, tin; New England, mid-19th century; $275–360 the pair.

Hog-scraper push-up candlestick, iron, with so-called wedding-ring brass banding; New Jersey, 19th century; $135–175.

Left: Candleholder, tin; Pennsylvania, mid-19th century; $35–45. *Right:* Spiral candleholder, wrought iron; East, 19th century; $75–105.

Left: Snuffer tray, tin; New England, 19th century; $30–50. Candle snuffer, iron; New England; $45–60. *Right:* Push-up candlestick, tin; New England; $25–45.

227

Iron push-up candlesticks; New England, 19th century. *Left:* Wedding ring; $90–120. *Center:* Wrought iron, spiral shaft; $125–160. *Right:* Plain hog scraper; $35–55.

Chamber sticks, New England, 19th century. *Left:* Tin; $25–35. *Top center:* Brass; $65–80. *Bottom center:* Pewter; $90–110. *Right:* Brass; $55–70.

Simple candleholder, tin with glass insert; Midwest, late 19th-early 20th century; $25–40.

Candlestick pewter; New England, first half 19th century; $100–145. Like most American pewter, this piece is unmarked.

Candle lamp in style of kerosene lamp, tin; New York, 19th century; $55–80.

Left: Candleholder with drip pan, tin; Maine, 19th century; $40–65. *Center:* Kerosene lamp, tin and iron with brass fittings; New Hampshire, 19th century; $25–40. *Right:* Large candleholder, tin, with extinguisher and drip pan; Maine, possibly Shaker, 19th century; $75–110.

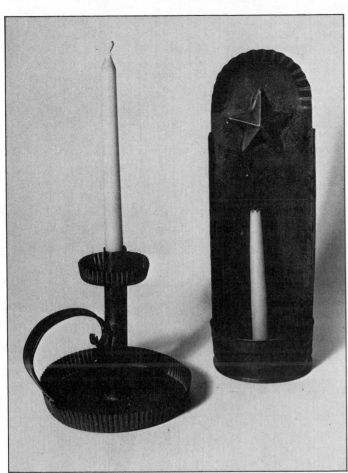

Left: Crimp-decorated candleholder with handle, tin; Maine, late 19th century; $45–70. *Right:* Candle sconce, tin, with stamped star decoration; New Hampshire, early 19th century; $250–325. Decorated sconces are not common.

Triple sconce, tin and iron; New York, early 19th century; $325–425.

Left and right: Pair of sconces, crimped tin; Maine, early 19th century; $275–375.
Center: Large sconce, crimped tin; Maine, 19th century; $220–290.

Very fine candle reflector, glass, mahogany and fruitwood inlay; New England, ca. 1800; $1,200–1,600.

Left: Candle lantern, tin and iron with punch decoration; Pennsylvania, early 19th century; $190–260. *Center:* Tin sconce with glass reflector; Massachusetts, first quarter 19th century; $310–390. *Right:* Candleholder, crimped tin; Maine, late 19th century; $35–60.

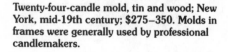

Twenty-four-candle mold, tin and wood; New York, mid-19th century; $275–350. Molds in frames were generally used by professional candlemakers.

Candle molds, tin; New England, 19th century. *Left to right:* $95–120; $80–100; $35–50.

Back left: Wall-hanging double match safe, tin, old black paint; $20–30. *Front left:* Pocket matchbox, tin; $15–25. *Center:* Pocket matchbox, tin with molded rim; $20–30. *Right:* Wall-hanging match safe, tole-decorated tin; $30–45. All, East, 19th century.

Two painted wall-hanging match safes, cast iron; late 19th century. *Left:* $25–35. *Right:* $30–45. Iron match safes were widely made in the Midwest.

Large wall-hanging match safe, tin; New York, 19th century; $15–25.

Wall-hanging candle box, tin; New England, mid-19th century; $250–325.

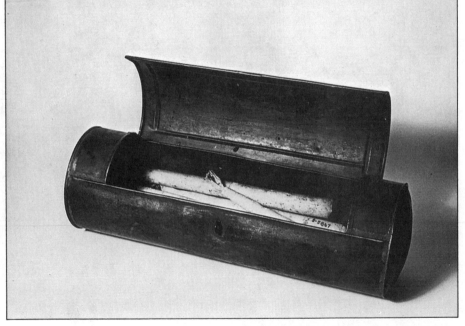

Tinderbox with candleholder, flint, and steel, tin; New York, early 19th century; $175–230.

Crusie lamp, wrought iron; New York early 19th century; $175–230.

231

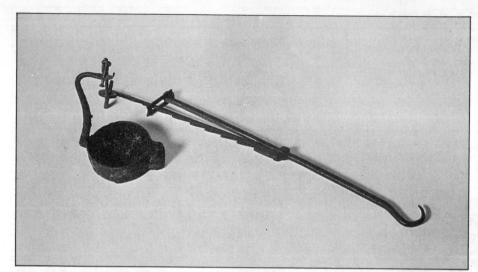

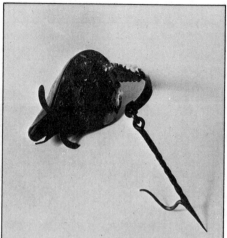

Crusie lamp, wrought iron with the early adjustable iron trammel; New England, late 18th-early 19th century; $360–440.

Betty lamp, wrought iron; Pennsylvania, early 19th century; $100–150. ▼

Left: Triple-burner fat lamp, tin; Pennsylvania, early 19th century; $150–200. *Right:* Double wall candleholder, toleware; East, mid-19th century; $125–155. Both are rare and possibly unique lighting devices.

Unusual hanging fat lamp, tin and brass; Connecticut, first half 19th century; $125–165.

Left: Fat lamp in unusual form, tin; East, early 19th century; $75–110. *Right:* Candleholder with matchbox attachment, tin; East, late 19th century; $100–135.

232

Left: Small camphene lamp, tin; Pennsylvania, mid-19th century; $45–65. *Right:* Fat lamp with handle, tin; East, early 19th century; $70–95.

Unusual fat lamp on stand, tin; New Jersey, early 19th century; $140–200.

Fat or whale-oil lamp on stand, tin; New England, first half 19th century; $175–240.

Tin lighting devices; East, mid- to late 19th century. *Left rear:* Kerosene lamp; $15–25. *Center rear:* Hanging fat lamp with pick; $60–85. *Right rear:* Parade torch; $50–75. *Front left:* Candle lamp; $65–105. *Front right:* Betty lamp with double reflectors; $90–135.

233

Two rare lighting devices. *Left:* Triple-burner camphene lamp, tin; New York, mid-19th century; $185–215. *Right:* Double-burner whale-oil lamp in sconce, tin; New England, ca. 1825; $180–230.

Reflector-mounted Argand lamp, tin; East, mid-19th century; $140–200. These lamps are uncommon.

Left: Tin candleholder; East, mid-19th century; $35–50. Iron snuffer; Pennsylvania, first half 19th century; $45–65. *Right:* Double-burner whale-oil lamp, tin; Massachusetts, ca. 1830; $85–125.

Double kerosene-lamp holder and reflector (lamps not shown), punch-decorated tin; Connecticut, mid-19th century; $175–225.

Very rare punch-decorated sconce with double burner whale-oil lamp, tin; New England; ca. 1830; $250–320.

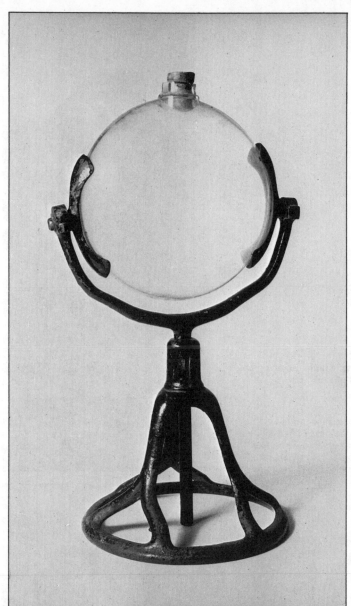

Lighting magnifier, cast iron and glass; Midwest, late 19th century; $45–65. This magnifier was filled with water to provide more light in a rural home.

Kerosene lamp with large reservoir, tin; Midwest, late 19th century; $35–60. Possibly used as a stove rather than for light.

Kerosene lamps, tin; Midwest, late 19th century. *Left:* $45–75. A homemade and possibly unique item. *Right:* $30–45.

Kerosene lamps, tin and glass; Midwest, late 19th century. *Left:* $20–30. *Right:* $25–40.

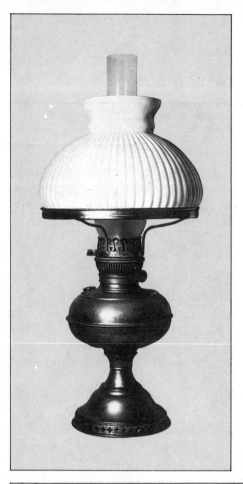

Attractive kerosene lamp, tin and glass; Maine, ca. 1870; $125–165.

Aladdin lamp, nickel-plated copper; Connecticut, late 19th century; $85–135. Lamps of this sort were very popular in late Victorian times and continue so today. Like this one, they are often electrified.

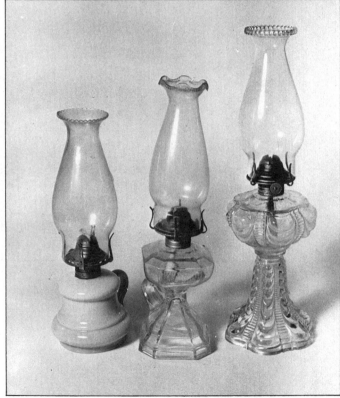

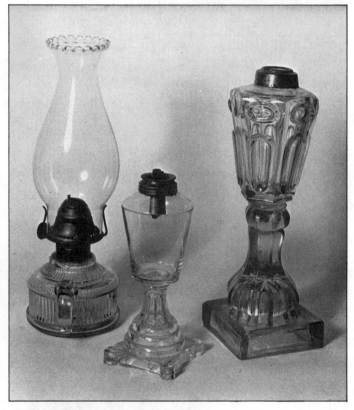

Pressed-glass kerosene lamps; New England, late 19th century. *Left:* Milk glass; $60–75. *Center:* Plain pressed; $25–45. *Right:* Lincoln drape pattern; $55–85.

Pressed-glass lamps; New England, 19th century. *Left:* Kerosene lamp, pattern glass; $40–65. *Center:* Whale-oil lamp with single burner; $85–135. *Right:* Whale-oil lamp; $80–120 (without burner).

Electric lamp, multicolored slag glass and white metal; East, 20th century; $400–650. Many glass lamps of this sort were made by Tiffany, and the general interest in Tiffany items has caused the prices of all such lamps to reach astronomical heights.

Electric counter lamp with stained-glass shade, designed as an advertising device for Whitman's Chocolates; 20th century; $350–450.

Electric lamp, pewter and slag glass; East, 20th century; $275–400. Another popular "new" antique.

Candle lantern of the sort commonly known as a Paul Revere lantern, punch-decorated tin; Pennsylvania, first half 19th century; $175–240. These lanterns are being reproduced.

Early candle lanterns; New England, late 18th-early 19th century. *Left:* Pierce-decorated with isinglass windows; $225–310. *Right:* Tin and glass; $150–210. Isinglass is rare in lanterns.

Hurricane lantern, tin and iron; New York, 19th century; $110–180.

Left: Dietz railroad kerosene lamp; Midwest, early 20th century; $30–45. *Center:* Barn or work lantern, sheet metal and glass; early 20th century; $25–40. *Right:* Candle lantern, punch-decorated tin; ca. 1850; $135–200. Both pieces at right are from New England.

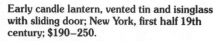

Candle lantern, tin and glass; Vermont, early 19th century; $220–310.

Early candle lantern, vented tin and isinglass with sliding door; New York, first half 19th century; $190–250.

Left: Candle lantern, tin and glass; Maine, ca. 1840; $180–240. *Center:* Wall-hanging match safe, cut and crimped tin; 19th century; $40–55. *Right:* Rare candle lantern, wood and glass; New Hampshire, mid-19th century; $250–350.

Double-candle lantern, tin and glass, black paint; New York, first quarter 19th century; $300–425. A rare and attractive lantern.

Kerosene barn lamp, tin and glass, black paint; New England, ca. 1880; $175–235.

Tiny house-shaped candle lantern, tole-decorated; New England, mid-19th century; $25–45.

Policeman's "bull's-eye" lantern with whale-oil burner, tin; New England, ca. 1850; $50–75.

Early kerosene railroad lantern, glass and sheet iron; Dressel, New York, first half 19th century; $75–110.

Dietz railroad lantern, glass and tin; East, or Midwest, early 20th century; $55–85.

Dietz kerosene railroad or construction lantern, sheet metal and glass; East, 20th century; $35–55.

Dietz railroad lantern, tin and colored glass; early 20th century; $50–80.

Kerosene dark lights in two sizes, tin, with original black paint; East, late 19th-early 20th century. *Left:* $35–50. *Right:* $50–$75.

13.
TOOLS

The collecting of tools has often been thought of as a particularly male pastime, probably because most of the objects sought are ones that have long been associated with such traditionally male occupations as carpentry, logging, and smithing. Until rather recently, interest was focused primarily on early hand-formed tools, those made by blacksmiths or in small two- or three-man shops during the period preceding the Civil War. However, it is now becoming fashionable to acquire factory-made objects of the late nineteenth and early twentieth centuries, such as those made by the Stanley Company and other early manufacturers.

There is no doubt that early tools have a charm and beauty exceeding that of later mass-produced wares. They were often made by, as well as for, the ultimate user and have a sense of personality—a decorative quality and a feeling of good workmanship—that is usually lacking in later production. On the other hand, there is some fascination in the complexity of the later pieces; and since they were produced in standardized forms, it is often possible to obtain complete sets of such tools as planes and chisels. The survival of several manufacturers' catalogs makes it possible to identify and date specimens with accuracy.

Tool collecting as a field is very broad. Carpenter's tools alone could occupy the collector for a lifetime. Axes are the choice items here, ranging from the hewing ax used to clear trees to the early and odd-shaped broadax with which the carpenter squared logs for house building. Like many tools, ax heads were hand-forged, and their wooden handles were made from patterns handed down from one generation to another. Several types of ax were used; there were also hatchets for shingling, lathing, and cooper's work.

Hammers are a second major category of carpenter's tools. Among them may be distinguished the ancient claw hammer, whose form can be traced back to Roman times, and the veneer hammer, as well as a variety of wooden mallets. All are relatively easy to find and are reasonably priced. Screwdrivers, braces, and bits are also common.

Perhaps the most popular of all carpenter's tools are planes. They exist in so many varieties that some enthusiasts limit their collections to them alone. Some planes are very small, and some are huge: the cooper's long jointer reaches a length of six feet; and the giant crown molding plane, which can cut a complete door- or window frame, requires two men for its operation. There were long planes called tryers, and jointers to smooth rough surfaces; rabbets to cut notches for the joining of cabinetry, and complex plow planes (most in demand) to cut a simple groove. Planes are for the most part relatively inexpensive.

Other carpenter's tools are less often seen, and their functions are sometimes little understood. The heavy adz, a flat-bladed tool, is used to smooth large surfaces such as floors; it is often mistaken for a hoe. The froe, used with a hammer to split shingles, looks like a crude knife. Scorpers, drawknives, and spokeshaves are all smoothing or finishing tools.

Less complex crafts employed a smaller variety of tools, and many of these items are as fascinating as they are rare. Loggers had felling axes, of course, but they also had the peavey—a device for pushing and pulling logs invented in the 1870s by a blacksmith named John Peavey—and the giant raft auger—five feet long and designed for drilling holes from a standing position. Loggers also employed many different kinds of chisels and the bucksaw.

The heart of the blacksmith's craft was his anvil, an instrument found in many variations. To hold and shape the hot iron, he also used hammers, chisels, tongs, and bits. The bellows to feed his fire might be four feet across; but the very few existing examples are rapidly finding their way into museum collections.

Wheelwrights made wagon and carriage wheels with the help of hammers and saws of various sorts. They also required the traveler, a wheel-shaped measuring device; the sturdy wooden wagon jack; and various awls, augers, and gouges to drill holes.

There were lesser-known crafts whose purpose and memory are today only dimly recalled. Farriers shoed horses and cared for their hooves with the help of chisels, pincers, and the odd-looking butteris, or hoof parer. Curriers owned a variety of knives and slickers with which they cleaned, scraped, and softened hides. Ice working as a craft no longer exists, since refrigeration has put an end to the need for vast amounts of cut and stored ice; but a century ago, thousands of men each winter swarmed upon the lakes and rivers of the north, cutting out ice blocks with special axes, chisels, and saws. The men now are gone; only the tools remain.

Other devices remain in use though somewhat altered in appearance. Bricklayers still use a special hammer and a brick ax, though the S-shaped raker that was used to remove old cement from around bricks is seldom seen. Farmers continue to find a purpose for the sickle and the scythe, but the old-fashioned hand seeder, the giant bull rake, and the odd-looking hay knife—designed for cutting hay out of a stack, not a field—have passed on.

The list could go on and on: shipwrights, machinists, foundrymen, plumbers, and stonecutters, all had tools particular to their craft or trade that are considered desirable by modern-day collectors. Often, an area of specialization is determined by the individual's own present trade or one that was or is pursued by a member of his family.

Fortunately, tools for the most part remain rather inexpensive and quite abundant. True, some, such as those used by whalemen, sailors, and early railroad workers, are rare and expensive. In general, though, the diligent collector in this field has an opportunity to find what he seeks. He may discover to his surprise, however, that he is competing not only with fellow antiques buffs, but also with carpenters and other craftsmen, who are also buying the old tools—for use on the job!

It should also be noted that since many tools, both metal and wood, bear manufacturers' marks, there exists a vast area for study in the identification and dating of thousands of early tools. Some work has been done in the field of planes and edge tools; but for the most part, very little research has been undertaken as yet, so that for each tool collector, there exists the exciting chance to become an authority in his own specialty.

Carpenter's T squares, wood and metal; 20th century. *Left to right:* $5–10; $5–10; $10–15; $25–35. Common examples of a common tool. Brass trim adds value to example at far right.

Iron calipers; 20th century. *Top:* For inside measurement; $50–75. *Bottom left and right:* For outside measurement; $20–35; $35–55.

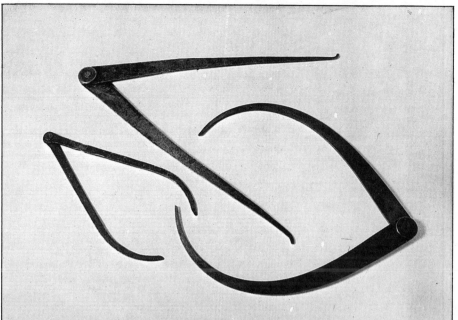

Top left: Cooper's croze, pine and ash; $35–55. *Top right:* Cooper's croze, pine and maple; $30–50. *Bottom:* Carpenter's marking scribe, pine and birch; $15–30. All, 19th century.

Left: Two marking gauges, pine and maple; late 19th century; $20–30. *Right:* Two travelers, iron; late 19th century; $45–60; $50–75. Traveler at center is of wrought iron.

Left: Carpet cutter, maple; 20th century; $15–25. *Right:* Cabinetmaker's veneer cutter, maple; late 19th century; $50–70.

Spokeshaves. *Left:* With adjustable screw; pine and iron; $25–35. *Center left:* Birch and iron; $20–30. *Center right:* Pine and iron; $15–20. *Right:* Pine and wrought iron; $35–55. All, 20th century, except piece at far right, which is mid-19th century.

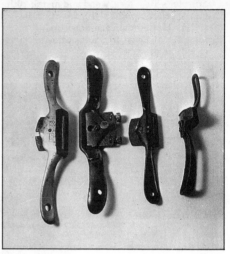

Patent spokeshaves, cast iron; 20th century. *Left to right:* $15–20; $25–35; $15–20; $10–15.

Left: Pruning hook, wrought iron; $25–40. *Center:* Curved pruning hook, wrought iron; $35–55. *Right:* Zake (a rare tile-roofing tool), wrought iron; $40–65. All, 19th century.

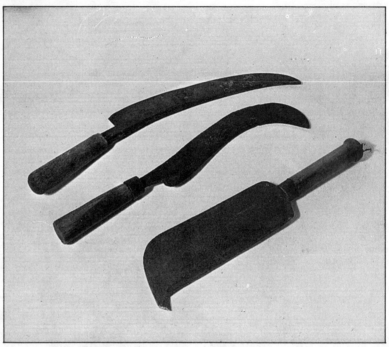

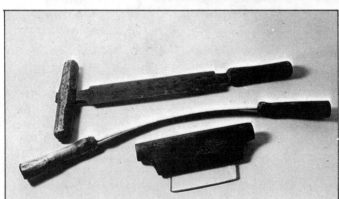

Top: Rare currier's knife, pine and wrought iron; $50–80. *Center:* Tanner's unhairing knife, pine and wrought iron; $45–75. *Bottom:* Tanner's slicker, pine and glass; $10–15. All, 19th century.

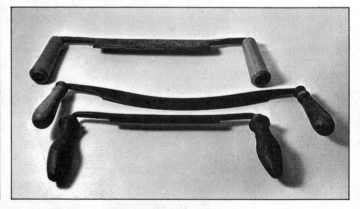

Drawknives. *Top and bottom:* Cooper's hardwood and wrought iron; $18–28; $20–32. *Center:* Coach maker's, hickory and wrought iron; $35–50. All, late 19th century.

Top: Froe club, pine; $12–20. *Center and bottom:* Two froes, hickory and iron; late 19th century. *Center:* $25–40. *Bottom:* $35–55.

Early hay knife, maple and wrought iron; $65–90. A less common variant dating from the 1840s.

Scorps. *Top:* Single handle, iron and pine; $20–30. *Bottom left and right:* Open scorps, iron and maple with brass fittings; $35–55; $40–65. All, 19th century.

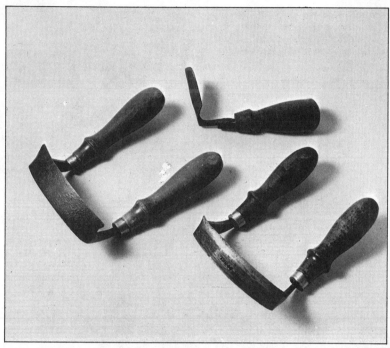

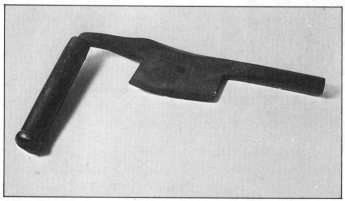

Chamfer knife, a cooper's tool, maple and pine; ca. 1850; $75–115. An uncommon piece with good form.

Hay knife, maple and wrought iron; mid-19th century; $38–58. Another tool with an attractive shape.

Two plow planes, maple; late 19th century; $25–50 each.

Plow planes, maple; late 19th-early 20th century; $25–45 each. Intended to cut a groove.

Patent scrapers, cast iron and steel; 20th century. *Left:* Veneer scraper; $30–45. *Center:* Cabinetmaker's scraper; $15–22. *Right:* Plane-style veneer scraper; $45–80.

Left: Wooden router, pine and wrought iron; late 19th century; $25–40. *Center:* Patent router, cast iron; 20th century; $15–25. *Right:* Stanley Patent all-purpose plane, cast iron; 20th century; $225–300. *Bottom:* Scraper, pine and cast iron; 20th century; $10–20.

Top left: Adjustable double-molding plane, maple; ca. 1870; $60–90. *Bottom:* Double-bladed dado plane, birch; late 19th century; $45–70. *Top right:* Bead plane, maple; early 20th century; $20–35.

Jointer plane, cast iron and steel; Stanley Patent, early 20th century; $75–105.

Group of planes. *Top left:* Compass plane, maple; late 19th century; $55–75. *Top right:* Round molding plane, pine; ca. 1850; $45–65. *Bottom:* Round molding plane, birch; 20th century; $20–35.

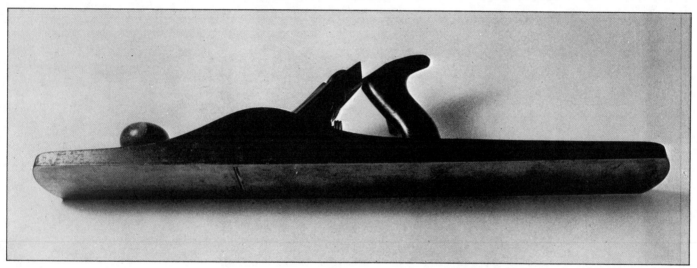

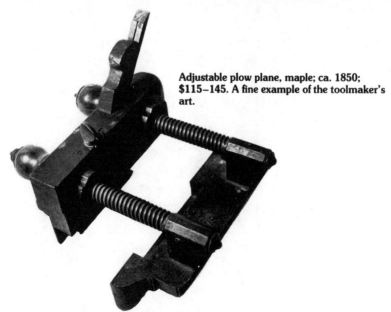

Adjustable plow plane, maple; ca. 1850; $115–145. A fine example of the toolmaker's art.

Two examples of Stanley Patent jack planes, cast iron and steel; 20th century. *Top:* $65–110. *Bottom:* 60–95.

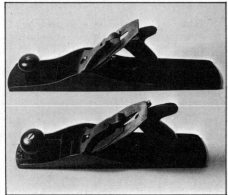

Top: Long jointer or floor plane, pine and maple; 19th century; $50–75. *Bottom:* Trying or trueing plane, pine and maple; 19th century; $45–60.

Top: Stanley Patent fore plane, cast iron, steel, and pine; $70–95. *Bottom:* Stanley Patent jack plane, cast iron, steel, and maple; $75–105. Both, early 20th century.

Two carpenter's clamps, maple and pine; 20th century. *Left:* $45–80. *Right:* $20–35. Prices depend on size, with largest and smallest examples most sought after.

Left: Early carpenter's vise, maple; $20–35. *Right:* File vise, pine and maple; $25–40. Both, 19th century.

Frame saw, maple with pegged joints and wrought-iron blade; first half 19th century; $65–100. Early and a fine form.

Common framed bucksaw of the sort still widely used to cut wood; late 19th-early 20th century; $20–30.

Two miter-box saws, pine and steel; factory made, 20th century. *Top:* $15–25. *Bottom:* $12–20.

Top: Early crosscut saw, pine and steel; $40–62. *Center:* Ripsaw, pine and steel; $28–42. *Bottom:* Pruning saw, maple and steel; $35–50. All, 19th century.

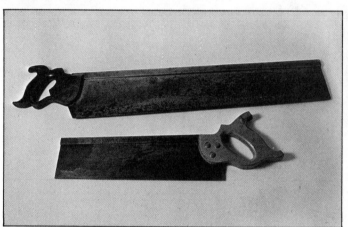

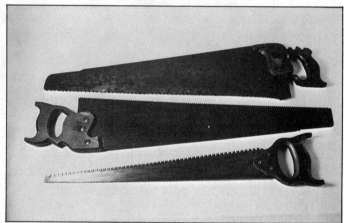

Keyhole saws. *Top to bottom:* Steel and cast iron; $10–15. Steel and pine; $5–12. Steel and pine; $12–24. Early steel and pine with unusual handle; $15–22. All, 20th century, except bottom saw, which is late 19th century. ▶

Broadaxes. *Top:* Maple and steel; ca. 1830; $85–135. *Bottom:* Hickory and steel; ca. 1880; $60–85.

Top left: Mortising hatchet, maple and steel; 19th century; $45–65. *Top right:* Standard factory-made hatchet; 20th century; $12–24. *Bottom:* Broad hatchet; 19th century; $35–55.

Top: Lathing hatchet, hickory and steel; 19th century; $25–37. *Center:* Patent wrecker's hatchet with pry bar, cast iron; $15–25. *Bottom:* Cast-iron hatchet; $10–20. Both, 20th century.

Left: Two shipbuilder's adzes, distinguished by spurlike nail punch; $75–120 each. *Right:* Two carpenter's adzes; $45–75; $50–85. All with hardwood handles and iron heads; 19th century.

Left: Hewing ax, maple and steel; $110–145. *Center left:* Mortising ax, ash and steel; $90–135. *Center right:* Broadax, ash and steel; $125–165. *Right:* Mortising ax, maple and steel; $80–125. All, 19th century.

Left: Tinner's hammer; $10–15. *Center:* Cooper's hammer; $8–13. *Right:* Tinner's hammer; $12–20.

Hammers, iron and hardwood. *Top:* Square-headed bricklayer's hammer; $18–27. *Center:* Cobbler's hammer; $15–25. *Bottom:* Blacksmith's hammer; $15–25. All, late 19th century.

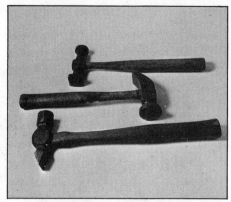

Left: Magnetic tack hammer; $5–10. *Center left:* House trimmer's hammer; $20–32. *Center right:* Machinist's hammer; $12–20. *Right:* Early tack hammer; $18–26. All, iron and hardwood; 20th century, except tack hammer, which dates from mid-19th century.

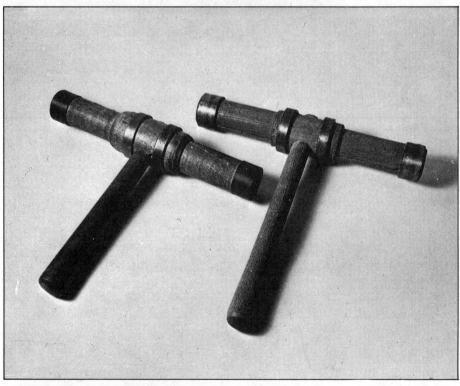

Two shipwright's caulking mallets, hickory with iron heads and brass fittings; both, late 19th century; $35–50 each.

19th-century mallets. *Left:* Maple; $8–15. *Center left:* Carpenter's, oak; $5–10. *Center right:* Oak; $5–10. *Right:* Wheelwright's, maple; $25–35.

251

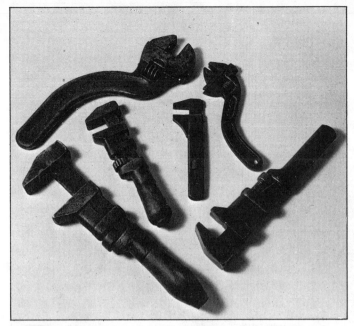

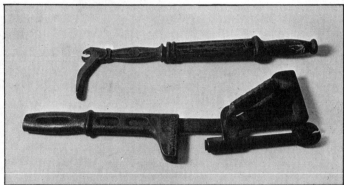

Patent clamp wrenches, cast iron; 20th century; $5–20 each, depending upon size and complexity of operation.

Patent nail pullers, cast iron; factory made, 20th century. *Top:* $22–34. *Bottom:* 32–46.

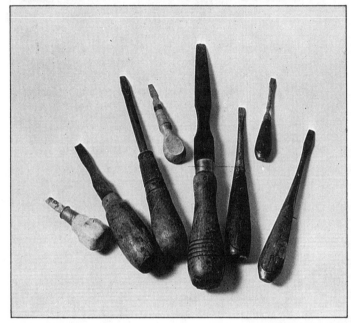

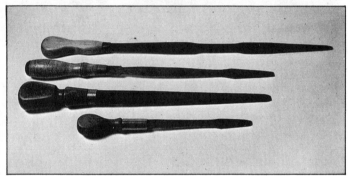

Machinist's screwdrivers, ranging in length from 12″ to 20″, iron with hardwood handles and brass fittings; 20th century. *Top to bottom:* $18–28; $16–24; $22–34; $20–30.

An assortment of iron and hardwood screwdrivers, some with brass fittings; 20th century; $2–20 each, depending on size and quality of workmanship.

Steel chisels with hardwood handles; late 19th-early 20th century. *Top:* Corner chisel; $15–30. *Center top:* Firmer, or forming chisel; $15–25. *Center bottom:* Rare curved gooseneck chisel; $38–54. *Bottom:* Framing chisel; $38–54.

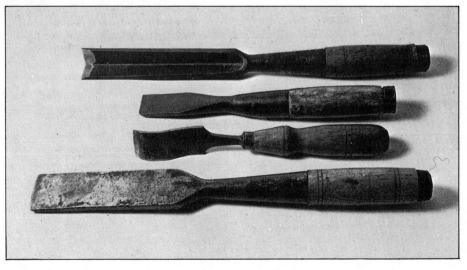

252

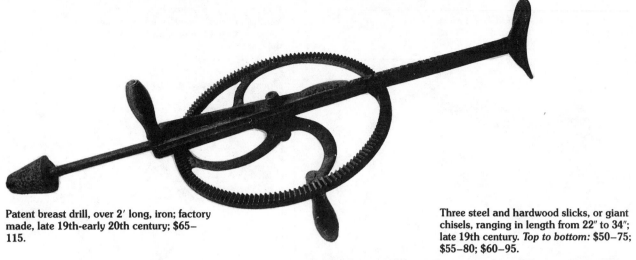

Patent breast drill, over 2′ long, iron; factory made, late 19th-early 20th century; $65–115.

Three steel and hardwood slicks, or giant chisels, ranging in length from 22″ to 34″; late 19th century. *Top to bottom:* $50–75; $55–80; $60–95.

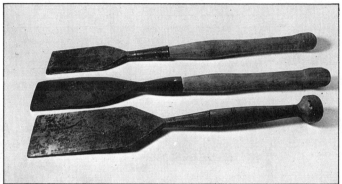

Three steel and hardwood gouges. *Top:* Late 19th century; $12–20. *Center:* With good brass fittings; late 19th century; $45–70. *Bottom:* Early wrought iron; ca. 1850; $30–45.

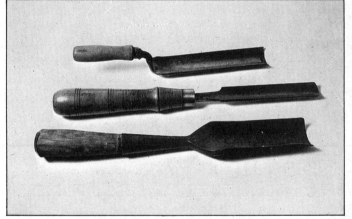

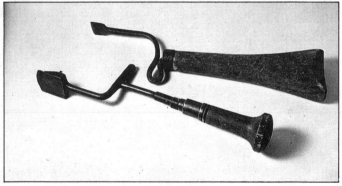

Two examples of the farrier's butteris, or hoof parer. *Top:* Early wrought iron and pine; ca. 1860; $48–64. *Bottom:* Maple and iron; ca. 1890; $36–52.

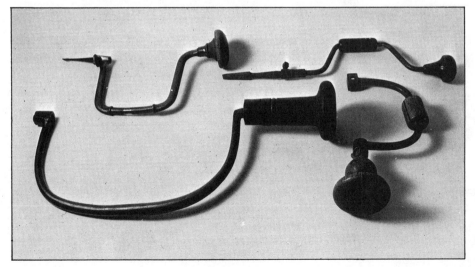

Top left: Brace and bit, brass iron, and pine; early 20th century; $55–80. *Top right:* Brace and bit, iron and pine; late 19th century; $45–70. *Bottom left:* Large brace, iron and pine; ca. 1850; $115–145. *Bottom right:* Brace, iron and pine; ca. 1870; $65–95.

Reamers, iron and hardwood; late 19th-early
20th century. *Top to bottom:* $17–27; $28–
42; $25–40.

Bale, or box, hooks, iron or iron and wood;
late 20th century; $5–15 each, depending on
workmanship. Common implements still in
daily use.

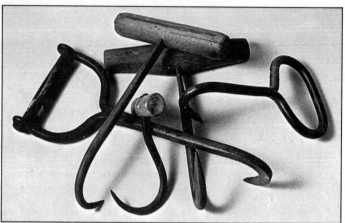

Group of augers, iron and hardwood; late
19th century; $10–35 each, depending upon
age, size, and quality of workmanship.

Wrought-iron blacksmith's tools; late 19th
century. *Top to bottom:* Flat bit; $16–28.
Pincer; $12–20; Hollow bit; $10–17. Round
bit; $14–24. Hammer tongs; $18–32. Long
pincers; 10–15.

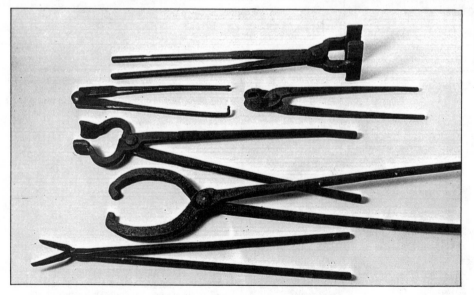

Iron anvils; 19th century. *Left:* 4" high; $45–60. *Center:* 14" high; $100–170. *Right:* 8" high; $60–85.

Cobbler's shoe forms, iron; 20th century. *Left:* $20–30. *Center:* $2–4. *Right:* $35–50.

Cobbler's vise, maple, traces of old paint; late 19th century; $75–110.

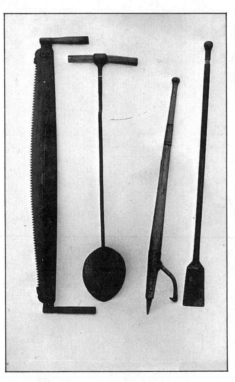

Left: Two-man crosscut saw, steel and maple; $25–40. *Center left:* Rare whale-blubber slick, iron and hickory; $220–300. *Center right:* Logger's peavey, iron and hickory; $20–35. *Right:* Ice chopper, iron; $25–40. All, mid-19th century.

Left: Potter's clay fork, ash and iron; $20–35. *Center:* Peat fork, ash and iron; $50–65. *Right:* Ice-cutting tool, iron and hickory; $40–55. All, mid-19th century. Uncommon tools of uncommon trades.

Top: Early shingling tool, wrought iron; mid-19th century; $45–85. *Bottom:* Knife sharpener, walnut and stone; late 19th century; $60–95.

Carpenter's nail and screw holder, cast iron; factory made, 20th century; $35–55.

Block and tackle; late 19th-early 20th century. *Left:* Iron and maple; $12–20. *Center left:* Cast iron; $8–16. *Center right:* With double tackle, iron and maple; $20–28. *Right:* Iron and pine; $10–17.

Instrument for capping bottles, iron and pine; late 19th-early 20th century; $35–50.

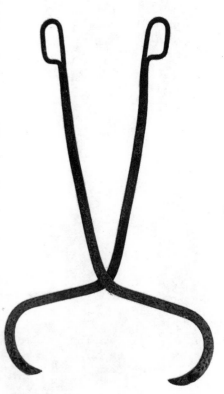

Ice-worker's tongs, wrought iron; early 20th century; $28–48.

Right: Top to bottom: Reverse-glass painting of Statue of Liberty; Massachusetts, ca. 1890; $100–135. Grain sieve; New York, early 20th century; $22–36. Decorated candlebox, pine; New York, late 19th century; $175–225. Small chest, pine, old red paint; Vermont, late 19th century; $65–90. Lap desk, pine, old red and black paint; Connecticut, late 19th century; $50–80. Country side chair, hickory, old blue paint; New York, ca. 1900; $75–125.

Opposite top: Harvest table, pine; Pennsylvania, ca. 1830; $1,800–2,500. Four of a set of eight matching fancy chairs, painted pine and hickory; Pennsylvania, ca. 1860; $1,750–2,400 the set. *Opposite bottom:* Library steps, oak; early 20th century; $125–180. Victorian double-drawer library desk, oak; late 19th century; $275–365. *On wall:* A group of tin and paper advertising signs; late 19th–early 20th century; $75–450. *Left:* Pewter cupboard, pine, old gray-green paint; late 18th–early 19th century; $1,000–1,500. A simple but good New England example.

Above right: Country Sheraton sofa; New England, early 18th century; $750–900. Fine pictorial hooked rug, wool on burlap; New York, late 19th century; $400–700. *Right:* Cupboard, pine and maple, old grain paint; Pennsylvania, mid-19th century; $1,400–1,700. A nicely made example of a common piece. *Opposite:* Open-top hutch, pine, old blue paint; New Jersey, mid-19th century; $700–850. Cricket stool, pine; New England, mid-19th century; $30–45.

Right: Middle shelves: Glass canning jars; late 19th century; $5–35. *Bottom shelf:* Redware and stoneware crockery; mid-19th century; $50–165. *Left, on wall:* Yellow tole salt holder; early 20th century; $35–55. All, East. *Below right: Left to right:* Cupboard pine, old black grain paint on red; East, mid-19th century; $450–650. Country bannister-back chair, pine and ash; New York, late 19th century; $40–70. Pie safe, pine, old red paint; East, mid-19th century; $350–500. *Opposite:* Pine harvest table; Pennsylvania, 1840–55; $1,200–1,500. Well-turned ladder-back side chairs, old paint; New England, 1830–50; $800–1,000 the set. *Page 264.* Victorian country mirror, painted pine; East, late 19th century; $85–115. Manganese-spotted redware bowl; New England, ca. 1850; $150–200. Lamp, brass and glass; early 20th century; $50–65. Country Empire desk, pine and maple; Pennsylvania, ca. 1840; $400–600. Ladder-back chair, pine and maple, traces of old red paint; New England, probably Shaker, ca. 1830; $250–375.

Cobbler's bench, pine; Maine, ca. 1875; $425–560. Typical of the utilitarian pieces now employed as furniture.

Wagon jack, hickory; late 19th century; $65–85. Despite its name, a device of this type was often used to move logs and rocks.

Tobacco cutter, iron and pine; late 19th century; $30–55. Less common and more desirable than the cast-iron factory-made examples.

Seeder, pine and maple; early 20th century; $40–65.

Wheelbarrow, pine and iron, traces of old blue paint; $30–50. Other than for use as planters, these tools are of little interest to most collectors.

265

14.
TOYS

Whether they serve as reminders of our lost innocence, or because they call us back to the playfulness and joy we only rarely experience as adults, old toys have become the object of one of our fastest growing national pastimes. The collecting of toys, however, differs in some respects from the collecting of other antiques.

First, few "old" American toys are really old. Until after the Civil War, most children in this country played with either imported or homemade toys, since there were only a small number of domestic toy manufacturers. Toy collectors are seldom troubled by this lack of age; in fact, some of the most eagerly sought specimens were made in the 1930s or even the 1940s. Furthermore, most collectors are not very interested in the older handmade toys; those they leave largely to the folk-art collector. The toy specialist usually confines himself to standard factory-made items. And as with other factory-made "antiques," one of the toy collector's objectives, besides the good condition and esthetic appeal of his examples, is to obtain complete sets or "runs" of a given type of toy, be it train, bank, or boat. In this respect, toy collecting, like tool collecting, resembles the collecting of stamps or coins.

The growing enthusiasm of collectors has created some problems in the field. To begin with, since there are simply not enough examples available to satisfy the demand, most old toys are now extremely expensive. Mass-produced, factory-made objects that sold originally for a few pennies now regularly change hands for hundreds of dollars. As often happens, the excess demand has given rise to reproductions and forgeries. There is no other area of American antiques where the inexperienced collector is so likely to make a poor buy.

The earliest toys made in this country were of wood or pottery. Dolls, boats, houses, and numerous toy animals were often made at home from material readily available in any woodlot, while the local potter turned out everything from marbles to banks to whistles. Many old homemade wood toys survive, but the pottery ones are relatively rare.

Little is known of the nonindustrial makers of wooden toys except for a few names. Wilhelm Schimmel and his pupil Aaron Mountz of Pennsylvania were itinerant carvers who wandered the nineteenth-century countryside whittling pull toys, bird figures, and Noah's arks for the families of their numerous hosts. Since their ware is highly individualistic, most of it has been bought by museums and is not accessible to the average collector. Factory-made wooden playthings are something else again. Push-and-pull toys such as those manufactured in the 1890s by the Gibbs Manufacturing Company of Canton, Ohio, are considered highly desirable, as are sleds, sleighs, and other toys of wood.

Much greater interest is focused on metal playthings, particularly those of a mechanical nature. The earliest are of tin and date to the 1830s. By 1848, the Philadelphia Tin Toy Manufactory was producing an extensive line of horse-drawn buses, trains, and wagons, which were either painted freehand or stenciled, in contrast to late nineteenth- and early twentieth-century tin, which was decorated by lithography. Another early maker was George W. Brown of Forestville, Connecticut. Existing sketchbooks used by this company indicate that a fascinating variety of tin pull toys was available to the child of the 1850s and 1860s.

Through the use of a clockwork mechanism, first employed in the 1870s by the Ives Company of Bridgeport, Connecticut, it became possible to produce tin toys that moved automatically. Some of them involve two or more separate figures and are remarkably complex—dancing figures, locomotives, and a rowboat that worked on water or land! They are among the most desirable of all early toys.

As a general rule, in tin toys, the larger sizes are the best, in both workmanship and detail. Many types, such as boats and wagons, were made in a range of sizes, with the largest always being the most complex—and most expensive, then and now.

Toys of cast iron were developed later than those of tin, with no significant production prior to the 1880s. In that decade the Hubley Manufacturing Company of Lancaster, Pennsylvania, came to the fore with a wide variety of mechanical and nonmechanical iron playthings. Other makers, such as the Kenton Hardware Company of Ohio, soon joined the field, and in the next sixty years thousands of different cast-iron toys appeared on the market.

Some of them, such as the horse-drawn fire engines, circus wagons, and sleighs, have proved to be so popular that they have been widely reproduced. Intentionally or otherwise, such reproductions are often offered for sale as originals. Since few of the new toys are marked (and marks, where existent, are readily removed), collectors of cast-iron toys must exercise considerable caution. Where possible, always buy from reputable sources that guarantee their goods. Moreover, while only long experience in the field will ensure complete safety in purchase, collectors can often learn to detect fakes. Try to locate original pieces in museums and private collections, and study them; avoid buying examples whose originals you have not seen. In examining a prospective purchase, observe its surface. Reproductions are often sand-cast from parts of original pieces, and individual units of the new models will show a rougher surface than the old. They will also be slightly smaller and will show a loss of clarity or sharpness in detail. Also, paint that looks "too good" for an old toy is probably just that—too good to be true. Nor is a rusty surface any assurance of age. Bright, flaky, red orange rust often indicates rapidly induced oxidation. Old rust is black and shiny, with a patina that can be acquired only through age and exposure.

These precautionary words, which apply primarily to cast-iron mechanical toys, also apply to toy banks, whether mechanical or not. The first children's banks were made of tin and were "still"; they had no moving parts. Examples from the last half of the nineteenth century are common, for manufacturers such as Stevens and Brown of Cromwell, Connecticut, turned out vast numbers of tin banks in the 1860s and 1870s. Several shapes were made, the most popular being the house; one example even had a porch complete with Victorian gingerbread trim. Decoration was applied by stencil and later by lithography.

Cast-iron still banks were also made in great quantity. The Hubley Company sold some in the 1890s in the shapes of mailboxes and cash registers; at a later date, the Williams Company of Ravenna, Ohio, specialized in banks representing cartoon characters, such as Mutt and Jeff or Little Orphan Annie.

Tin and iron still banks, while popular enough, are not in such great demand as to encourage fakery, and they can still be bought at reasonable prices.

Mechanical cast-iron banks are quite a different matter. In the 1870s, Stevens and other companies brought out banks incorporating figures that would spring into action when a coin was deposited—an Indian that would shoot a bear, for instance, or a prizefighter that would strike his opponent. The many figures and actions depicted are delightfully inventive, with the result that these banks are in great demand; mechanicals such as Jonah and the Whale or William Tell are valued in the hundreds of dollars. As a secondary result, large numbers of them have been issued in modern reproduction, and the prospective collector would do well to observe all the precautions previously discussed in regard to buying iron toys.

Trains, both tin and cast, are a highly specialized branch of toy collecting. The earliest successful mass producer was the Ives Company, and that firm's products are most often sought. Other desirable makers are W. B. Carpenter, Hubley, and the Wilkins Toy Manufacturing Company of Medford, Massachusetts, all of which manufactured cast-iron pull trains or tin and iron windup trains. Electric trains came later, and they also are in great demand. There has as yet been little intentional production of forgeries in this field, but prices are extremely high, particularly for the earlier models.

Various steam-driven toys were also popular at the turn of the century. The Weeden Manufacturing Company of New Bedford, Massachusetts, produced several steam engines as well as belt-driven mechanical toys, such as organ-grinders, knife sharpeners, and wood sawyers, that could be set in motion by attaching them to the engines. Weeden steam engines were given away as premiums by *Youth's Companion* magazine in the 1880s. They are well made and attractive and for the most part reasonably priced at present.

Toy weapons and military miniatures appeal to a special, and large, group of collectors. The army of toy soldier enthusiasts alone numbers in the thousands. While there are some early paper, wood, and metal soldiers of American manufacture, most interest today is centered on the lead and cast-iron examples made in the period between the two world wars. These are abundant, attractive, and fairly priced. Cannons, a related item, were made in many sizes, from tiny companion pieces for the soldiers to large outdoor guns for holiday celebrations. The larger pieces have attracted the most attention.

Cap pistols have been made in the United States since Civil War times, and many variations are encountered, though most collectors have taken little interest in them. An exception is the animated cap pistol, a device incorporating one or more figures that are activated when the pistol hammer is struck. There are not many of these toys, and they are eagerly sought.

For the quiet hours, Victorian children (and their parents) had many different board games, which were made of cardboard and wood and packaged in chromolithographed boxes. In addition to providing amusement, they were often intended to educate the young in the strict moral values of the day. It would have been difficult, indeed, to take the wrong side in a game titled "Pope and Pagan, or the Missionary Campaign; or the Siege of the Stronghold of Satan by the Christian Army." That tongue twister was issued in 1844 by W. and B. Ives of Salem, Massachusetts, one of the most prolific games producers. Board games haven't yet caught on with collectors—in part, perhaps, because they are seldom found intact or in good condition—so they represent a relatively inexpensive area of toy collecting.

Dolls and their accessories have always held a strong fascination for American collectors. While many of the dolls cherished now—as then—were imported from Europe, there was a strong tradition of American manufacture. The first dolls produced here were undoubtedly made at home of carved wood and rags, generally unbleached cotton or linen stuffed with sawdust. Their features were hand painted, and their hairstyles are often a clue to their age.

Ludwig Greiner of Philadelphia was among the first of many factory-based dollmakers. In 1858, he took out the initial patent for a papier-mâché doll head. Such heads were sold through shopkeepers to individual customers, who then added bodies of their own making, usually of wood or kidskin.

Born of England's "penny woodens"—simple, unpainted wooden dolls—the wooden doll tradition continued long in this country. The earliest examples were rigid until a Vermonter, Joel Ellis, patented a jointed wooden doll in 1873; an improved version was marketed by a neighbor, F. D. Martin, in 1879. The Schoenhut Company of Philadelphia later put out a similar doll with ball-and-socket joints.

Dolls were made of other materials as well, including wax-headed figures, popular during the 1870s and 1880s, and rubber dolls, which made their first appearance in the same period. Ceramic and celluloid figures were also popular.

By the middle of the nineteenth century, many dolls were beginning to assume a distinct form and image. Previously, doll faces had impersonal features, but now attempts were made to give them individual traits—in some cases those of real people, such as Jenny Lind or President Lincoln. In the twentieth century, this custom has continued. Betty Boop, Little Orphan Annie, Alice and a whole cast of characters from Wonderland, and Charlie Chaplin are just a few of the many so-called celebrity dolls manufactured in the last seventy years. Indeed, some of the later creations are among the most popular and expensive of all.

American children have always taken great delight in dollhouses and doll furniture, and for many grown-ups the charm continues to exert its hold. Most of the early examples have disappeared, but dollhouses from the Victorian era are plentiful, and furniture may be found in every style from the Queen Anne period on. Miniature furniture of any age is today extremely expensive, but child-size pieces (eighteen to thirty inches high) are surprisingly cheap, though not especially common.

Much like the larger furniture are such working miniatures of adult household objects as musical instruments, some of which were extremely well made. Schoenhut made children's pianos of fine tone in the 1870s, and there were whole orchestras of toy musical instruments.

For as long as children have existed, there have been many other toys of every description. Indoor and outdoor activities of all sorts had special equipment, just as they do today. Sleds, skates, tops, marbles, hoops, balls, bats, and numerous others may be found to satisfy the desires of every grown-up lover of toys.

Fire engine drawn by three horses, cast iron;
ca. 1880; $350–450. Addition of tin and
wood parts mark this as a rare and early
piece.

Horse-drawn hook and ladder, cast iron; by
Kenton, ca. 1922; $200–275. Very large with
excellent design.

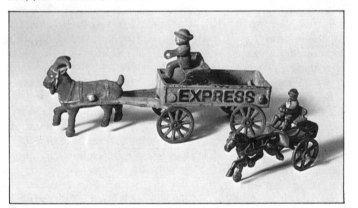

Horse-drawn sleigh with female occupant,
cast iron; by Hubley, ca. 1920; $300–375.

Rear: Express wagon drawn by goat, cast
iron; $110–160. *Front:* Horse and sulky, cast
iron; $75–110. Both, ca. 1920.

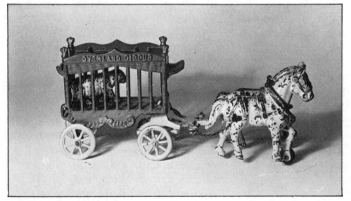

Cast-iron automobiles; ca. 1920. *Rear:* Ford
touring car; $150–200. *Front:* Coupe with
rumble seat; $90–120.

Horse-drawn Overland Circus, cast iron;
Kenton, 1940s; $180–270.

Left: Rare dirigible, cast iron, silver paint; $90–120. *Right:* Airplane marked "Lindy," cast iron; $110–135. Mark on plane is a reference to Charles A. Lindbergh, who made his historic flight in 1927. Both, 1920s.

Fordson tractor, cast iron; 1924; $100–135.

Motorcycle and rider marked "Harley Davidson," cast iron; ca. 1925; $175–225.

Oil truck marked "Champion Case & Motor Oil," cast iron; ca. 1920; $135–185.

Hubley Popeye "Spinach Cycle," cast iron, rubber tires; ca. 1930; $260–350. Figure has movable arms. A large and most attractive piece.

Mechanical bank, Indian shooting bear, cast iron; ca. 1910; $225–345. Like many mechanical banks, this one has been issued in modern reproduction.

Locomotive and cars, cast iron with silver finish; ca. 1920; $120–165.

Early locomotive and cars, cast iron; by Carpenter, ca. 1880; $275–400.

Electric trains, tin and iron; by Ives, ca. 1890; $250–400. An early example of the electrically powered train.

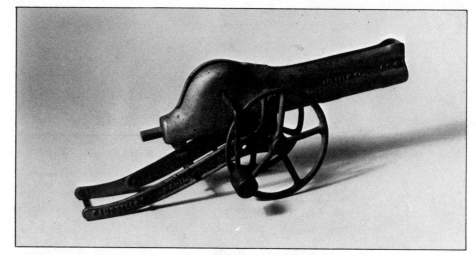

Toy cannon, marked "Campbells Rapid Fire Gun," cast iron; patented 1907; $65–95. A mechanical toy that can shoot pellets.

Selection of cast-iron soldiers painted olive drab; ca. 1930; $5–8 each, depending on type.

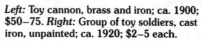

Left: Toy cannon, brass and iron; ca. 1900; $50–75. *Right:* Group of toy soldiers, cast iron, unpainted; ca. 1920; $2–5 each.

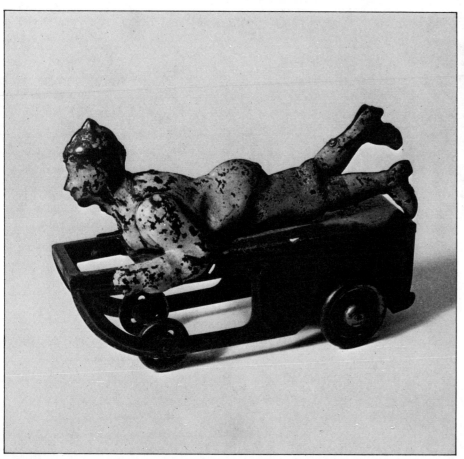

Pull toy with three bells, tin, steel, and iron; ca. 1900; $80–105.

Boy on sled, painted tin and cast iron; ca.1910; $95–115.

271

Very large friction-powered toy locomotive,
tin and iron; ca. 1935; $100–165.

Unusual friction toy, Hansom cab, tin and
iron; ca. 1897; $180–225.

Left: Toonerville Trolley, cast lead; 1923;
$65–80. *Right:* Wind-up Toonerville Trolley,
tin and iron; Fontaine-Fox, ca. 1922; $250–
325.

Delivery wagon and horse, marked "Hygeia Ice," tin; ca. 1920; $90–135.

Strauss Inter-State bus, tin with lithographed decoration and excellent detail; ca. 1935; $250–375.

Fine early balance toy, tin, with excellent detail on the figures; ca. 1910; $150–210.

Wind-up toy, Fresh-Air Taxicab, tin; ca. 1930; $450–650. One of the many toys inspired by once-popular radio programs.

Wind-up toy, Blondie's Jalopy, tin; ca. 1935; $275–360. Occupants' heads nod when toy is set in motion.

Tin and sheet-metal spaceships; late 1930s. *Front left:* Pull toy with rubber tires; $35–45. *Rear:* Wind-up Rocket Fighter; by Marx; $175–250. *Right:* Wind-up Buck Rogers; $90–135.

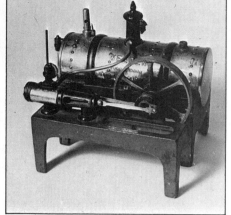

Mechanical Charlie McCarthy car, tin; by Marx, late 1930s; $275–350.

Mechanical Dogpatch Band, tin; by Unique Art, ca. 1945; $300–375.

Horizontal steam engine, iron and brass; by Weeden, ca. 1903; $75–125. A working model.

Mechanical knife sharpener at work, tin, ca. 1930; $95–125. Much more sophisticated than the average mechanical toy of the period.

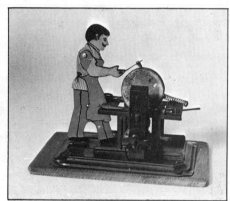

Mechanical Popeye figures, tin; 1930s. *Left:* With punching bag; $165–210. *Right:* With pet parrot; $140–185. These are among the most popular of the comic-inspired toys.

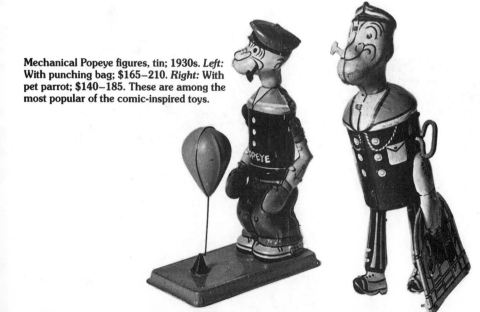

Doepke mechanical sand conveyor, tin and steel; ca. 1935; $130–180. An example of the many working models of earth-moving machines produced by Buddy-L and other manufacturers.

275

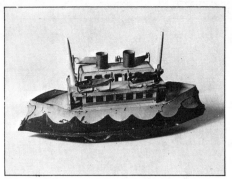

Steamship pull toy, steel and tin; ca. 1900; $130–180.

Mechanical submarine, steel and tin; by Wolverine, ca. 1940; $60–80.

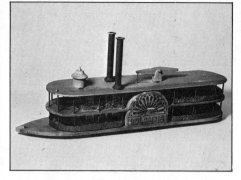

Early wood side-wheeler, the *Columbia*; ca. 1890; $350–550.

Mechanical battleship, tin and steel with lithographed decoration; ca. 1910; $750–1,200.

Barney Google and Spark Plug, jointed wood and cloth; ca. 1930; $250–325 the set.

Gypsy wagon, wood, with two stamped-wood horses; Sears-Roebuck, 1912; $125–175.

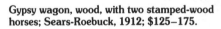

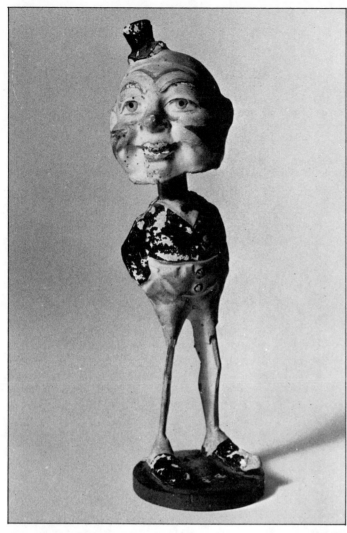

Unusual and extremely well-done nodding doll, plaster and wood; ca. 1910; $75–100. Items of this sort are rarely duplicated.

Chinese acrobat, celluloid and wood balance toy; ca. 1930; $50–75.

Wooden tops; early 20th century. *Left:* $15–22. *Right:* $5–10.

Ferdinand the Bull, composition wood, jointed; late 1930s; $50–75.

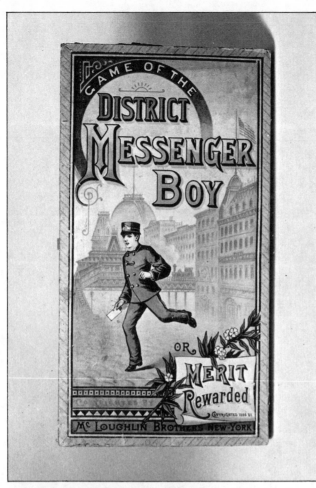

District Messenger Boy, board game; by McLoughlin Brothers, New York, patented 1886; $35–55. An example of Victorian children's games intended to promote hard work and adherence to traditional values.

Excelsior Paint Box, wood with an excellent lithographed cover; ca. 1900; $30–55.

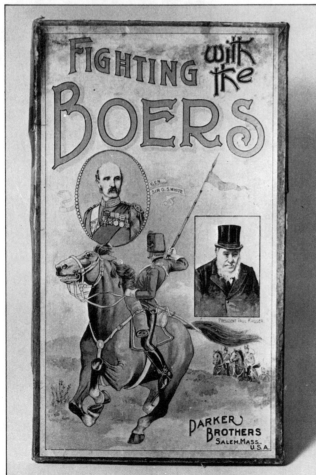

Magnetic Fish Pond; by McLoughlin Brothers, New York, patented 1891; $40–65.

Board game, Fighting with the Boers; by Parker Brothers, Salem, Mass., ca. 1900; $65–85. Board-game prices have not kept pace with the general sharp increase in toy prices; they offer a good area for purchase.

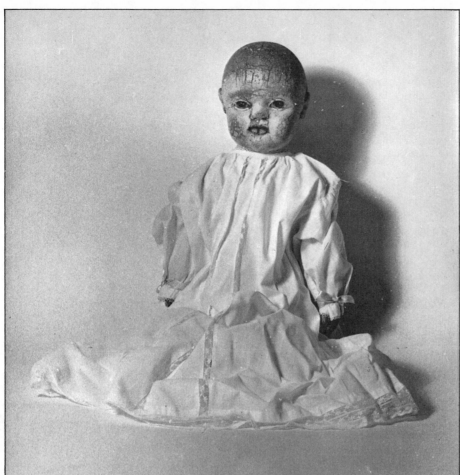

Philadelphia Baby doll, rag body; J. B. Shepherd and Co., ca. 1860; $550–750.

Two jointed dolls, wood with pewter hands and feet. *Left:* By Mason-Taylor, ca. 1878; $425–550. *Right:* By Joel Ellis, Springfield, Vt., ca. 1873; $350–450.

Greiner doll, papier-mâché head, kid body; ▲ patented 1893; $475–625. A popular early-American doll type.

Unusual black doll, gutta-percha; Kentucky, ca. 1865; $350–500.

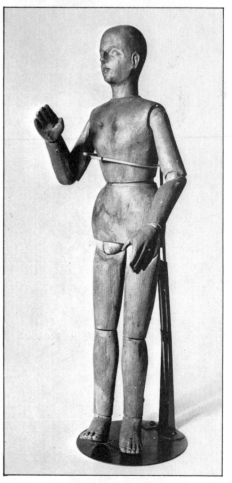

Jointed figurine, a "Lay" stick figure, wood; mid-19th century; $350–550. These were often used as artist's models.

Boy doll in sailor suit, known as "Tootsie Wootsie"; by Schoenhut, Philadelphia, early 20th century; $500–650.

Two wood dolls; by Schoenhut, Philadelphia, ca. 1911. *Left:* Rare baby doll; $900–1,400. *Right:* Standing doll; $500–625.

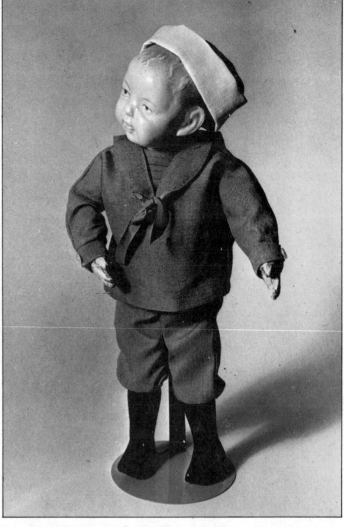

Large jointed doll; by Fulper, New Jersey, ca. 1917; $325–425. A fine-quality doll produced in response to the cutoff of European imports during the First World War.

Bylo dolls; ca. 1923. *Left:* Laughing Bylo; $550–700. *Right:* With composition body; $450–550.

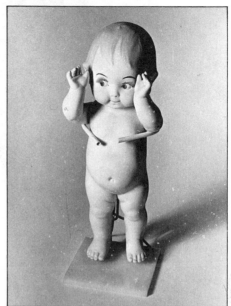

Peterkins; by Fulper, New Jersey, ca. 1919; $300–400. A small porcelain bisque figure designed by the well-known Helen Trowbridge.

Rare set of Alice-in-Wonderland figures; by Martha Chase, ca. 1905; $2,750–3,200 the set. Only six complete sets are known.

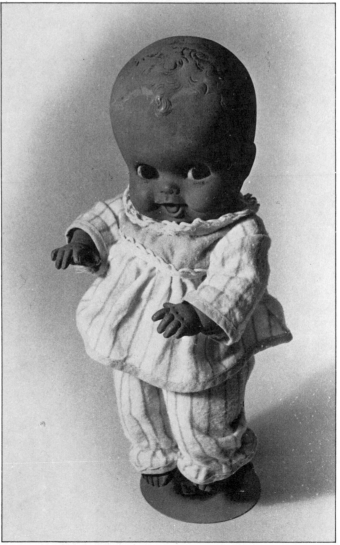

Betty Boop Doll; by Kallus, ca. 1932; $200–325. Inspired by the cartoon figure, this doll once sold for $1.

Amos Andria, black rubber character doll; Sun Rubber Co., ca. 1940; $50–85.

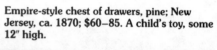

Empire-style toy chest of drawers with mirror, pine, 16″ high; ca. 1860; $80–120.

Early Teddy Bear, stuffed with straw; $235–300. Countless variations of this toy were inspired by the story of President Theodore Roosevelt in which he spared a small bear while on a hunting trip.

Empire-style chest of drawers, pine; New Jersey, ca. 1870; $60–85. A child's toy, some 12″ high.

Victorian toy chest of drawers with mirror, pine, 18″ high; Midwest, ca. 1900; $70–115.

Toy kitchen cabinet, pine; by Cass, ca. 1940; $35–60. A factory-made piece.

Victorian spool-turned toy bed, maple, with quilt and coverlet; Maine, ca. 1880; $75–120.

Country Sheraton toy rope bed, pine and maple; New Hampshire, ca. 1840; $175–250. A fine early piece.

Excelsior washing set, pine; East, ca 1920; $50–75.

Schoenhut toy piano and stool, walnut; ca. 1910; $250–325. A working model with excellent detail.

Empire-style child's music box in form of a piano, walnut and iron; East, ca. 1860; $275–350.

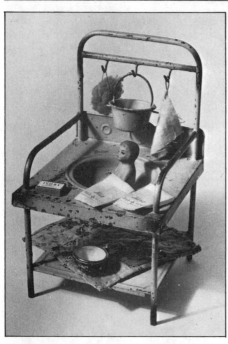

Doll's bathing set, ceramic, tin, and iron; ca. 1910; $125–160.

Toy stove and accessories, cast iron; by Royal, ca. 1935; $115–145. Stoves of this sort could actually hold a small fire.

Little Orphan Annie electric stove; ca. 1940; $45–60. A working model.

Extremely stylish Victorian doll's carriage, wicker and iron; East, ca. 1870; $275–360. Rare and fine.

Early three-wheeled doll carriage, pine, canvas, and iron, with stencil decoration in gold on green; Vermont, ca. 1860; $225–310.

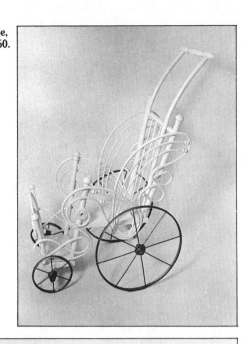

Child's sleigh, pine and iron, with overstuffed upholstered interior; Vermont, ca. 1880; $185–245.

Toy sled, pine, only 1' long, dovetailed, with traces of old red paint; Maine, ca. 1860; $20–40.

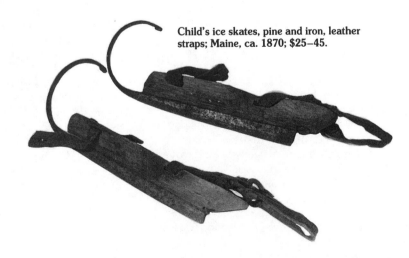

Child's ice skates, pine and iron, leather straps; Maine, ca. 1870; $25–45.

15

DECOYS

It was many years ago—a thousand at least—that men learned how to lure flying wild fowl to their doom through the use of decoys. That this method works is because of the gregariousness of certain species. Ducks, geese, and various small shorebirds tend to seek out their own and to rest or feed where they see others of their species. The American Indian knew of this characteristic and used grass, wood, rushes, bird feathers, and even mud to shape forms that from a distance might be taken for resting wild fowl. Such decoys were in no sense true replicas of the birds they were intended to lure but were more in the nature of symbols—they resembled the species sufficiently to be able to deceive.

At first, the colonial settlers copied Indian decoys. There was no European tradition in this area, and the settlers had to learn from experience. By the 1800s, there were so many hunters working the inland and coastal waterways that the birds were becoming shy, and it became necessary to devise more efficient decoys. At this time, two distinct types emerged. The first, and probably the oldest, was the stickup, a birdlike figure mounted on a rod or rodlike legs so that it could be stuck into mud or a sandbank. Examples of stickup decoys in the guise of ducks and geese are known, but the form proved more suitable to the smaller shorebirds that habitually roamed the tidal flats seeking food—mostly because the greater weight required for a model of the large birds caused the stickup to sink into the mud, giving the decoy an unnatural posture.

To lure the larger wild fowl—which tended to land, feed, and rest on the water—hunters created floating decoys in a vast array of shapes and sizes. Unlike the symbolic decoys employed by the Indians, both the floaters and the stickups were meant to be replicas, imitating more or less exactly the shape and plumage of a particular bird.

For most collectors, floaters are the only type of decoy. Shorebird stickups were never widely made beyond the Atlantic coastal area, and in 1918 a Federal law forbade shooting of the diminutive shorebirds, bringing to an end any need for new stickup decoys. Floating decoys, on the other hand, are still made and used today.

There are many species of duck, and

for each species decoys have been created. The so-called sea ducks are those that feed and rest almost exclusively on salt water: bays, estuaries, and even the open ocean. They include the whistler, canvasback, bluebill, bufflehead, scoter, coot, redhead, eider, ruddy duck, and old squaw. Decoys for these birds tend to be large and sturdily built so that they might be seen from a distance and could withstand rough weather.

Marsh ducks, such as the mallard, black, pintail, widgeon, and teal, frequent the calmer waters of inland ponds and rivers. For them the decoy need not be so large nor so sturdy.

Other and even larger birds are or have been lured with decoys. The great Canada goose is eagerly sought, and many variations of the goose decoy may be found, with the rarest being the feeding and sleeping versions. Before the taking of plumage for hats and garments was outlawed, hunters sought the swan, the crane, the loon, the heron, the gull, and the egret, and lifelike models of these species are also available. It was also known that the sight of wily birds like the swan and the gull gave flying ducks a feeling of security when they were looking for a place to land, so that even after swans and gulls could not be taken for their feathers, they were copied and used as "confidence" decoys. Nevertheless, in numbers, decoys of the plumage birds cannot be compared with ducks, and the former generally sell for a good deal more money.

At least 90 percent of all decoys are made of wood, chiefly pine, though cedar, basswood, cottonwood, cork, and balsa have also been employed. The making of such a lure generally takes the following course. A log or wooden block is split in two to provide material for two bodies. Each of the resulting pieces is pointed at one end for a tail and rounded at the other to simulate the breast. The head is carved from a separate piece of wood and then inserted into a hole drilled into the body. Most decoys are then painted and, as a final step, rigged with ballast (so that they will float properly), a mooring line, and an anchor. Today's decoy collectors are not necessarily hunters (indeed, they often oppose the sport), and they often overlook the fact that until the advent in recent years of the

"art," or model, decoy, all decoys were intended to be used; thus, their ability to float properly was a far more critical factor than good paint or an artfully carved head.

The decoy maker employs few tools: an ax, a drawknife, a gouge, a jackknife for whittling heads, and a piece or two of sandpaper. He may have cardboard patterns from which to model heads, but more often than not, these are done freehand. Most available decoys were made by unknown workers who produced a few each year for their own use or for sale to fellow sportsmen. A certain number of craftsmen in each area of the country did become full-time professional carvers, producing hundreds of birds to sell to gunning clubs or to commercial hunters, who, before the outlawing of their trade, would use a hundred or more decoys in a single rig for hunting sea ducks. Most professional carvers marked their birds, but decoys can also be identified by style. The work of these makers is now extremely valuable and may sell for thousands of dollars apiece; examples by such men as Elmer Crowell of East Harwich, Massachusetts, Albert Laing and Charles "Shang" Wheeler of Stratford, Connecticut, and Nathan Cobb of Chincoteague, Virginia, are highly prized. The collector should bear in mind, though, that most decoys carry no maker's mark, and that a well-made example may be a splendid piece of folk art even though it remains anonymous. It may also be a lot easier on the purse.

The great demand for decoys during the last years of the nineteenth and first decades of the twentieth centuries led to the development of decoy factories. Here the bodies were formed on duplicating lathes, but the painting and finishing was done by hand—thus the pieces may still be thought of as handmade. Perhaps the best-known commercial decoy manufacturer was the Mason Decoy Company of Detroit, Michigan. Mason produced four grades of birds, all of which were of high quality and are avidly collected today: Premier, Challenge, Detroit, and Fourth. Another well-known producer of commercial decoys was the Wildfowler Company of Saybrook, Connecticut.

The great majority of wood-bodied decoys are made with solid bodies, but hollow types may be found. These were harder to make but were preferred by sportsmen because of their light weight. The same rationale explains the existence of cork and balsa examples. Also, where dealing with very large forms such as the goose or swan, the craftsman might resort to a frame body covered with canvas. At a later period, the slat frame was replaced by one of heavy wire. The same need to reduce weight explains, in part, the existence of the extremely simple decoys known as shadows. These are simply flat boards cut in the general shape of a duck and given a coat of paint. At a distance they do appear birdlike, and they are a lot easier to carry long distances over mud flats. At the opposite end of the spectrum are those gunners who used decoys made from cement or even cast iron. These were generally employed in floating shooting boxes called batteries; and the individual decoys often might weigh as much as forty pounds. Such birds are rarely found today.

Stickup decoys for shorebirds and other species can present a sticky problem for the collector. Since no legal working models have been made for nearly sixty years and since so many were destroyed when the prohibitory laws went into effect, good-quality authentic examples are not common. The gap has, unfortunately, been filled with many fakes and reproductions, some of which are difficult to spot.

There are several types of small birds that frequent marshy coastal areas, including the plover, yellowlegs, curlew, sandpiper, ruddy turnstone, willet,

dowitcher, and knot. Decoys have been made for all. Since the birds are small, seldom more than six inches long, the decoys are tiny and often carefully painted, with a hole in the bottom into which a standing rod may be placed. Both size and quality of decoration make these "peeps," as they are called, extremely suitable for table or shelf display. They have, accordingly, been collected for some years not only by decoy enthusiasts but also by general collectors of folk art. As a result, prices are high. Shorebirds by Elmer Crowell may go for as much as seven thousand dollars, while ordinary unmarked examples often bring several hundred dollars apiece.

Not all stickups were made of wood. One frequently encounters lithographed tin examples that were produced in factories at the end of the nineteenth century. These are often very attractive, and specimens retaining a good coat of paint are not cheap. Papier-mâché was also used to make peeps, as was balsa. Both are light, and their fragility did not present as great a problem as it would have for floating decoys. Stickups were also used in hunting inland species, such as crows, pigeons, and doves. Few of these decoys were modeled; with the maker contenting himself with a flat, painted shadow. Tin was also used to make these decoys, as was rubber, particularly as the twentieth century advanced. Rubber decoys seem singularly mass-produced and unattractive, being more a matter for

curiosity than anything else. They are said, however, to draw crows well.

In collecting decoys one should look for two things: good form and old paint. Form is the more important factor. A well-shaped lure is a piece of sculpture and should be revered as such; no amount of paint will hide an ugly and ill-proportioned body. Also, good original paint is rare on working decoys. Wind, rain, and water soon put an end to even the hardest finish, and many wild fowlers habitually repainted their decoys each year. Since it was not often that the owner was as competent a craftsman as the maker, subsequent coats of paint are usually indifferent work at best. A good early coat of paint is a blessing to be treasured.

Marks are, of course, very important. Some can greatly increase the value of a decoy. However, as noted, most decoys (including some of the most artistic) are not marked, or they bear names that cannot be found in books on decoy makers. Often, this just means that the bird was stamped by its previous owner. It could, however, mean that the piece is by a previously unknown craftsman. A lot of men made and sold decoys, and new makers are coming to light all the time. It is always possible to find a specimen by someone who in time will be regarded as another "Shang" Wheeler or Elmer Crowell. If possible, the collector should track down the unidentified names that appear on his pieces. It's fun, and it could be profitable.

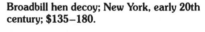

Broadbill hen decoy; New York, early 20th century; $135–180.

Rare stickup duck decoy, probably a brant; Maine, late 19th century; $220–275.

Shorebird stickup decoy, probably a yellowlegs; New England, late 19th century; $265–345.

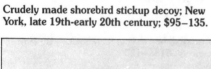

Sanderling stickup decoy; New York, early 20th century; $80–115.

Crudely made shorebird stickup decoy; New York, late 19th-early 20th century; $95–135.

Pair of very well-made snipe stickup decoys; Long Island, N.Y., late 19th century; $1,200–1,700 the pair.

Yellowlegs stickup decoy; New England, late 19th century; $450–575.

Sanderling stickup decoy, cork body; early 20th century; $75–110.

Crow stickup decoy, with wire legs; Connecticut, late 19th century; $170–230.

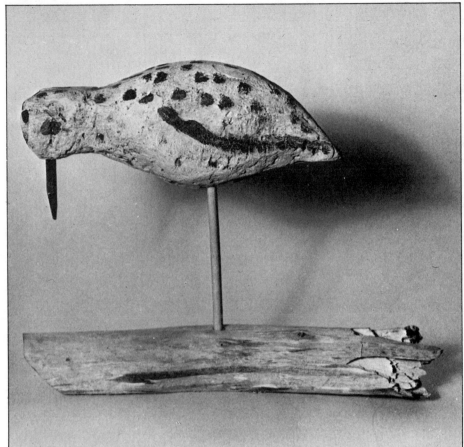

Uncommon factory-made pigeon stickup decoy, rubber; East, early 20th century; $40–65.

Black duck shadow decoy; Pennsylvania, 20th century; $35–60.

Interesting crow shadow decoy; New York, 20th century; $55–85.

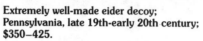

Extremely well-made eider decoy;
Pennsylvania, late 19th-early 20th century;
$350–425.

Redhead drake decoy, pine; New Jersey,
early 20th century; $95–125.

Teal decoy, pine; New York, 20th century;
$105–140.

Broadbil decoy, hollow carved pine; Midwest,
20th century; $80–110.

Bluebill drake decoy; East, 20th century;
$135–175.

Widgeon decoy, pine; Ontario River region of
New York, 20th century; $135–185.

Primitive decoy, probably a black duck; late
19th-early 20th century; $50–70.

Well-done canvasback decoy, with good original paint; East, early 20th century; $140–190.

Merganser decoy, pine; New York, late 19th century; $75–115.

Scoter decoy; Stevens Factory, early 20th century; $200–275.

Bluebill hen decoy, pine; East, 20th century; $90–135.

Canvasback decoy, pine; Illinois, early 20th century; $125–175.

Black duck decoy; New England, late 19th century; $175–235.

Broadbil drake decoy, with original paint; Upper New York State, ca. 1920; $120–165.

Black duck decoy; Wildfowler Decoy Company, Connecticut, 20th century; $115–145.

Whistler hen decoy; East, early 20th century; $50–65. Recent painting, such as this, always decreases the value of a decoy.

Fine brant decoy; East, late 19th century; $350–500. This decoy was in the well-known Mackey collection, and such a history always boosts the price.

Primitive redhead decoys, male and female, pine; New England, late 19th century; $165–245 the pair.

Oversize canvasback decoy; Virginia, late 19th-early 20th century; $125–165. ◄

Crude goldeneye decoy, pine; East, late 19th century; $45–65.

Black duck decoy; Mason Decoy Co., Detroit, Mich., early 20th century; $215–265.

Well-painted Canada goose decoy; New York, late 19th-early 20th century; $200–275. Goose and swan decoys are generally high-priced.

Broadbil hen decoy; East, 20th century; $75–115.

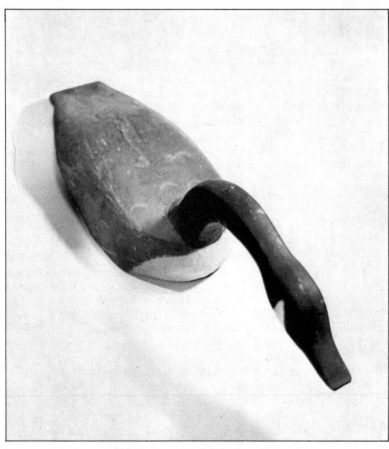

White-winged scoter decoy, cork body; East; late 19th century; $60–85.

Extremely rare and very large (3½') Canada goose decoy in the feeding position; made and marked by William Holzman, Long Island, N.Y., 20th century; $350–500.

Bluebill hen decoy, so-called Victor type; Mississippi, 20th century; $65–90.

16

WEATHERVANES AND WHIRLIGIGS

Weathervanes

Weathervanes and whirligigs today are regarded as interesting and valuable examples of American folk art. Not too long ago, they served an important function, too, as adjuncts to every person's own weather service. In the days before radio and its daily or even hourly weather forecast, nearly everyone was a weatherman. Sailors and farmers were the people most critically affected by sudden changes in weather, and they strove always to predict the weather and thereby keep ahead of it. It has long been known that changes in wind direction presage weather changes, both the long-term seasonal type and, more immediately, those short-range shifts that mean rain or storm.

At its simplest—a flat board mounted on a swivel rod—the weathervane could record those changes. It is, therefore, hardly surprising that vanes are known to have existed even in the days of the ancient Greeks and that they are among the earliest of American antiques. Some have survived from the seventeenth century, including a wooden fish studded with copper nails that once topped the roof of a Massachusetts copper shop. The first known vanemaker in America, Shem Drowne of Boston, created several vanes in the 1740s that still stand in that city. Best known of these is the copper grasshopper that graces old Faneuil Hall; it has survived several disasters, including earthquake, fire, and assorted hurricanes.

The earliest weathervanes were made of wood, and that medium is still employed by some makers. It is relatively simple to saw or chisel a vane from a board, and the silhouette thus produced stands out well against the sky. More sophisticated workers, who wanted to achieve an illusion of depth, carved vanes in the round, creating a full-bodied animal or other form. Wood used for this purpose has a serious defect, however: with daily exposure, even the stoutest piece is vulnerable to the elements. It is therefore understandable that artisans soon turned to other mediums. Iron, either wrought or cut from a solid sheet, has often been employed in the construction of weathervanes, and some of the most interesting examples are found in this medium. Iron will

eventually rust, however; more important, it is heavy, which makes it an impractical material for the very large weathervanes that were often mounted atop public buildings. By the middle of the nineteenth century, copper had been found to serve the purpose best. The bulk of the weathervanes collected today were made of copper by professional manufacturers during the period from 1870 to 1920.

In order to make a copper vane, the craftsman first carves a wooden form and from this casts an iron mold. The mold is cut into workable sections, which are hinged together to facilitate removal of the completed vane. Next, the worker fills the mold with molten lead, which contracts when cool, leaving a space between it and the wall of the iron mold. A sheet of copper is sandwiched into this area, and by pounding on the lead, the craftsman causes the copper to conform to the shape of the mold. The individual sections of the vane are then soldered together to produce a full-bodied hollow form. Even today, weathervanes are made in essentially this manner; and though produced in a factory, they may be said to be handcrafted.

Copper is light and extremely weather resistant. By the second half of the nineteenth century, nearly all major weathervane manufacturers were using it almost exclusively for their products. The variety of forms they produced was truly astonishing, particularly in the light of the fact that for hundreds of years there had been only two: the cock and the banneret. The figure of the crowing rooster appeared early and became traditional when, in the ninth century, a papal decree required that all churches employ this form of weathervane in order to remind the faithful of Peter's denial of Christ and the penalty for abandoning the dogma. So universal was the use of the cock that in England and New England the term *weathercock* was synonymous with *weathervane.*

The banneret is a flat, more or less rectangular metal piece that customarily terminates in an arrow. It may be as much as four feet long, with names or initials cut into the body so that they may be seen against the sky. The form may be traced to the heraldic banners flown from medieval castles.

Even in Shem Drowne's time,

vanemakers had gone well beyond these basic forms, and by the 1880s, manufacturers' imaginations were running rampant. Animals were always most popular, reflecting, no doubt, the fact that the farmer and stock man was always the vanemaker's best customer. Horses appear in many forms, including "portrait" examples of such great racing horses as the trotters Hambletonian and Nancy Hanks and the flat racer Dexter. Inspiration for most of the horse, horse-and-buggy, and horse-and-rider weathervanes appears to have been provided by popular lithographs, such as those printed by Currier and Ives. Today, the horse is by far the most desirable antique weathervane, although the deer and the eagle are also in great demand. Of farm stock, one can list cows, bulls, hogs, sheep, chickens, and rabbits. The fox may be found as well as the pigeon, the bear, and the swan. There are also many exotics not likely to be found on most farms—elephants, dragons, boars, lions, buffalo, peacocks, ostriches, and tigers. Not to be forgotten is man's best friend, the dog, as well as his constant prey, the squirrel. Many of these forms are exceedingly scarce and when offered for sale may bring thousands of dollars.

The number of vanes in existence whose forms are associated with a particular craft makes it evident that workmen and shopkeepers found the weathervane a handy advertising device. To the farmer's (or plowmaker's) plow, one may add the blacksmith's anvil, the shoemaker's shoe, the cigar and tobacco leaf of the local cigar store, and the carpenter's saw. Also found are wheels for wagonmakers, the writing master's pen, and the malt shovel and barrel that marked the local brewery.

Other less readily identifiable symbols were employed in weathervanes. Arrows, the sunflower, the bicycle, Indian chiefs and maidens, fish (chiefly the cod and the mackerel), and even the butterfly appear. Some of these may have had social or fraternal significance. Certainly, the Liberty Cap and the various representations of the Goddess of Liberty and the Statue of Liberty were patriotic in intent.

As new modes of transportation appeared in the late nineteenth and early twentieth centuries, they too were immortalized in copper. The sailing ship vanes, always popular in coastal towns, gave way to steamships and ferryboats. The horsecar was succeeded by the trolley. Locomotives of various types were available, as were many different examples of firefighting apparatus. These, along with the fireman's hat and trumpet, were frequently seen atop turn-of-the-century firehouses. Cannons and the soldier's cap and gun were placed above the local armory, and by 1920 a new airport might boast its own weathervane in the form of the current model of flying machine.

These are but a portion of the various vane types one may expect to encounter about the country. In addition, new specimens are still appearing, for not all the old weathervane manufacturers went out of business. Two of the most famous nineteenth-century companies, J. W. Fisk and E. G. Washington of Danvers, Massachusetts, are still making vanes in the same old way. As one might suspect, this presents problems for the collector. The makers offer their vanes as new, but they often employ the old molds and the same materials as those found in vanes a hundred years old. With a little "weathering," a new vane can look pretty old. That such faking can take place is understandable in light of the fact that weathervanes are one of the most popular items on the current antiques market. Even the little eight-inch cows and horses once given away by feed and milk companies sell for a hundred dollars or so, and any full-size vane will bring anywhere from several hundred to several thousand dollars, depending on type and size.

One of the saddest side effects of the weathervane craze is the gradual disappearance of these noble symbols from the American skyline. Either lured by the value they possess to sell them or driven to hide them away by fear of thieves (who in recent years have resorted to helicopters to seek out their prey), owners are taking down the old vanes. It is a sad commentary on the state of our society that such beautiful and useful objects are not even safe on rooftops.

Whirligigs

Whirligigs are, in essence, wind toys, although those that are mounted on a free-moving shaft can serve also as weathervanes. The basic and earliest form is that of a figure with paddlelike arms, which are set on and revolve about a shaft running through the shoulders. When the wind blows, the arms turn like propellers. Traditionally, the first American examples were models of Hessian soldiers and were supposedly made by Pennsylvania settlers of German origin in mockery of the German mercenaries employed by the British during the Revolutionary War. There is little support for this story, but there is no doubt that the whirligig was known and made in Europe long before the settlement of this continent.

Few whirligigs are made of any substance other than wood, though they may often have various metal accessories. This is especially true of the late nineteenth- and twentieth-century examples, which are far more complex than the traditional models. These more recent wind toys often have several moving parts, so that when motivated, they can perform various functions. A sawyer may saw a log, a blacksmith may strike his anvil, or a whole group of people may perform a jerky dance. Such compositions are aptly termed "twentieth-century folk art" by collectors, for few of the devices date prior to 1900. They are eagerly sought today despite their rather recent vintage, and the collector will be well advised to watch for them at country yard sales and auctions. Unlike weathervanes, whirligigs can often be purchased for next to nothing.

The very simplicity and crudeness of the average whirligig make it fair game for the faker. With a little paint, some old wood, and a few bits of iron, someone with ingenuity can put together a representative example. New examples do appear regularly, but so far they seem to lack the sophistication of reproductions in other fields. The paint is generally too new, and there is little sign of the weathering that should be present on an object that has been outdoors for a few years. If prices go up in the field, no doubt more skilled operators will enter the arena.

Pig weathervane, painted pine; New York, 20th century; $350–500. Good form and color in a late adaptation of an old favorite.

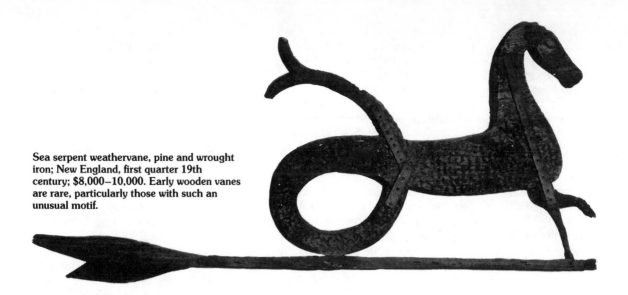

Sea serpent weathervane, pine and wrought iron; New England, first quarter 19th century; $8,000–10,000. Early wooden vanes are rare, particularly those with such an unusual motif.

Mare and foal weathervane, painted pine; Rhode Island, mid-19th century; $750–900. A simple saw-cut vane of a type still made today.

Crude fish weathervane, pine; New England, late 19th century; $400–500.

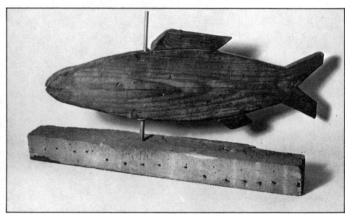

Eagle or buzzard weathervane, painted pine; East, late 19th century; $700–950. The head on this piece is particularly well done and sets it apart from most sawed wood eagles.

Full-bodied Angel Gabriel weathervane, molded and rounded polychromed pine; New York, mid-19th century; $4,500–6,000. A fine example of the carver's art.

Heron weathervane, painted pine; New York, 20th century; $700–875. Not very old but extremely well done.

Horse and rider weathervane, painted sheet iron; New York, mid-19th century; $1,000–1,250. Though much of the original painting has been worn away, enough remains to indicate that it was of unusually high quality.

Horse weathervane, painted sheet iron; East, late 19th century; $450–600.

Horse and rider weathervane, tin with traces of original paint; Rhode Island, ca. 1840; $1,500–2,500. An example of an early full-bodied vane.

Carved wood form for weathervane; East, late 19th century; $1,300–1,800. Used to prepare the molds from which copper vanes were made; few of these forms survive.

Rooster weathervane, cast iron with tail of sheet iron; Massachusetts, last quarter 19th century; $1,700–2,300.

Rooster weathervane, copper, New England, late 19th-early 20th century; $850–1,200. An example of a common full-bodied form.

Rooster on arrow weathervane, strongly molded copper; East, last quarter 19th century; $975–1,350.

Prancing horse weathervane, copper and iron; East, 19th century; $1,000–1,750. A spirited steed; the disheveled mane is rather unusual for an American-made piece.

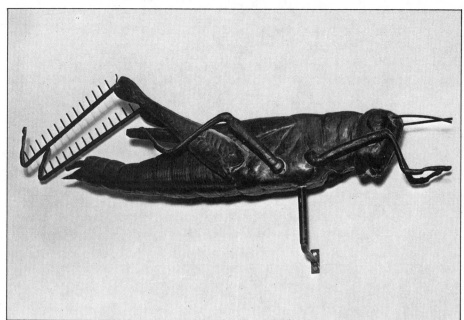

Grasshopper weathervane, copper; New England, last quarter 19th century; $8,000–10,000. An old and prized type.

Eagle on orb weathervane, copper; New England, late 19th century; $3,000–3,750.

Sailing ship weathervane, tin and wood; Maine, 20th century; $2,200–3,000. A fine specimen of a 20th-century craftsman's work.

Goddess of Liberty weathervane, copper with traces of gilding; New England, 1858; $3,500–4,750. This is a small version of a popular vane, which in the 3′ or 4′ size may bring over 10,000 dollars.

Writing quill weathervane, copper and sheet iron; New York, late 19th century; $1,000–1,300.

Cow weathervane, gilded tin, approximately 8″ long; East, early 20th century; $275–365. Small vanes of this sort were given away as premiums by companies that sold grain or purchased raw milk.

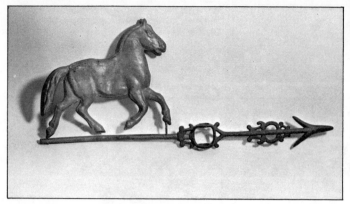

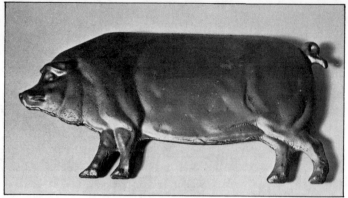

Horse weathervane, gilded tin; New England, 20th century; $245–285. Another small vane used as a premium.

Pig weathervane, gilded copper; New England, late 19th century; $125–165. This vane is only 6″ long.

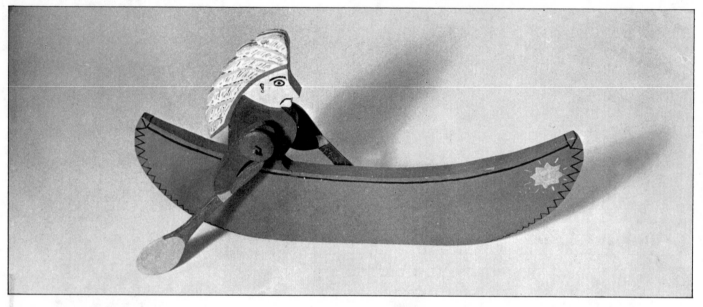

Indian in canoe whirligig, painted pine; New York, early 20th century; $60–90.

Man and propeller whirligig, painted pine; East, early 20th century; $175–250. A very well-done piece.
◄

Airplane whirligig, painted pine; 20th century; $300–425. A large and interesting piece, though not very old.

Helicopter whirligig, pine and tin; New York, 20th century; $125–175.

Sulky and trotter whirligig, painted pine and iron; New England, late 19th-early 20th century; $400–650. Complex movable whirligigs of this sort are attracting increasing collector attention.

Windmill whirligig, painted tin; East, late 19th-early 20th century; $135–185.

17.
TRAMP ART

Few areas of American folk art have slumbered unnoticed for as long as tramp art. A wide variety of objects was made in this distinctive style for well over a half century, but it was not until very recently that more than a few astute dealers and collectors began to appreciate the form.

The term *tramp art* refers to objects made by a specific technique that produces a unique style. Construction is characterized by gluing or nailing together layers of thin board, usually obtained by dismantling old cigar boxes or fruit crates. By gradating the size and shape of the layers, it is possible to create depth and varying perspective, which could otherwise be achieved only by very sophisticated deep carving. Combined with layering is the ancient art of chip, or notch, carving, the cutting of V- or Z-shaped notches into the surface of the wooden components. Changing the number and placement of the notches greatly alters the appearance of the object. Layering and chipping can be combined in an infinite number of ways to create objects with highly decorative surfaces and considerable individuality. No two pieces of tramp art are exactly alike.

The origin of the craft is unclear. Its name reflects a general supposition that the objects were made by itinerant carvers—hoboes, perhaps—who made pieces to sell or to barter for food and shelter as they wandered from town to town. Certainly, some work may well have been done in this manner. Many of the pieces are small enough to have been made on the move, and their materials were readily obtainable. A knife for carving was a standard item carried by itinerants, and the wood—mahogany or cedar from cigar boxes, pine from packing cases—could be picked up along the way, in public dumps or at stores where discards were stacked high in the alleys. But such an origin could account for only a portion of the output. Hoboes were hardly likely to have made large items such as beds and bureaus. Moreover, many pieces show the mark of cutting tools other than the knife—fretsaws, gouges, and chisels, unlikely possessions for a drifter.

Recent research has indicated a much more complex development for this craft than was originally supposed. Chip carving itself is characteristic of early American decorative woodworking as well as German and Scandinavian art from the seventeenth century on. The earliest dated tramp art in America is from the 1860s, which coincides with the period of great immigration from these areas. This and the fact that tramp work has been found in Germany strongly indicates that the style was brought to the United States by immigrants, probably itinerant craftsmen or apprentices who carved as they traveled and spread the technique by example. Unfortunately, there is little reliable oral tradition associated with the work, and no written references exist prior to the 1920s, a time when it was already on the wane, driven out by new uses for leisure time and a declining interest in cigar smoking, which reduced the availability of material.

At its zenith, tramp art must have been extremely popular. It was made in jails (though apparently only as a time killer, not for public sale), in lumber camps, by members of the military, and at public schools, where it appears to have been at one time part of shop courses. Pieces that can be attributed to a definite source are few, however; the great bulk of the ware remains unidentifiable.

This anonymity is particularly surprising in light of the fact that known specimens cover such a wide range of forms and styles. Yet there was much, much more. In a very real way, tramp art mirrors the changes in popular taste. The earlier work is strongly Victorian with a lavish busyness that is almost a parody of its inspirational source. As the twentieth century progressed, Deco influences crept in. Always, while remaining individualistic, the work is responsive to current styles.

The variety of forms in the medium is very great, and new types keep appearing. Picture frames, boxes, and mirrors are the most common items. Large pieces of case furniture, though hardly common, are found often enough to lead one to suspect that many others have been consigned to the woodshed. Full-size chests of drawers, cupboards, sideboards, sofas, and desks are known. There is even at least one floor-model radio cabinet! Many smaller household objects were made as well: coatracks, hanging wall pockets, plant stands, and tables; birdcages, ashtray holders, comb cases, pincushions, and barometer boxes; and a variety of clock cases ranging from a stately grandfather to wall and shelf models. Toys were also made in this style, and more than one child thrilled to the sight of a tramp-work miniature chest of drawers, cradle, rocker, or table. Hardest to come by are the whimsies, one-time projects that are unique and cannot be duplicated. Among the known examples are a model of the Brooklyn Bridge, a church, and a boxed wooden turtle.

Besides layering and chip carving, these pieces frequently display other decoration. Certain symbols occur repeatedly as decorative motifs: stars, hearts, flowers, birds, fish, deer, and various geometric forms. In addition, glass fragments, brass tacks, porcelain knobs, bits of colored stone or paper, and even complete lithographed pictures may be pasted onto the composition. While most tramp ware was left in the natural state or shellacked, some specimens were painted. Where present, the color is often highly fanciful. Bright reds, blues, greens, and yellows were applied indiscriminately, producing an effect that once must have been garish in the extreme. Fortunately, the natural fading with the passage of time has often transformed these to more subtle hues, which appeal to the modern eye.

Tramp art is rarely signed or otherwise specifically identifiable. Some pieces may be dated approximately, by determining the dates of operation of the cigar company or fruit packer from whose wood the ware was made. However, since by its nature the art was anonymous, it is not especially important to know the date or maker—to know the work is enough.

Prices in the field have risen steadily over the past five years. Smaller and more common examples such as frames seem a bit high at present, but one can hardly quarrel with the sums asked for the larger, rarer specimens. These are, in large part, unique or nearly so, and to own one is a rare privilege.

Left: Pinchusion; $45–60. *Center:* Penny bank; $80–120. *Right:* Lift-top box; $30–50. All, 20th century.

Left: Small pedestal box with star motif; $90–115. *Right:* Mirrored lift-top box; $60–90. Good examples of inexpensive 20th-century tramp art.

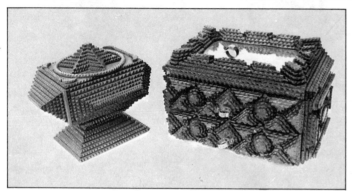

Left: Unusual layered bank; $80–125. *Right:* Lift-top box with heart motif and red satin interior; $65–115. Both, early 20th century.

Box with two drawers concealed behind hinged panel; late 19th century; $90–140.

Octagonal storage box in shape of minaret; late 19th century; $325–400.

Extremely well-done double-pedestal storage box with handle; late 19th century; $280–350. Only a few tramp art boxes have more than one pedestal.

Left: Large, well-done pedestal box; $125–165. *Right:* Humidor; $135–175. Both, late 19th-early 20th century.

Gold-painted box with mirrored top and sides, containing man's shaving set; late 19th century; $200–300.

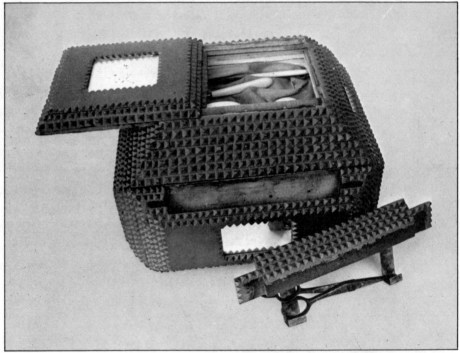

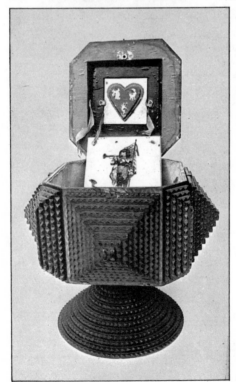

Pedestal box with multicolor decorated interior; early 20th century; $200–285. A very unusual piece.

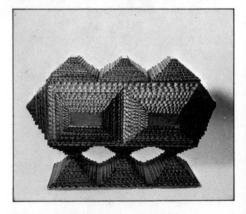

Triple-pedestal storage box; late 19th century; $350–450.

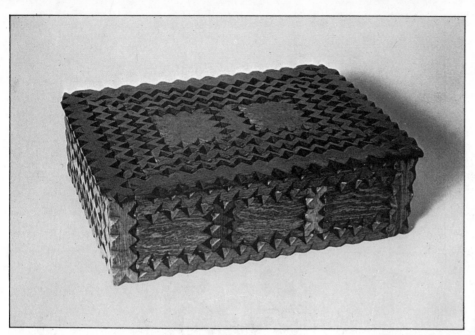

Simple lift-top storage box; 20th century; $30–45. This box is typical of the simple and inexpensive items in this line.

Interesting lift-top boxes. *Left:* With clasped hands and lover's message; $175–250. *Right:* With painted blue interior; $60–85. Both, late 19th-early 20th century.

Well-decorated hanging cupboard or spice chest; late 19th-early 20th century; $175–225.

Sewing box in old red paint, 20th century; $180–260. Note use of cheeseboxes as drawers.

Complexly cut wall pouch with rare cutout figure of a man; late 19th century; $550–750.

Wall box and mirror with motif; dated 1912; $200–285. In this area, as in others, dated pieces are prized.

Wall pockets. *Left:* With incised representation of flag; 20th century; $75–125. *Right:* Late 19th century; $35–50.

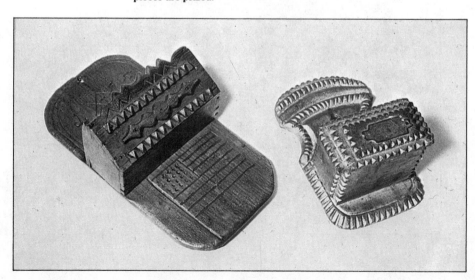

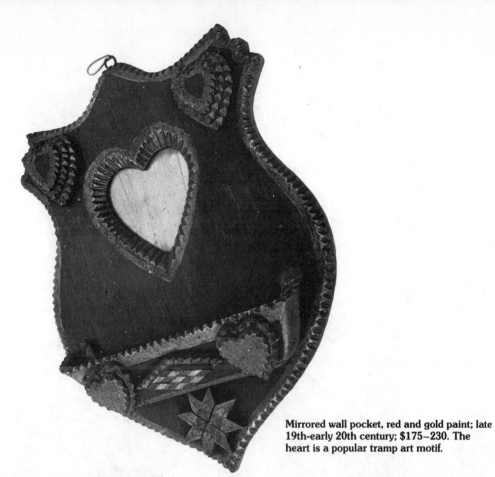

Mirrored wall pocket, red and gold paint; late 19th-early 20th century; $175–230. The heart is a popular tramp art motif.

Elaborate mirrored wall pocket with acorn, leaf, and heart devices, gold trim; possibly Canadian, 20th century; $200–260.

Mirrored wall box with elaborate carving and layering; late 19th-early 20th century; $275–350.

Presentation wall box, black and gold paint; dated 1919; $350–500. Photos and initials of donor and receiver may be seen on this choice piece.

Wall pocket with shield device and porcelain button trim; early 20th century; $175–220.

Gothic-style multicolored wall mirror; late 19th century; $200–275.

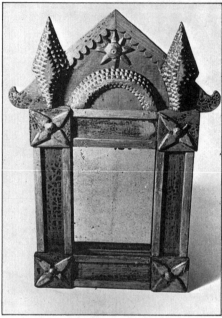

Small wall mirror in shape of a star; late 19th century; $165–230.

Round wall mirror with hearts-and-flowers motifs; late 19th century; $300–400. A rare and beautiful piece.

Small, nicely carved wall mirror; late 19th century; $90–130.

Wall mirror with representations of eagle and eaglets, silver paint; early 20th century; $350–450.

Full-size grandfather's clock elaborately decorated with numerous tramp art motifs; late 19th century; $1,500–2,000. An extremely rare example.

Two small wall mirrors nicely painted in red, green, and gold; 20th century; $75–115 each.

Standing clock case with lower shelf, drawer, and mirror; early 20th century; $350–500.

Nicely carved clock case; 20th century; $225–300.

Cross on pedestal; 20th century; $70–110.
Tramp art crosses are common, particularly
in Canada.

Left: Cross in shrine; $60–95. *Right:* Cross
on pedestal; $75–100. Both, late 19th-early
20th century.

Cross-decorated picture frame with cut-
paper representation of the Garden of Eden;
late 19th-early 20th century; $275–375.

Lady's vanity mirror with interesting chip
carving; late 19th century; $300–400.

Picture frame in form of a heart; late 19th century; $126–165.

Bureau-top mirror; late 19th century; $150–230.

Hanging frame for family record in form of ▶ tramp art house; two silhouettes and six daguerreotypes included; $1,300–1,700. A possibly unique example from the 19th century.

Picture frame, pine; Midwest, late 19th–early 20th century; $110–160. An unusual four-frame form.

Large flower pot, gold paint; 20th century; $200–275.

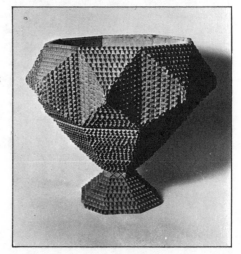

Plaque with depictions of first twenty-five presidents and facsimile of Declaration of Independence; ca. 1900; $1,500–2,100. Almost certainly a unique commemorative piece.

Carved pedestal for lamp or vase; late 19th-early 20th century; $215–275.

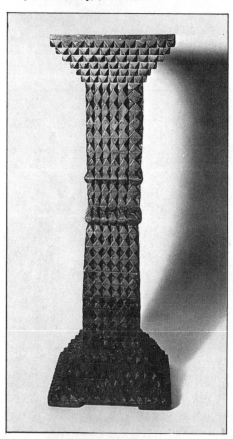

Elaborately decorated plant stand, multicolored; early 20th century; $900–1,200. An outstanding example.

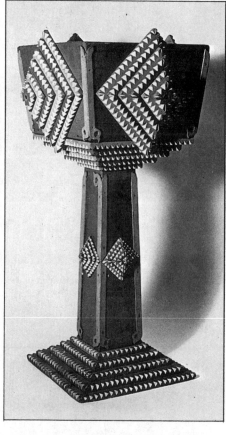

Carved plant stand; 20th century; $400–500.

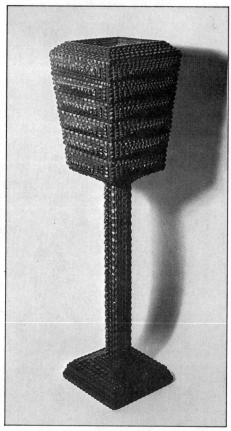

Unusual double-pocket plant stand on elaborate base; early 20th century; $750–1,100. Tramp art's answer to the wicker craze.

Very large multilevel candle lamp, purple and gold paint; 20th century; $450–575.

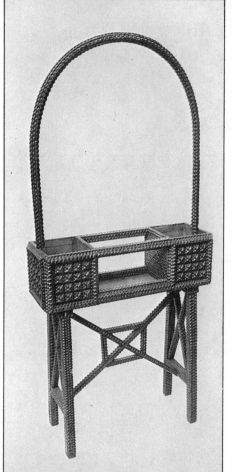

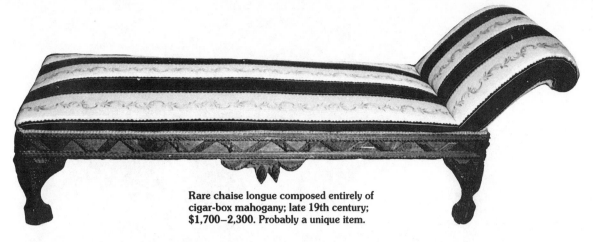

Rare chaise longue composed entirely of cigar-box mahogany; late 19th century; $1,700–2,300. Probably a unique item.

Dome-top trunk decorated with tramp art motifs; early 20th century; $200–250.

Unusual lamp; 20th century; $900–1,100.

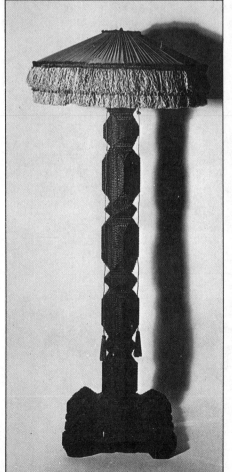

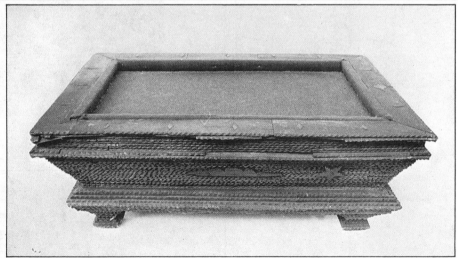

Miniature billiards table; late 19th-early 20th century; $800–1,000.

Radio cabinet in elaborate tramp art style creating the impression of a church; 20th century; $1,400–1,900.

Ashtray on pedestal; 20th century; $175–235. A rare piece.

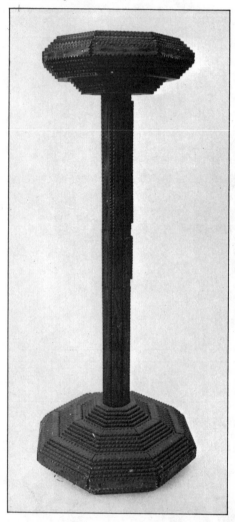

Foot stool, white paint; late 19th-early 20th century; $55–80.

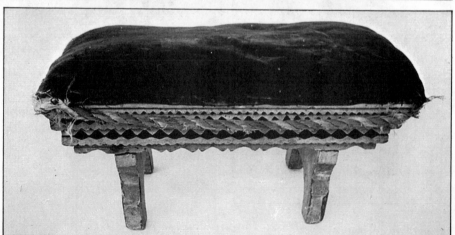

Elaborately decorated Victorian bureau, gold paint; late 19th-early 20th century; $1,850–2,000.

Two-shelf stand, white paint; 20th century; $150–250.

◄
Child's chest of drawers with porcelain knobs; early 20th century; $275–375.

Panel from large tramp art cupboard with extraordinary design and workmanship; late 19th century; $1,500–2,100.

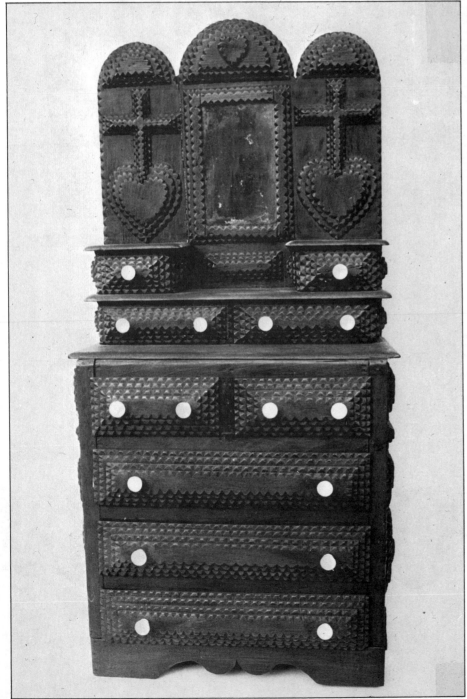

Child's chest of drawers with elaborate decoration, ceramic tile inlay, and bureau-top boxes; late 19th-early 20th century; $425–500. A little bit of everything.

Dollhouse, 20th century; $450–575. These are not common.

Child's toy cupboard; early 20th century; $215–285.

Set of doll furniture; 20th century; $135–185 the set.

Victorian-style overstuffed doll furniture; late 19th-early 20th century; $300–425 the set.

Victorian carved whimsey; late 19th century; $175–235.

Glass box for ship model in tramp art technique known as Crown of Thorns; early 20th century; $240–295.

Elaborate birdcage; late 19th-early 20th century; $400–550.

Unusual representation of a bridge, believed to be a model of the Brooklyn Bridge; late 19th century; $1,500–2,200. Unique.

18.
SCRIMSHAW

To a lover of the sea or to someone fascinated by the life of the early sailor, no antique art form better expresses this aspect of American folk history than scrimshaw. But good scrimshaw is rare and expensive, and reproductions and outright fakes abound.

Knowing something about the background of the craft will help the collector distinguish the good from the bad. Most simply stated, scrimshaw is bone—usually that of a whale—that has been carved or on which a design has been scratched or engraved. This work appears to have been done exclusively by sailors, who could easily obtain the preferred material and whose long sailing trips gave them ample leisure to perform this very detailed and time-consuming work; however, decorative carving of bone was not unique to American sailors, nor to sailors in general. It was known in prehistoric times; and in the modern era it was common in Africa and among the Eskimos and the natives of the South Pacific. Since American sailors had contact with these cultures, it is reasonable to assume that their work was influenced by earlier efforts.

The making of American scrimshaw took place over a relatively brief period, one that coincided with the most prosperous years of the whaling trade. Colonial sailors were seeking the whale throughout the eighteenth century, but there are few dated examples of scrimshaw from that era. A whalebone tooth, marked 1790, with an engraving of Boston harbor seems to be the earliest piece that is clearly native. The great bulk of existing specimens are from the period 1820 to 1890. By the later date, whaling had declined, and with it the whaler's art.

The relationship between whaling and scrimshaw is clear. Bone such as ivory that was available for carving and decoration in other cultures was not readily available to the sailor. He soon learned, however, that the teeth and jawbone of the sperm whale, as well as the pan bone (the hinged end of the jaw) of other whales, could be employed with equal effectiveness. Not all sailors, of course, sailed aboard whalers; but it was not difficult for those who didn't to buy or swap for the necessary material at a seaport. As long as the supply of bone remained constant, scrimshaw was made.

The creation of a piece of scrimshaw began with killing the whale. Once the usable portions of bone were removed from the carcass, they were divided among the crew. Each sailor scraped his bone clean with a sharp knife and then ground it smooth with sandpaper or sharkskin. It was then buffed to a high polish with ashes from the ship's fire. As final preparation, each was soaked to an appropriate softness for cutting.

Scrimshaw work itself included both carving and engraving. Many items, such as the tiny jagging or crimping wheels used to crimp the edges of pies, required shaping and fitting. After a piece was assembled, it might or might not be decorated. The lack of decoration on a piece of whalebone does not disqualify it as scrimshaw. Decoration was a long and tedious process feasible only because the crew on sailing ships had large blocks of free time in their work schedules.

The decoration found on scrimshaw is of two types. The earliest, and some of the best, was done freehand. The sailor simply scratched out a picture or various decorative devices on the bone surface and then gradually deepened the scratches. Pieces done in this manner may be crude, but they also often have the power and vitality of true folk art. More common is pattern-based decoration. This technique called for the sailor to paste to the bone surface an oiled pattern, usually made from a picture cut from a popular periodical; he would then carefully prick out with a steel pin those portions of the pattern he wished to incorporate into his design. The pinpricks would be joined and deepened by scratching, and a recognizable picture would emerge.

For this work the mariner would employ a surprisingly large array of tools. The jackknife was the basic tool, but iron needles of various sorts, awls, files, gimlets, and various polishing devices were also employed.

Once the line work was completed, the design would be darkened by rubbing grease, lampblack, or India ink into the scratches. Infrequently, other colors were used, most commonly red, green, and blue. Finer pieces or those designed as gifts might be further embellished by silver or wooden fittings or inlay in mother-of-pearl.

The subject matter found on decorated whalebone varies, but certain motifs predominate.

Many different scrimshaw items are available. Decorated teeth are in greatest demand, and these present the most problems for the collector. Throughout the twentieth century, various engravers have tried their hands at scrimshaw. Much of this work is intended to look old and is deliberately aged or is done on old blank teeth. Differences in style, methods of cutting, and lack of wear may help to distinguish the late from the early; but the best guide is an honest dealer.

Large pan-bone wall engravings, often of naval actions, are found, but they are rare and expensive. More readily and reasonably obtained are small worked objects, such as jagging wheels (of which there are a great number), corset busks, rulers, rolling pins, napkin rings, cane heads, whistles, needle cases, clothespins, sewing bodkins, and cribbage, chess, and checkers sets. Prices for these items will vary depending on the amount and quality of decoration. Rarer or more complex items such as bootjacks, swifts, and elaborate work or sewing boxes will be more expensive. Sailors' work items such as fids or marlinespikes, planes, sail seam rubbers, and measuring devices are not especially common and are much sought after by collectors of nautical antiques. Most of these items have not been reproduced, but the abundance of fakes in the scrimshaw field dictates that an enthusiast should proceed with caution. There are, fortunately, a number of good public scrimshaw collections, notably at the Kendall Whaling Museum in Sharon, Massachusetts; the New Bedford Whaling Museum in New Bedford, Massachusetts; and the Mystic Seaport Marine Historical Association in Mystic, Connecticut. Examination of examples in these collections will enable the collector to familiarize himself with the types and decorative techniques involved in scrimshaw and thus avoid making unwise purchases.

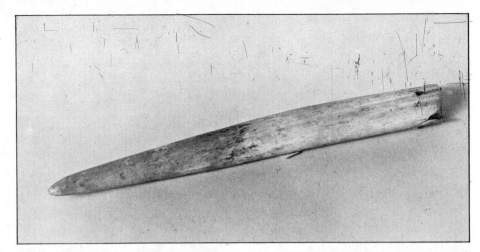

Old, uncarved walrus tusk; $50–90. Bone of this sort is eagerly sought for reproduction carving.

Extremely fine carved whale nearly 10″ long, whalebone; New England, 19th century; $650–775. Possibly used as a paperweight.

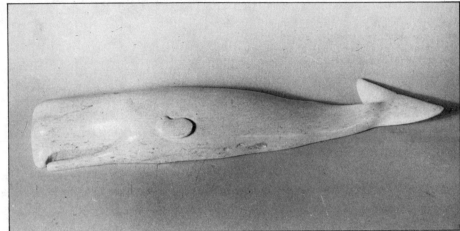

Pie crimper, or jagging wheel, in shape of a whale, whalebone; late 19th century; $200–325. Jagging wheels are among the most common of scrimshaw; this is a crude but strongly shaped piece.

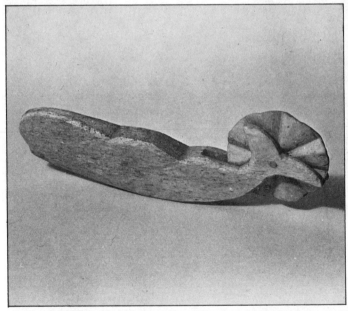

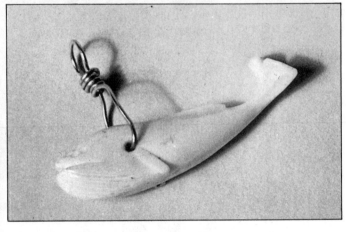

Watch fob or charm, whalebone or tooth with gold-wire clasp; New England, late 19th century; $150–220.

Harpoon, whalebone, 6″ long; late 19th–early 20th century; $365–435.

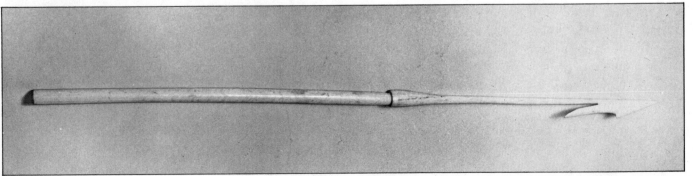

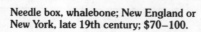
Needle box, whalebone; New England or New York, late 19th century; $70-100.

Spouting whale, engraved on sperm-whale tooth; New England, mid-19th century; $800-1,100.

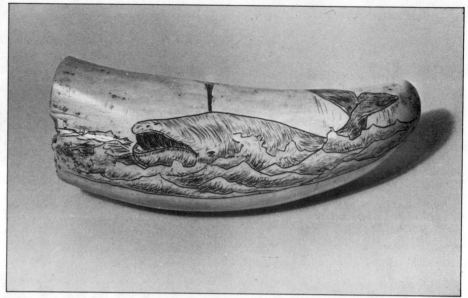

Whalebone stamp used to indicate lost whales in ship's log; New England, mid-19th century; $265-345. A very unusual piece.

Whaling ship and whales, engraved on a whale tooth and mounted on mahogany stand; New England, 19th century; $600-850.

Well-worked representation of the sailing ship *W. R. Grace*, engraved on whale tooth; $900-1,300. East, 19th century.

Battle between the *Essex* and the *Alert*, engraved on whale tooth; New England, early 19th century; $1,400–2,100.

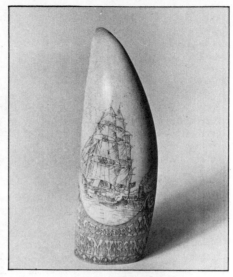

Representation of the Civil War battle between the U.S.S. *Cumberland* and the Confederate States' ram *Virginia*, engraved on whale tooth; East, 1860s; $1,200–1,600. The piece is more highly decorated than usual.

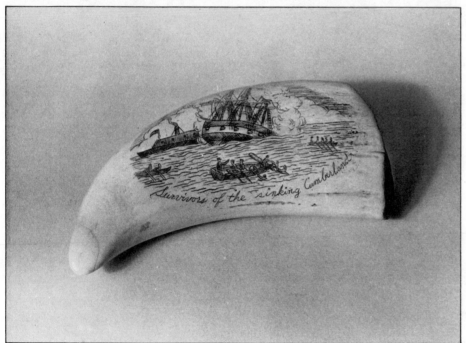

Depiction of the sinking of the *Cumberland* following its battle with the *Virginia*, engraved on sperm-whale tooth; East, 1860s; $750–1000.

Portrait of Captain Maffitt of the Confederate Navy, commander of the warship *Florida*, engraved on whale tooth; Southeast, 1860s; $450–650.

Portrait of Admiral Farragut, Civil War naval hero, engraved on whale tooth; New England, 1860s; $550–750.

321

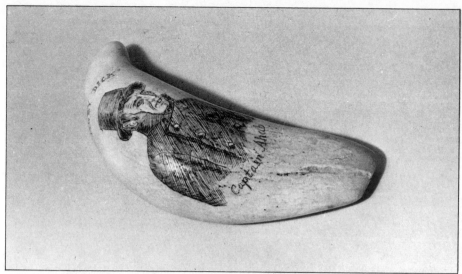

Representation of Captain Ahab, famous character in Herman Melville's *Moby Dick*, engraved on whale tooth; East, 20th century; $225–300.

Seated Liberty or Columbia, engraved on whale tooth; 19th century; $425–525.

Early, crudely engraved eagle and shield, on whale tooth; East, first half 19th century; $575–725.

Representation of a Victorian lady, engraved on sperm-whale tooth; East, second half 19th century; $500–650.

Carved whistles, whalebone engraved with sailing ships; New England, 19th century; $260–230 each.

Unusual storage container of the type commonly called a ditty box, carved and engraved baleen and whalebone; New England, mid-19th century; $1,000–1,400. Baleen, a coarse, flexible membrane found in the whale's throat, was used in the construction of boxes and corset stays.

Well-carved cane head in the form of a fist, whalebone, with engraving; New England, mid-19th century; $275–350.

Watch fob engraved with a dolphin, whalebone or tooth mounted in silver; New England, 19th century; $160–235.

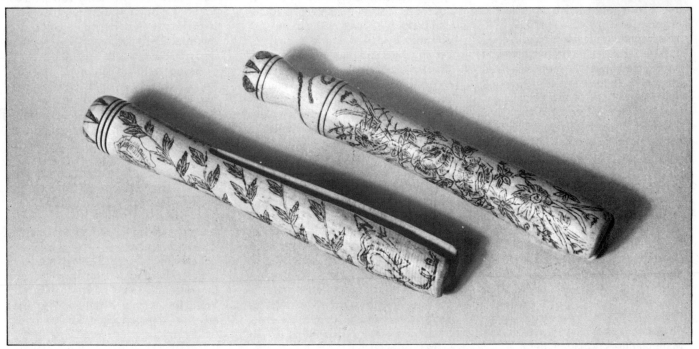

Intricately engraved clothespins, whalebone; East, 19th century. *Top:* 125–165. *Bottom:* 110–140.

Cane head or umbrella handle, whalebone with carved knot work and engraved representations of whales; New England, mid-19th century; $275–325.

19

ADVERTISING MEMORABILIA

Although most advertising antiques date from the very late nineteenth and the twentieth centuries, the concept of advertising is much older. On this continent, the manufacturers of patent medicines were advertising their wares in local papers during the 1700s, and by 1810 they were marketing their concoctions in bottles embossed with company names.

Trade cards—small pieces of stiff paper printed with the name, address, and product of a craftsman—are the most abundant of the early advertising devices. Specimens from before 1850 are relatively uncommon, but by the end of the Civil War, the widespread use of lithography led to a proliferation of trade cards. Hand-colored lithographed trade cards exist in great numbers. Everything from whiskey to sewing machines was promoted in this manner, with the cards being handed out at stores or given away on the streets by boys. Prices are moderate, with only the earliest or rarest types selling for more than ten dollars apiece, and many cards are available for no more than a dollar.

Paper was utilized for other advertising devices. The boxes and other containers in which products were sold were printed with eye-catching designs. The labels on fruit and vegetable crates are particularly appealing to collectors. Cardboard fans, given out at country fairs and in hotels prior to the days of air conditioning, were used to promote anything from funeral parlors to ice-cream parlors. Manufacturers provided their distributors with large lithographed paper and cardboard posters extolling the virtues of their wares. Other paper memorabilia include beer coasters, seed packs, and a vast number of other decorated containers. Cigarette and cigar packs are a particularly popular and interesting area. Everything from beautiful ladies to war planes appears, and the collector's cards given away in some packs provide an added bonus.

It didn't take long for advertisers to figure out that if an attractive design and catchy slogan would draw business, a useful gadget would do even better. Such items were distributed at two levels. First, manufacturers sold, leased, or gave to their distributors such things as lamps, shop signs, and cigar lighters or cutters. These served a purpose, and

they also carried the painted or embossed slogan of the manufacturer. In addition, any number of household aids were given away to consumers or offered as premiums. The list is endless, including wooden cutting boards, tin scoops, bottle openers, buttonhooks, pokers, ice picks, pie plates, graters, goblets, and knickknack containers. All carried somewhere on their surface the advertiser's message, and all are today of great interest to collectors.

Tin advertising trays were widely distributed during the period 1890 to 1940. Beer, whiskey, soft drink, and mineral water makers provided them for their clients, and they came in several sizes. Large sixteen-inch wall plaques can be found as well as the more common twelve- to fourteen-inch serving trays and the tiny round or·oval tip trays. All bear lithographed designs or pictures and, of course, the name of the distributor. Perhaps the best known are Coke trays, which today may fetch several hundred dollars for certain hard-to-find examples.

The most outstanding example of the advertising antique—and perhaps the most familiar—is the cigar-store Indian. Trade figures of various sorts were quite common in the nineteenth century: purveyors of nautical goods might have a statue of a sailor outside the shop; a bakery might feature a jolly representation of the man in the white cap and apron. But by far the most popular were the hand-carved figures of Indian chiefs and maidens that were associated with tobacco shops. These were produced in large numbers during the period 1850 to 1890. The Indians, which were nearly life-size, were traditionally placed outside the shop, where they might attract the attention of passersby but where they were also exposed to wind and weather. Over the years, most have fallen prey to fire, theft, or general deterioration. The few hundred remaining examples are in great demand. The whereabouts of most are known, and when one changes hands, the sale price is usually around five thousand dollars.

One must be extremely wary of modern reproductions. High demand has led to sophisticated faking in this area, with expert carvers copying known genuine pieces and employing old wood and techniques. Cigar-store Indians should be purchased only from

reputable dealers who can provide an authenticated history and a money-back guarantee.

There were other figures, many of them Indians, that stood inside shops on a table or counter. These are usually two or three feet high and may be of plaster of Paris, iron, or wood. These are more common and less expensive than their big brothers.

If the seller of tobacco or liquor directed his advertising primarily to men, the lady of the house was certainly not ignored by other merchants. Perfume, cologne, and toiletries distributors regaled her with a variety of eye-catching enticements. Small mirrors for pocket or purse were popular. These were round, oval, or square and usually incorporated a lithograph of a beautiful and obviously wealthy woman.

As the twentieth century advanced and women added smoking cigarettes and wearing makeup to their life-styles, advertisers adjusted the pitch. Attractive lighters and cigarette cases carried the commercial message as did a variety of cosmetic cases. For those of more conservative taste, there were still the traditional give-aways. Maxwell House coffee offered cups and saucers emblazoned with the firm name. Egg beaters extolled the virtues of, naturally, an egg company.

Many of these small articles are inexpensive and offer an appealing area for collectors. Good mirrors can be found for less than twenty dollars, and advertising paperweights, at five to ten dollars apiece, seem somewhat underpriced considering their quality and the fact that many date from the nineteenth century. Compacts and lighters are somewhat higher but also seem to be a good buy at present.

If one is interested in an area that allows for an infinitely expanding collection, the previously mentioned trade cards are available. There are also tin tobacco tags. These were introduced in the 1880s by the Lorillard Company and were provided with prongs with which they were clamped into plugs of chewing tobacco. Originally, these tiny pieces of tin were intended by the manufacturers to be redeemed for various premiums. They were, however, interesting in their own right, often being cut in the shape of hatchets, stars, guns, crosses, and the like. Accordingly, they were frequently accumulated rather than redeemed, and large collections are often found.

Another major collector interest in this field is "tins," various lithographed tin containers not unlike the ones seen in stores today. The earlier examples are much more elaborately decorated, though, and contained such things as gunpowder, rat poison, and stove polish, none of which would be packaged in this way today. Shapes and sizes vary greatly, ranging from large round or bin-shaped coffee and tea dispensers to tiny rectangular cigarette boxes. The qualities that determine price are the degree of rarity and

attractiveness. For most collectors, the latter is of major importance. Good lithographed design is a plus, and the quainter the better. Rarity can lead to very high prices, but only among a small group of very sophisticated collectors. For most, the decoration is the thing. Decorated tin containers of this sort have been on a spectacular price rise for the past five to ten years. Even certain recent tins, such as those of Sir Walter Raleigh pipe tobacco and du Maurier cigarettes, are worth a few dollars, and earlier examples frequently sell in the tens of dollars. A great deal of material is available here, though, and it is possible

to amass a representative grouping without spending a great deal, particularly if one frequents yard sales and country fairs where tins often are sold for just a few cents.

Advertising antiques is one of the largest fields of antiques collecting, and the definition of the category is constantly being expanded. For example, attention is now for the first time being directed to lithographed box tops. Though fragile, these are a good buy. Old newspapers are filled with advertisements, many of them illustrated with woodcuts; and these are a virtually untouched area.

Lift-top tobacco box, lithographed tin; Illinois, late 19th century; $150–210.

Storage and dispensing box, lithographed tin; Midwest, late 19th century; $200–275. One of the best of its type, this is one of a series depicting the ships of America's famed "White Squadron." Shown here is the U.S.S. *Chicago*.

Cut-plug box with bail handle, lithographed tin; East, 20th century; $20–35.

Packing case, lithographed tin; New Jersey, late 19th century; $75–125.

Tobacco packing box, lithographed tin; Michigan, early 20th century; $50–70.

Tea canisters, lithographed tin; 20th century. *Left:* Wells Tea; New York; $15–25. *Center:* Tetley Tea; East; $5-15. *Right:* Family Tea; Midwest; $15–25.

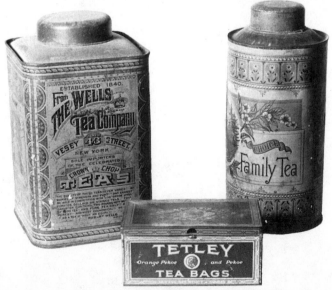
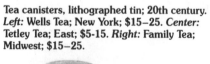

Peanut roaster, tin and sheet iron; East, early 20th century; $175–275.

Hinged coffee bin, lithographed tin, paper label; East, early 20th century; $45–60.

Storage canister, wood, lithographed paper label; New Jersey, late 19th century; $75–100.

Storage canister, wood, lithographed paper label; New York, late 19th century; $35–65.

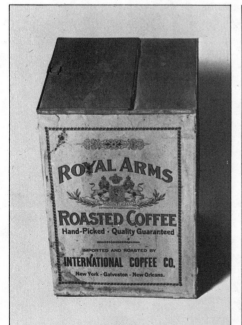

327

Wall-hanging ruler, tin, reverse has 6″ rule; Valentine and Co., Varnish Manufacturers, Delaware, late 19th century; $25–40.

Cottolene Shortening pie plate, graniteware, white with blue trim; East, early 20th century; $5–10.

Serving tray, lithographed tin; Midwest, 20th century; $50–65.

Glass paperweight with lithographed advertisement of Babcock Manufacturing Co.; Connecticut, late 19th century; $20–35. Paperweights of this sort come in a wide variety and are a good investment in the advertiques area.

Advertising pin, lithographed tin; East, early 20th century; $25–45.

Serving tray, lithographed tin; New York, 20th century; $75–125.

Advertising pin, lithographed tin; New England, early 20th century; $30–55.

Pill boxes, lithographed cardboard; East, late 19th century. *Left:* Ma-Le-Na Liver Pills; $6–9. *Center:* Fellow's Liver Pills; $3–5. *Right:* Dr. White's Liver Pills; $7–15.

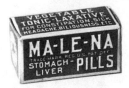

Handkerchief box, lithographed cardboard; ca. 1870; $10–20.

Tobacco packages, lithographed paper, late 19th–early 20th century. *Left:* Veteran; $10–15. *Center:* Lucky Curve; $30–45. *Right:* Luxury; $15–22.

Underwear packing box, lithographed cardboard; New England, ca. 1920; $15–25.
▼

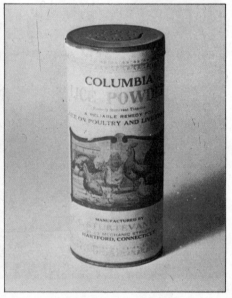

Columbia Flea Powder, lithographed paper, ▲ cardboard, and tin; Connecticut, early 20th century; $5–15.

Three examples of seed packages, lithographed paper; Midwest, 20th century; $5–12 each.

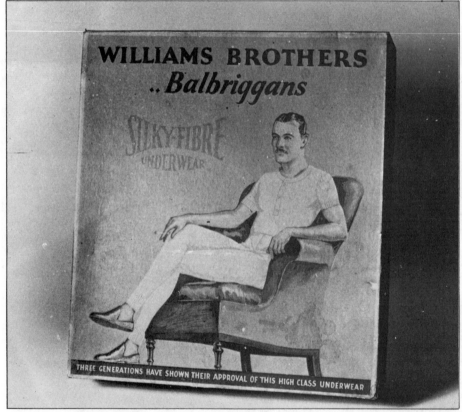

Packing boxes, wood, lithographed paper labels; New England, late 19th century. *Above:* Defiance Mustard; $25–35. *Below:* Welcome soap; $55–80. The more decorative the detail, the higher the price.

Packing box, wood, multicolored lithographed labels; New York, late 19th century; $75–125.

Diamond Dyes display case, lithographed tin and wood; East, late 19th century; $285–365. One of the most desirable advertiques.

Revolving store rack, lithographed tin; New England, late 19th century; $135–195.

Penny match dispenser, cast iron; New England, late 19th century; $150–220. Advertiser's name appears on side.

Rare cast-iron Jaxon soap pot, gold paint; Midwest, late 19th century; $80–120.

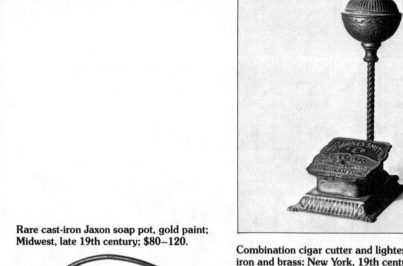

Combination cigar cutter and lighter, cast iron and brass; New York, 19th century; $125–160. Another advertising store fixture.

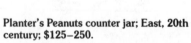

Planter's Peanuts counter jar; East, 20th century; $125–250.

Store coffee grinder, cast-iron and lithographed tin; "Hunters' Cabinet Coffee Mill, Patent 1888," Midwest; $65–90.

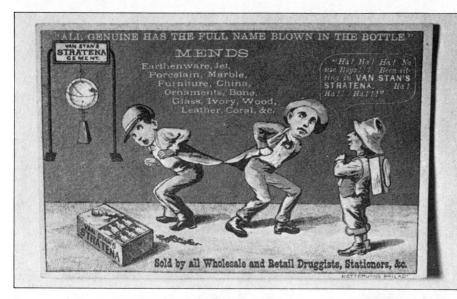

Trade card, lithographed cardboard; Pennsylvania, late 19th century; $15–22. An example of inexpensive and very popular advertising items.

Trade cards, lithographed cardboard; East, late 19th century. *Left:* Ammen's Cough Syrup; $5–9. *Right:* Pinkham's medicines; $4–8.

Lithographed cardboard trade cards in the form of sailing ships, issued by the Honest Cut Plug chewing tobacco company; New York, 19th century. *Left:* $17–25. *Right:* $18–28. These cards came with the tobacco and were intended to be collected in a series.

Ayer's trade card, lithographed cardboard; Lowell, Mass., late 19th century; $10–17. For obvious reasons, one of the most popular cards.

Trade cards, lithographed cardboard; late 19th century. *Left:* Brown's Bitters; $5–9. *Right:* Melvin's Nerve Liniment; $4–8.

Trade cards, lithographed cardboard; late 19th century. *Left:* Pond's Extract; $4–7. *Right:* Morse Dock Root Syrup; $4–7. Bottle collectors often collect proprietary medicine trade cards such as these as "go withs."

Trade cards, lithographed cardboard; New England, late 19th century. *Left:* Hire's Cough Cure; $4–8. *Center:* Florida Water; $3–6. *Right:* Tarrant's Aperient; $3–6.

Trade card, lithographed cardboard; New York, late 19th century; $3–7. Merchants as well as manufacturers issued trade cards.

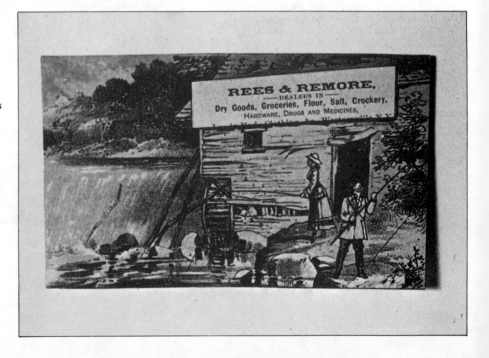

Maccoboy snuff jar, stoneware with applied lithographed label; New Jersey, 19th century; $75–105.

Vinegar jug, stoneware; New Jersey, late 19th century; $75–135.

Stamford Hotel spittoon, stoneware; Stamford, N.Y., ca. 1870; $175–250.

Covered cheese crock, stoneware; Wisconsin, 20th century; $4–7.

Advertising picture for Weyman's Snuff, lithographed paper on board; Pennsylvania, 19th century; $170–240. One of the best of its type.

Sample bean pot, redware; Massachusetts, late 19th-early 20th century; $12–20. Advertising pottery in redware is uncommon.

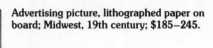

Advertising picture, lithographed paper on board; Midwest, 19th century; $185–245.

Advertising picture, paper on board; Midwest, late 19th century; $160–220.

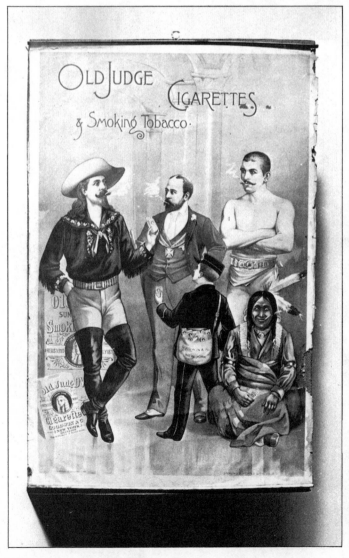

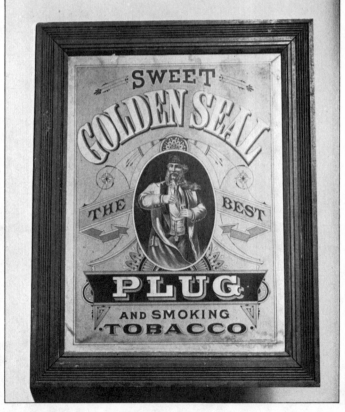

Advertising picture, paper on board; East, late 19th century; $175–235.

Illustration from lithographed paper advertising calendar; New York, late 19th century; $190–280. Figures include Buffalo Bill, Prince Albert, John L. Sullivan, and an unknown Indian.

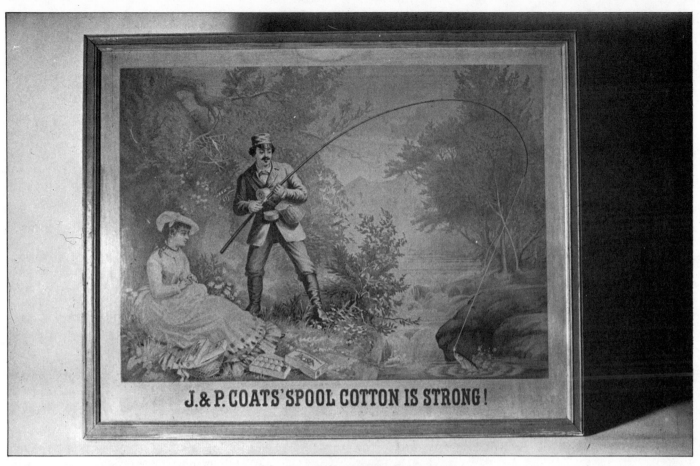

Advertising picture, lithographed paper on
wood; East, late 19th century; $150–200.

Advertising picture, lithographed paper on
wood; New York, ca. 1891; $135–190.

Advertising picture, lithographed paper on
wood; Massachusetts, 1884; $200–275.

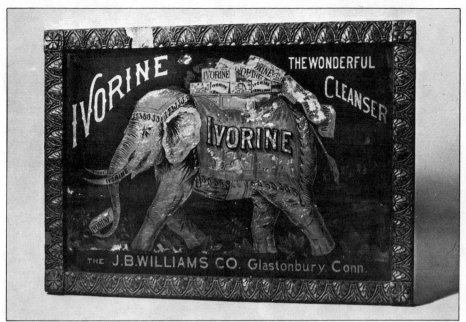

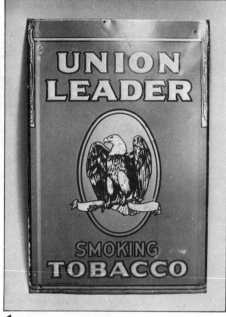

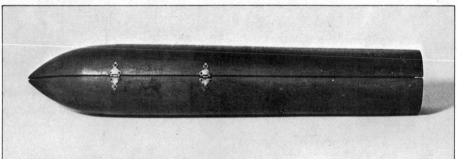

◄

Trade sign, sheet iron with traces of old paint; East, 1825–45; $950–1,350. Figure on horse is believed to be Andrew Jackson.

Counter-top-size cigar-store Indian, plaster of Paris; East, early 20th century; $125–300.

Hand-carved life-size cigar-store Indian, polychrome paint; New England, ca. 1880; $9,000–14,000. These figures are rare and in demand.

Barber pole, polychromed wood; New York State, ca. 1880; $500–850.

20

PHOTOGRAPHIC MEMORABILIA

The collecting of photographic memorabilia—photographs, cameras, and auxiliary equipment—is a rather recent American interest. There were few large collections prior to 1900, and the majority of the important collections have been assembled since the 1930s.

Photography itself can hardly be called new. Daguerreotypes, the most popular form of photograph collected today, were developed in 1839 by the Frenchman Louis Daguerre. Though few daguerreotypes were made before 1841, the art was well developed by 1853, when it was estimated that 3 million such images were produced annually in the United States alone.

The daguerreotype is a photograph taken by exposing a silver-coated copper plate in the camera. This plate is a positive image, not a negative; since no duplicate prints can be made of it, each daguerreotype is unique. Moreover, like a mirror image, the daguerreotype image is the reverse of what the camera sees, a characteristic shared by the later ambrotypes and tintypes. Techniques for coloring or tinting the images were introduced as early as 1842, and many show such features as pink cheeks and lips, but the color is often poor. Daguerreotypes are fragile, and vast numbers have been destroyed, either through carelessness or in an effort simply to obtain the minute amount of copper in each plate. They must be handled with care and cannot be cleaned or polished.

Daguerreotypes were housed in small hinged cases usually made of wood covered with embossed paper or, at a later date, a plasticlike substance mistakenly referred to as gutta-percha. Case sizes were varied to fit the images, which ranged from one and one-half by one and three-quarter inches, the ninth plate, to eight and one-half by thirteen inches, the double whole plate. In general, the larger the image, the more valuable is the daguerreotype, since the great majority was quite small.

Ambrotypes, which were invented by F. Scott Archer of England in 1852, differ from the earlier daguerreotypes only in that the image is taken, or "secured," on glass rather than on a copper plate. To most people the two products look much alike. They can be distinguished, however, by holding an example of each up to a bright light and turning it slowly to the side. The

daguerreotype will reflect the light, while the ambrotype will not. Like its predecessor, the ambrotype is a unique positive image, not a negative, and cannot be duplicated. In order to be seen, the image must be backed with varnish or black paint.

Ambrotypes were somewhat cheaper to produce than daguerreotypes, and they were extremely popular during the period 1854 to 1865. Among the vast quantity made were the photographs in the first "rogues gallery" established by the New York City Police Department in the 1860s.

The prices of daguerreotypes and ambrotypes depend on several factors. As previously mentioned, larger examples are hard to come by and command a higher price. Subject matter is also very important. Images of famous persons can be very valuable—in 1973, a half-plate daguerreotype of Edgar Allan Poe sold for nine thousand dollars. Most images, though, are of ordinary men and women. But something may take them out of the ordinary and thus elevate the price; this could be the clothing the subject is wearing, some props, or anything else that might reveal information about the person. Photographs of cowboys, Indians, workmen with tools, gold miners, soldiers or other men with weapons, and nudes, for example, are all eagerly sought. A few people even share the Victorians' morbid preoccupation with death and collect images of the dead.

Far less common than likenesses of individuals are cased daguerreotype or ambrotype views of buildings or localities. Such views of Washington, D.C, were first discovered in the 1970s, but so far none of New York City has been found, though it is known that several series on the city were prepared. In perhaps no other area of antiques does such a distinct possibility exist of finding something truly rare and valuable.

Other elements may affect price to a lesser extent than those so far discussed. The work of certain photographers who have obtained posthumous fame commands a premium. Mathew Brady, for instance, the great Civil War photographer, placed his name on thousands of images, which are now of substantial value; some even remain to be discovered. The photographer's

name generally appears on the front matting or the case of an ambrotype or daguerreotype, and new acquisitions should always be examined with this factor in mind. The quality of the image is also a consideration, although a lesser one, in price. Good, sharp reproductions, which are the exceptions in both techniques, will bring more than the standard images.

The cases in which these images were housed are also collected. The first mass-produced containers, which appeared in the 1840s, were made of wood with an embossed paper covering. Between five and six hundred different patterns appear on the embossings, mostly falling in one of three categories: birds, flowers, or fruit. The cases are in general rather ordinary and are of minor interest to most collectors. However, certain unusual types, produced mostly during the 1850s, are exceptions to the rule. The Mascher-type case, which incorporated a lens to enable one to view the image stereoscopically, is rare and choice, as are those papier-mâché specimens that were inlaid with mother-of-pearl.

The bulk of collector interest focuses on the so-called Union cases, which were made of a mixture of sawdust and colored shellac and compressed in a powerful mold to produce a fairly hard finished product. There are over eight hundred different case-cover designs in the Union category, mostly related to nature, religion, history, or patriotic events. Among the most popular are those that portray Washington crossing the Delaware to attack Trenton and Columbus landing in the Americas. Neither is rare, but both sell for well over a hundred dollars. Other designs are less common, and all are eagerly sought by collectors.

The introduction of the tintype in 1856 revolutionized photography, making available, for the first time, a cheap and relatively rapid method for the production of multiple images. The tintype is made by exposing in the camera a varnished iron plate. Its invention coincided with development of the multiple-lens camera; by employing a tintype plate in this new camera, it was possible to expose as many as four 2½- by 3½-inch images on a single plate, which after being developed could be cut apart.

Tintype "galleries" sprang up all over

the country during the 1860s, offering photographic portraits—though rather inferior ones—for as little as twenty-five cents per shot. Because they were so cheap, they were seldom enclosed in cases, and most are found loose today.

On the whole, tintypes are neither as popular as daguerreotypes or ambrotypes, nor as expensive. Images of famous persons are seldom found, since they preferred the traditional forms of photography. Some of the popular tintype subjects are Indians, soldiers, and artisans. In addition, a number of outdoor scenes and interesting interiors are found; they are the most expensive tintypes. Prices in this area, in general, are moderate, and it offers a good field for the new collector.

Another mass photographic device was the carte de visite, or visiting card, which received a French patent in 1854 and quickly gained international popularity. The visiting card is a piece of photographic paper showing a bust or full-length portrait of an individual on photographic paper, mounted on cardboard; the average size is 2¼ to 3¾ inches. It was produced in a multiple-lens camera by exposing a glass negative, from which a contact print with from four to eight photos was made. These were then cut apart to make individual photographs.

During the period of their greatest popularity, 1860 to 1885, millions of visiting cards were manufactured. Over a hundred thousand copies of a single photograph of Abraham Lincoln were made for the election of 1860 alone. Yet that card, like others of celebrities, is hard to find today. A card with the bust of Alfred Lord Tennyson sold recently for three hundred dollars, and other comparable portraits are equally expensive. As in earlier photographic mediums, the unusual sells best. The common, anonymous family portrait is of little value, but outdoor scenes, animals, Indians, machinery, and other unusual images command substantial sums.

Similar to visiting cards were cabinet cards. They were made in essentially the same way but in a larger size, the average being 3¾ by 5½ inches. The peak of their popularity was from 1867

until just after 1900, during which time large quantities appeared on the market. More sophisticated lighting, methods of posing, and background materials were employed in an effort to make each cabinet card a work of art. Today, the best portraits of famous individuals may sell for several hundred dollars apiece.

Stereographs, or stereo views, were a popular form of nineteenth-century entertainment. First developed in 1851, they consist of paired views of the same subject, which, when viewed through a stereoscopic viewer, show a single three-dimensional image. The first stereo views were taken by two cameras mounted side by side, but photographers soon adopted the dual-lens, or binocular, camera for this purpose. Daguerreotype and ambrotype stereographs were made in large numbers, primarily in Europe, while American manufacturers turned first to glass views and then to card stereographs, which were produced here in vast numbers from the 1850s on. By 1862, one stereo view manufacturer, Edward Anthony of New York, could boast of an output numbering in the hundreds of thousands. Many other companies joined the business, including mail-order houses such as Montgomery Ward and Sears Roebuck.

Lithoprints, or multicolored stereographs, were developed at the close of the nineteenth century, and they quickly gained public acceptance. Lithos were made from photographs or artist's renderings and often had as their subject humorous or sentimental themes.

Stereographs today are quite reasonably priced. Those that are among the oldest or that depict famous events, locales, disasters, or famous people are expensive enough, ranging upward from a hundred dollars. But most stereographs do not fall within these categories, and it is still possible to purchase interesting views or genre scenes for a few dollars or even less.

What we think of today as photographs—that is, images secured on paper, with film negatives—are the end product of extensive experimentation with various

techniques. The first of these involved the calotype, invented in England in 1841. There followed in rapid order salt prints (so called for the salt solution in which the photographic paper was dipped before printing), albumen prints (where the print paper was coated with albumen, or egg white), and emulsion prints. The use of gelatine bromide emulsion on photographic paper enabled photographers to greatly increase the rapidity with which prints could be made from a negative and heralded the introduction of modern photographic methods.

The result of these advances was a vast number of paper-backed photographs, most of which until recently have been of little interest to collectors of photographic memorabilia. In the 1970s, though, as the supply of inexpensive daguerreotypes, ambrotypes, and other early forms has dwindled, photograph enthusiasts have turned their attention to the later images. The choice is so great that, at present, most collectors are seeking either prints by famous photographers or photographs with unusual subjects—famous personages, events, or localities. Prices vary greatly. Interesting photos may be purchased for less than a dollar, while those bearing the mark of renowned photographers such as Alfred Steiglitz may sell for hundreds of dollars. Only the collector's inclination and his pocketbook will determine what he will collect.

Photographic equipment, cameras, and the like have their devoted enthusiasts, though in number they hardly compare to those who collect images. There are several reasons for this. Early cameras, particularly those used prior to 1900, are scarce and expensive. Many are found in damaged condition, and restoration is expensive. Camera equipment is more difficult to store and to display than photographs. because equipment requires more space.

Despite these problems, the number of collectors interested in cameras appears to be growing. Early Kodaks and other mass-produced and relatively common cameras may be obtained for well under a hundred dollars; and a group of them can form the nucleus for an expanding collection.

Sixth-plate daguerreotype of a woman, with tinted features; 1850s; $10–20.

Quarter-plate daguerreotype of two children; 1850s; $35–45.

Rare ninth-plate daguerreotype of a primitive painting of a woman, papier-mâché case; 1850s. The daguerreotype is worth $60–95; the painting, if found, perhaps a hundred times that!

Sixth-plate daguerreotype of a nun; 1850s; $45–65.

Ninth-plate daguerreotype of a child in unusual Mascher magnifying viewer case; 1850s; $125–175.

Set of nine daguerreotypes in a walnut ogee frame; late 19th century; $250–400.

▼

Half-plate ambrotype in wood and paper case; mid-19th century; $500–625. Unusual view of western gold miners and rare gold tint applied to rocks give the plate its high price.

Quarter-plate ambrotype of four children; 1850s; $35–55.

Quarter-plate ambrotype of little boy, wood and paper case, dress tinted yellow; 1850s; $45–70.

Half-plate ambrotype of New England building, Union case; mid-19th century; $165–225. The larger the plate size, the more valuable the ambrotype.

Quarter-plate ambrotype of Civil War soldier in wood and paper case; early 1860s; $60–85. A pink tint has been applied to man's cheeks.

Cartes de visite from the 1860s. *Left:* General Banks, by Mathew Brady; $20–35. *Right:* Civil War soldier; $15–25. Photographic material by a leading photographer like Brady is always desirable.

Carte de visite of Niagara Falls; last quarter 19th century; $15–30. Scenic views are relatively uncommon in this medium.

Sixth-plate ambrotype of boy in school uniform, cheeks tinted pink; 1850s; $10–15. An example of the inexpensive ambrotype.

Rare two-sided ambrotype of woman by Mathew Brady; mid-19th century; $150–200.

Commodore Nutt and Miss Minnie Warren.

Carte de visite of the famous midgets Commodore Nutt and Minnie Warren; 1860s; $35–55. Midgets and circus freaks were popular material for cartes de visite.

Carte de visite of a woman; 1860s; $2–5. Inexpensive pieces like this one are a good buy at present.

Tintype of a crippled young man in the standard 2″ x 3″ size; second half 19th century; $20–40. The unusual subject matter makes for a higher price.

Tintype of a man in standard 2″ x 3″ size; second half 19th century; $2–5. Tintypes in standard size are moderately priced; the larger sizes are rare and more costly.

Stereoscopic view of the ruins of the Great Chicago Fire; ca. 1871; $10–18.

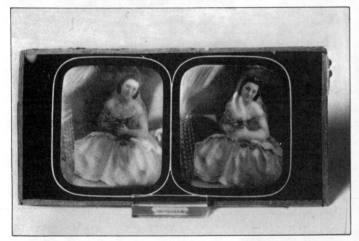

Extremely rare stereoscopic daguerreotype; 1850s; $450–600.

Stereoscopic view of buildings in Buffalo, N.Y.; second half 19th century; $5–8. Collecting stereo cards is becoming a major American hobby.

Stereoscopic view of destruction caused by the Johnstown, Pa., flood in 1889; $10–20. Stereoscopic views of disasters were very popular. The "dead" body in foreground is probably posed.

Top: Stereoscopic view of risqué ladies; 1890s; $15–30. *Below:* Stereoscopic view of Indian woman; Nevada, late 19th century; $60–95.

Two examples of the less-expensive Keystone-type stereoscopic views; 1890s. *Top:* View of Missouri zinc mine; $2–5. *Below:* Steamboat; $10–20.

"Love Reigns Supreme," colored or tinted stereoscopic view of the sort popular at the turn of the century; $3–6.

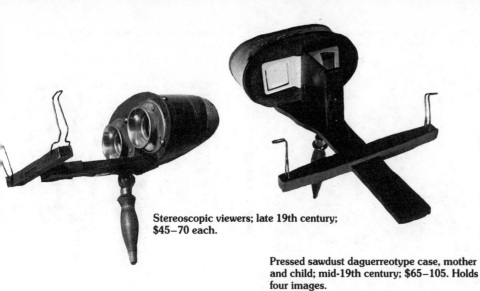

Stereoscopic viewers; late 19th century; $45–70 each.

Pressed sawdust daguerreotype case, mother and child; mid-19th century; $65–105. Holds four images.

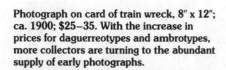

Pressed sawdust daguerreotype case, seated Liberty; mid-19th century; $45–75. Many people make a collection solely of these attractive cases.

Photograph on card of train wreck, 8″ x 12″; ca. 1900; $25–35. With the increase in prices for daguerreotypes and ambrotypes, more collectors are turning to the abundant supply of early photographs.

Pressed sawdust daguerreotype case, "Capture of Major Andre"; mid-19th century; $75–120.

Cabinet photograph of Prairie Flower, Indian show woman and sharpshooter; late 19th century; $55–85. Disaster and personality photographs, like this one, rate high with collectors of old photos.

Photograph of early American hotel, 10″ x 12″; late 19th century; $65–90.

Photograph of the warship *Columbia*, 6″ x 8″; late 19th century; $15–25.

Photograph of a wagon shop, 6″ x 8″; late 19th century; $20–35.

Photograph of a group of World War I soldiers, 4″ x 6″; ca. 1917; $10–20.

Photograph of two women on horseback, 8″ x1 0″; early 20th century; $5–15.

Photograph of a large summer hotel, 8″ x 10″; early 20th century; $10–18.

The Quad camera, a mechanical plate camera; ca. 1896; $65–100.

Photograph stand, ebony inlaid with mother-of-pearl late 19th century; $35–55.

Victorian photogaph album of the type once owned by every family; late 19th century; $20–45. The albums are attractive with or without pictures.

Pocket Kodak folding camera with wooden interior; early 20th century; $25–40.

◄ Folding Pony Premo A, plate camera; early 20th century; $75–100.

21.
POSTERS, POSTCARDS, AND OTHER PRINTED MATERIALS

The amount of antique paper material of interest to collectors is so extensive that most people specialize in one particular type, be it posters, postcards, or magazines. As might be expected from its fragile nature, most collectible paper is of rather recent vintage (post-1900), though a surprisingly large number of earlier examples do exist.

The earliest widely collected form is the broadside, a single sheet of rag-based paper crudely printed in black and often decorated with primitive wood-block designs—a coach and horse team, for example, on a sheet advertising a stage line. Like the modern poster, broadsides were intended to convey quickly a brief message; they were passed out on the street or pasted up on walls, and few survived for any length of time. As a consequence, they are not common today and, when offered on the market, can command a good price. The form generally disappeared with the widespread use of lithography, and most specimens found today date from before 1850.

Lithography was invented in 1796 by Alois Senefelder. Despite its advantages over the earlier art of engraving, as a quicker and cheaper means of reproduction, it spread slowly, and it was not used to any extent in the United States until after 1825. The earliest lithographs were simple monochromatic line drawings, usually in black, but it soon became customary to add color. This was done by hand on a production line, where women and older children, seated at a long table, would each tint certain areas of a lithograph before passing it on to the next person to tint certain other areas. It is rare in early pieces to find more than four colors: gold, black, blue, and green.

The first known American lithographers were Barnet and Doolittle of New York City, active from 1821 to 1822. They were followed by a host of imitators. By far the best known of them is the firm of Currier and Ives, which was established in 1833 by Nathaniel Currier, joined by James Ives as partner in 1857, and flourished in New York City until 1906.

The secret of Currier and Ives's success was two-fold: they employed the best artists available, and they had

an uncanny knack for spotting what the public would like. In the days before radio, television, and journalistic photography, they illustrated for America the major events of the period: the Civil War, the opening of the Indian Territories, the glories of the great American West, and the triumphs of leading sports figures from boxers to horses. They also published religious lithographs and nostalgic scenes, such as the beloved *Home for Thanksgiving*. Today, some Currier and Ives lithographs are worth hundreds or even thousands of dollars—not bad for a mass-produced item.

In collecting Currier and Ives prints, one should keep in mind that the popular (and valuable) prints have been reproduced many times, so that it is not always easy to distinguish the originals from the later prints. Furthermore, the name alone, even on an original print, is not enough to ensure a profitable investment. Certain Currier and Ives lithographs, primarily the religious scenes, don't sell. They can be had at auction for ten or twelve dollars and are worth little more retail.

As popular and long-lived as they were, Currier and Ives were just one of many nineteenth-century lithograph publishers. Peter Mavrick, H. R. Robinson, Imbert and Company of New York; Moors Lithography Company of Boston; and Edward Webber of Baltimore, to name but a few, also produced many high-quality lithographs, which are often available at a fraction of the cost of a Currier and Ives. A form particularly in demand, but still inexpensive, is the fashion illustration found in such early magazines as *Godey's Lady's Book*. Hand-tinted lithographs, they accurately portray women's and children's styles for several decades of the nineteenth century, and they are of great interest to students of design. At a later date, when the invention of chromolithography made it possible to print a full-color illustration rather than coloring by hand, lithographers such as Louis Prang of Boston turned out a whole array of multicolored lithographed items, from framed mottoes for the home to postcards. All are highly collectible today.

The development of chromolithography also gave rise to the advertising poster of the twentieth century, a form that came into its own during World War I. At that time, posters ranging in size from the standard single sheet (twenty-eight inches by forty inches) to twenty-four-sheet billboard fillers were widely used in publicizing the four great Liberty Loan campaigns. Such well-known artists of the era as Charles Gibson and James Montgomery Flagg collaborated in the creation of some two thousand different designs from which, it is estimated, over 20 million posters were printed. A similar effort during the Second World War produced another imposing array of political posters. While the later examples are not as yet widely collected, World War I posters are in great demand. Some rare or particularly well-done pieces go for several hundred dollars, and even ordinary ones bring from twenty-five to seventy-five dollars if in good condition.

In no area did chromolithography have greater effect than in that of postcard art. Prior to the twentieth century, postcards, while important as a means of communication, were severely limited in their use by postal regulations. When the Post Office Department in 1907 amended its rules to allow writing a message on the back of the penny postcard (where previously only an address was permissible), the door was opened to rapid expansion of the postcard industry. During the years from 1907 to 1918, the height of the craze, thousands of different colored postcards were produced, many by German lithographers for sale in this country.

Collectors have been actively seeking these cards for some years, and now postcards may be said to be one of the more popular collecting categories. Most enthusiasts favor a single type of card—patriotics, for example, which were commonly exchanged on the Fourth of July, Lincoln's or Washington's Birthday, and Memorial Day. At present, no less than five hundred different patriotic designs are known. Disaster cards offer another interesting area. They were reproduced primarily from photographs and offer views of such assorted unpleasantnesses as the Johnstown Flood, the San Francisco Earthquake, and a variety of fires and train wrecks. On a more peaceful and bucolic note, there are scenes from the national forests or depictions of famous buildings and historic sites. The categories may be limited, but the number of postcards seems limitless, with new finds being made constantly in every area. Best of all, most cards can still be obtained for a dollar or two, or even less, except for those with rare views or those done and signed by such well-known postcard artists as Bernhardt Wall and Frances Brundage.

For many people the most interesting type of paper memorabilia is the greeting card, foremost among which is the valentine. The tradition of giving valentines to loved ones on Valentine's Day is very old. At least as early as 1750, Americans were exchanging handmade cards exhibiting fine scissor-cut decoration and elaborate watercolors. Valentines from this period are, of course, rare; but commercially manufactured cards, which first appeared in the 1840s, are generally available. Though some valentines made before 1900 were engraved, the great majority were lithographed and then carefully tinted by hand. They were never inexpensive, even when new. T. W. Strong of New York, a major producer in the 1840s, advertised in 1848 that he had cards "to suit all tastes and customs, prices ranging from six cents to ten dollars." This was at a time when a working man might make no more than a dollar for a day's labor!

As the nineteenth century advanced and handwork gave way to mechanical construction, valentines became increasingly more elaborate. In the 1850s, tiny daguerreotypes or tintype photographs were sometimes added to the cards. Silk pillow centers and textile netting appeared in the 1860s; and later Victorian examples, from about 1870 to 1890, might feature stand-up figures, mechanical devices, feathers, and mother-of-pearl inlay. The less common

and more elaborate of these valentines are far from inexpensive. Fortunately, though, it is possible for the collector to acquire attractive lacy valentines with interesting features for prices seldom in excess of twenty dollars. Earlier examples and those made by hand will, of course, go for much more.

On a somewhat more prosaic level are paper materials printed for commercial purposes, such as almanacs and trade catalogs. Almanacs contain a calendar along with a variety of useful information about the weather, care for illnesses, cooking, and any number of other concerns. Since they were nearly all advertising gimmicks issued by patent medicine firms, they contain a plethora of testimonials from satisfied users of whatever concoction might have sponsored the publication. As such, they are historical documents that provide interesting insight into the customs and attitudes of earlier generations, and they are worth preserving. Prices at present are extremely reasonable, particularly since some of the cover illustrations are superb.

Trade catalogs are an even more important piece of Americana. It was not until late in the eighteenth century that American businesses were wealthy enough to produce catalogs, and only after 1850 did these publications appear in any abundance. Even then, they were usually jobbers' or distributors' catalogs, since few manufacturers had an extensive enough inventory to justify printing a catalog for the public. Catalogs are significant both as research tools and for their often high-quality engravings or lithographs. Their appeal to the general public is evident from the spectacular sales of the reproductions of early Sears-Roebuck catalogs. In general, the most valuable catalogs are first editions: the first ice-box catalog, the first color-illustrated catalog, the first catalog by a prominent firm such as Montgomery-Ward. There is much interest in this field at present, and prices are climbing steadily. On the other

hand, many catalogs undoubtedly lie yet undiscovered, and it is possible to pick up good examples at country shops or in box lots to be found at auctions.

Cookbooks were also given away in large quantities as an advertising device. They contained recipes as well as household hints and cures and often were illustrated by such well-known commercial artists as Maxfield Parrish and Grace Drayton, whose Campbell Kids worked for Campbell Soup. Since Jell-O alone produced a quarter million recipe books during the period 1900 to 1925, most types cannot be said to be rare. Nevertheless, the high quality of their illustrations and the historical or social insights they provide make them a valuable addition to any paper collection.

Illustrations are also the key to the increasing interest in old magazines. Such publications as *The Country Gentleman* and *The Delineator,* which could hardly be given away a few years ago, are valued today for their fine illustrations and sell for three dollars or more apiece. If the cover happens to be by an artist such as Norman Rockwell, the magazine may go for fifteen dollars. Cover art is, in fact, becoming so important that desirable covers are being framed and sold like prints.

Beyond the realm of literature but within the realm of paper is the bandbox, a storage box popular during the period 1800 to 1850. Usually oval, bandboxes were used to hold such articles as hats, sashes, and collars. They were made of wood or cardboard and were covered with lithographed or block-printed paper much like wallpaper (and frequently made by wallpaper manufacturers, though to a different size). The current interest in American bandboxes and the resulting high prices are explained both by their extremely attractive colors and by the fact that they often portray early American scenes—particularly those illustrating various modes of transportation—current at the time the boxes were made.

Hand-tinted lithograph of the wreck of the steamboat *Swallow;* New York, ca. 1845; $165–235.

Printed broadside; New York, 1841; $150–220. Though abundant in their day, these broadsides are now uncommon.

Hand-tinted illustration; from *Godey's Lady's Book,* ca. 1880; $10–15. These magazine illustrations are now being mounted and sold individually.

Chromolithograph; by Prang, New York, late 19th century; $45–65.

Hand-tinted lithograph; by Kellogg and Thayer, New York, ca. 1860; $15–30. Though of the same genre as Currier and Ives prints, these sentimental lithographs have attracted less attention.

Chromolithograph motto; East, late 19th century; $15–25. Framed mottoes of this sort are attracting collector interest.

Chromolithograph of the centennial of the British evacuation of New York City; by J. Koehler, New York, ca. 1883; $175–250.

"Spirit of America," by Howard Chandler Christy, 20″ x 30″; 1919; $125–175. An extremely well-done poster of the World War I era by a famous artist.

"Keep Him Free," by Charles L. Bull; 20″ x 30″; ca. 1919; $110–165. One of the most famous of all American posters from the World War I era.

"Weapons for Liberty," by J. C. Leyendecker, 20″ x 30″; World War I era; $135–215.

"Boys and Girls!" by James Montgomery Flagg, 20″ x 30″; ca. 1919; $115–145. ▲

"This is the Enemy," 20″ x 30″; World War II poster, ca. 1943; $60–85.

World War II poster, early 1940s; $35–60. War-time posters are increasing in value.

Years of Dust," by Ben Shahn, 25″ x 38″; ca. 1936; $1,250–1,750. One of the finest posters created in the 20th century by the well-known artist.

Advertising poster for *Harper's* magazine, by Edward Penfield, 12″ x 18″; 1895; $125–155.

"Thurston, World's Famous Magician," 27″ x 41″; $165–215. A show-business poster typical of the late 19th-early 20th century.

Advertising poster for the book *Miss Träumerei*, by Ethel Reed, one of the early female illustrators, 14″ x 22″; ca. 1895; $225–275.

Advertising poster for Chesterfield cigarettes, by C. E. Chambers, 14″ x 30″; ca. 1929; $70–95.

Three late 19th century postcards of a sort now sought by collectors. *Left:* $1–2. *Right:* $2–3. *Below:* $1–2.

Well-done Art Nouveau greeting postcard; ca. 1900; $3–5.

Three good examples of the greeting postcards popular in the late 19th-early 20th century. *Left and center:* $1–2 each. *Right:* By Frances Brundage; $4–7.

Scenic postcards; late 19th-early 20th century; $2–3.

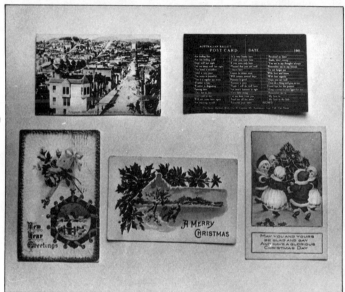

Seasonal and novelty postcards; late 19th-early 20th century; $2–3.

Seasonal greeting postcards; early 20th century; $2–3 each, except lower right, by Frances Brundage, $4–7.

Punched gilt valentine paper; late 19th century; $15–30.

Lacy valentine with chromolithographed insert; 1880–90; $25–40.

Excellent lacy valentine with chromolithographed inserts; 1870–80; $35–55.

Lacy valentine with chromolithographed inserts; 1870–80; $35–60.

Lacy valentine with chromolithographed inserts; 1870; $35–60.

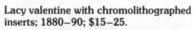

Lacy valentine designed to hold sachet;
1860–70; $35–50.

▲ Embossed lace and mesh valentine with gilt
inserts; 1850–60; $55–80.

Lacy valentine with chromolithographed
inserts; 1880–90; $15–25.

Embossed lacy valentine; 1880–90; $25–35.

Almanac; by Dr. Kilmer's Swamp-Root patent medicine; New York, early 20th century; $10–17.

Recipe book by Crisco, the sort given away as an advertising device; early 20th century; $5–10.

Joke book given away as an advertising device by the Alka Selzer Company; ca. 1924; $5–9.

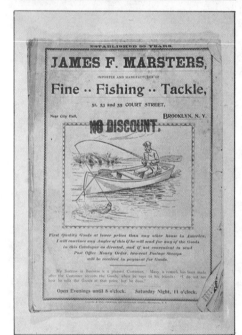

Trade catalog from a fishing tackle manufacturer; New York, late 19th century; $22–34.

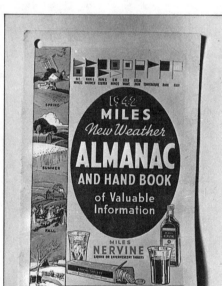

Almanac; by Miles Nervine patent medicine; Indiana, 1942; $3–6.

Trade catalog; from E. T. Barnum Iron and Wire Works, Michigan, ca. 1923; $15–30.

Woman's Home Companion; 1922; $5–12. Their elaborate covers and interesting illustrations have made early 20th-century magazines a paper collector's favorite.

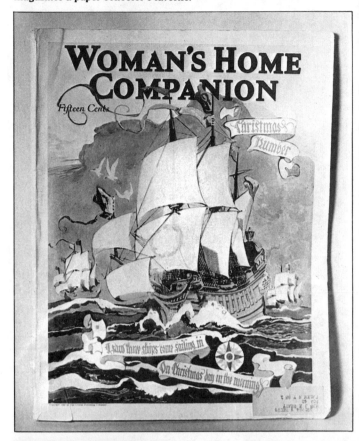

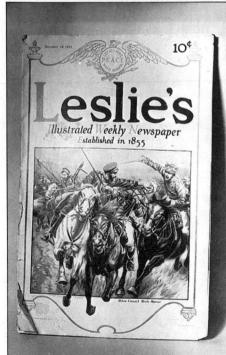

Leslie's Illustrated Weekly Newspaper; 1914; $7–13.

Interior illustration from *Leslie's;* 1914; $7–13.

The Saturday Evening Post; 1909; $6–9.

McCall's Magazine; 1914; $9–14.

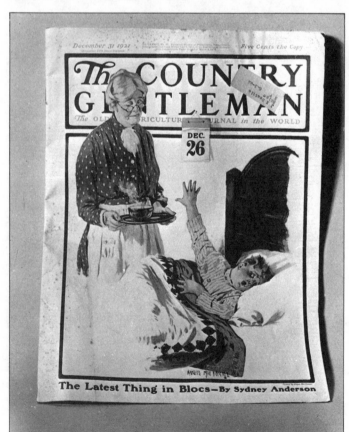

The Country Gentleman; 1921; $12–18.

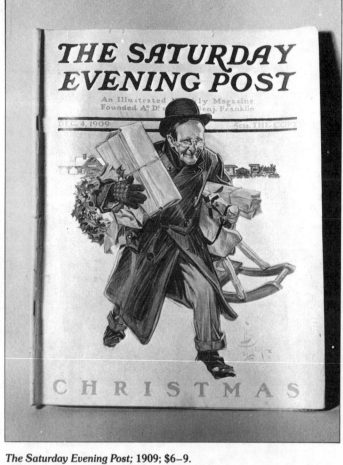

The Country Gentleman, with cover by
Norman Rockwell; 1921; $25–32. A
Rockwell cover boosts the price of any
magazine.

"The Delineator; 1911; $7–12.

Collier's; 1904; $5–8.

Good Housekeeping; 1926; $6–9.

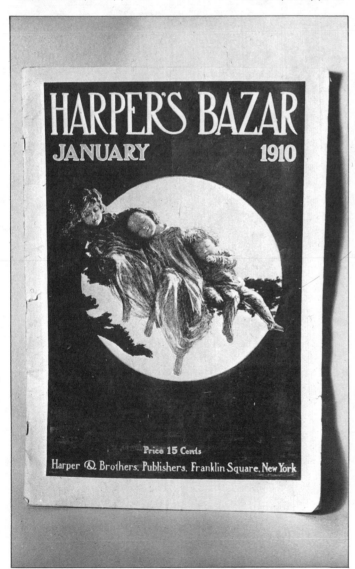

Harper's Bazar; 1910; $8–13.

The Ladies' Home Journal; 1914; $7–12.
This magazine frequently carried Kewpie-doll
cutouts, and their presence brings the price
per copy to $40–65.

Wallpaper-covered bandbox; New York, ca. 1850; $90–130.

Wallpaper-covered bandbox; Connecticut, ca. 1840; $110–150.

Wallpaper-covered bandbox, decorated with flowers and peacocks; New England, ca. 1840; $135–175.

Wallpaper-covered bandbox, floral decoration; New England, ca. 1840; $115–150.

Wallpaper-covered bandbox depicting
various sailing ships and steamboats; New
York, ca. 1840; $220–275.

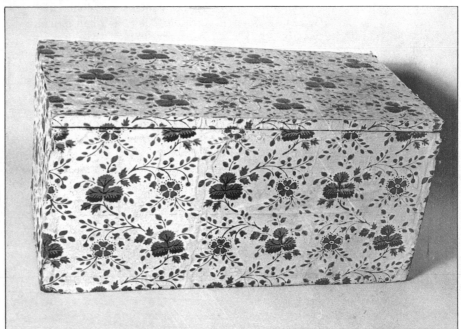

Rectangular wooden box covered with block-
printed wallpaper; New England, ca. 1850;
$125–160.

Papier-mâché dog, probably a toy; New York,
ca. 1870; $65–95.

22

POLITICAL MEMORABILIA

For several reasons, political memorabilia comprise a rather young and small group of collector's items. For one thing, electoral campaigning as we know it today—with its buttons and banners and its widespread attempts to influence the votes of millions—did not exist before the second quarter of the nineteenth century. Before that time, voting in the United States—whether for national or local candidates—was mostly the privilege of the wealthy few. But by the mid-1830s, the right to vote had been extended to all white adult males, more than tripling the size of the voting population of the preceding decade; and more and more candidates of national importance were being elected directly by these voters, instead of being chosen in limited party caucuses. The result was an intense rivalry between the political parties to stimulate and sway voter opinion. Then, as now, one of the methods they used to promote their cause was the distribution of various articles bearing the name or likeness of their candidate and perhaps a slogan reflecting the currently contested issue.

However, few political artifacts survive from before the middle of the nineteenth century. This is not so surprising, for such items are transitory by their very nature. Not only are they fragile—being made of paper or other nondurable material—but also, unlike almost all other antiques, they were intended to serve only the shortest-lived of purposes—the few months required to conduct a political campaign. Most political mementos were cheaply produced, because although intended for a mass audience, they were not meant to last; they were often destroyed in use, were discarded immediately, or perished from neglect once their purpose had been served.

Fortunate exceptions are the parade lanterns and torches that were used in traditional nighttime parades prior to the advent of electricity. In the mid-nineteenth century, it was customary for marching clubs to be formed among the politically like-minded in militia battalions or volunteer fire departments for the purpose of conducting ceremonial parades, especially in support of their candidates at election time. To heighten the drama of the occasion, and thus create a greater impression on their fellow citizens, the members would carry large numbers of tin and glass lanterns and torches, which they carefully preserved, to be used again from year to year. As a result, large numbers of such parade lights have come down to us, and many may be found in public and private collections.

Another exception is political whiskey flasks, which, judging by the large numbers that survive, seem to have been prized as much by their original owners as they are today. Until the 1870s, it was the custom to pass out free liquor at political rallies and parades. Wise candidates saw to it that their gifts were bottled in pint or half-pint flasks embossed with their own portrait—often linked with that of an earlier patriot such as Washington, to heighten their own prestige. Today, these flasks are in great demand, and their prices are quite high. (Samples of them are illustrated in Chapter 4.)

The largest collector interest in political memorabilia centers on political buttons and ribbons, items that were far from common prior to the last years of the nineteenth century. One of the oldest political mementos to come on the market in recent years is a brass button cast for Washington's inauguration in 1789. It was dug up in Virginia and sold at auction for four hundred dollars. Such buttons appear to have been quite popular in the early 1800s. So were brass or bronze medallions, which were cast with the likeness of the candidate and had a small hole through which a ribbon might be strung, to be worn around the neck or arm.

Just before the Civil War, lapel and breast pins appeared. They consisted of a circular brass frame within which was mounted a tintype or ambrotype picture of the candidate. Some were pierced for stringing, but others bore the first spring-wire pins. Also popular in the 1850s and 1860s were cartes de visite, or photographs on cardboard, of candidates.

The button collector did not truly come into his own until the election of 1896. At that time, celluloid—which had been invented in 1869—was first combined with a patented pin-back attachment to create the celluloid pin-back button. The manufacturing process was quite simple. A picture or slogan printed on paper was covered with a piece of hard, clear celluloid; then both were wrapped about a round tin shell and fixed in place with a stamped metal collar to which the spring-wire pin was attached. The technique revolutionized political button manufacture. It was quick and relatively inexpensive, and enabled anything that could be printed to be placed on a button. Whitehead and Hoag of New Jersey was the most active early producer of these buttons, but by 1900 dozens of companies were in the business. During the two McKinley-Bryan campaigns alone (1896 and 1900), it is estimated that nearly two thousand different campaign buttons were turned out.

During their period of most active use, 1896 to 1920, thousands of celluloid political buttons appeared. Most were made in vast quantities and are, even today, relatively easy to obtain. But for one reason or another, some were produced in a limited edition and are, accordingly, both rare and expensive. As a general rule, these include odd sizes, both large and small; third-party buttons; and those issued in support of a cause (such as the Women's Vote) rather than a candidate. Jugate buttons, which picture the presidential and vice-presidential candidates side by side, are a special favorite with collectors and may often sell for more than less-common non-presidential items. At present, the rarest jugate and the most valuable of all celluloid pin backs is the Cox–Roosevelt button issued by the Democrats during the 1920 campaign.

In 1920, lithographed tin political buttons made their first appearance and quickly replaced celluloid pin backs, which today are made only in special editions. The tin pin is easier to produce and much cheaper than its predecessor. It is manufactured with a die press, which can shape and stamp a large sheet of tin in one operation, to produce multiple images of the same design. As is the case with so much modern technology, though, something is lost in the process. Tin pins are easily scratched, so that few undamaged examples are found. Moreover, economic practicalities limit the number of colors that may be used, a factor of no consideration in celluloid buttons since printing was done separately on the paper insert. As a whole, the quality of political buttons has declined since 1920; though with the renewed interest in all slogan buttons during the 1960s, some interesting designs have begun to appear.

Though most buttons were used alone, they were sometimes combined with ribbons of various size. In fact, ribbons bearing the printed names of candidates were widely used in the nineteenth century. Tintype picture buttons and ribbons were combined during the Lincoln campaign of 1864, and both ribbons and sashes dating back to the 1820s may be found. The practice has continued in the twentieth century with interesting additions, such as the felt sunflower backing used for Alf Landon's buttons in 1936. (Landon, the Republican candidate in that year, was a native of Kansas, the sunflower state.)

Over the years a variety of other political mementos has been produced, in nearly every medium imaginable. In the 1870s and 1880s, comic statuary was popular, and more than one politician was unhappy to find himself the subject of a comic jug or mug turned out at a pottery such as the one at Anna, Illinois. Tin and other metals were effectively employed not only for buttons and medallions but also for such useful objects as match safes. An extremely desirable political item is the pewter match safe shaped as a bust of General Grant, the Republican candidate in 1868. Tin whistles and horns used at rallies and parades are also in demand, particularly if they incorporate interesting slogans or pictures. In the days when men used pocket watches, they often carried a decorative watch fob with the likeness of their favorite candidate; these may be obtained in silver, pewter, or bronze.

Pressed-glass beer mugs, cups, and saucers were also embellished with the features or names of political figures, both active and deceased. In the twentieth century, the art of decalcomania is utilized to produce these pieces, while in the nineteenth century, such items were made primarily of pattern glass.

Perhaps the most common material employed in political advertising has been paper, since it is so inexpensive. Paper banners and streamers have traditionally decorated the halls where rallies are held; the partisans wear paper hats or beanies; and great posters of the candidates look down on the faithful assembled at their feet. Unfortunately, paper is fragile and very expendable. Vast quantities have been thrown away after every election, so that today, paper political memorabilia in good condition that predates 1900 is extremely hard to come by. Some things, of course, are harder to find than others. Life-size posters and large banners are rare, but sheet music, such as the "rousing" "Keep Cool with Coolidge," is relatively plentiful, and the same may be said of printed speeches and general propaganda. Of course, given the politician's fondness for talk, one may safely conclude that the existence of so many speeches, like the tip of an iceberg, gives only an inkling of what once must have existed.

Various slogan buttons related to the Franklin D. Roosevelt campaign of 1940; $8–15 each.

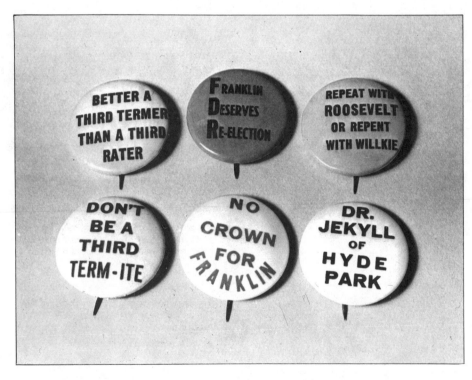

Pocket card, Cleveland-Stevenson; 1885;
$20–32.

Delegate's badge, Cleveland-Stevenson
Democratic Convention; 1892; $45–70

Bronze medallion, William Henry Harrison;
1841; $35–50. Medallions of this sort were
forerunners of the modern political button.

Brass-bound ambrotypes of Lincoln; 1860.
Both $150–200. Example at right shows
early pin back.

Lincoln ambrotype button with multicolored
ribbons; 1864; $350–425.

Early ambrotype of Jefferson Davis, president
of the Confederacy; ca. 1862; $300–450.
Among the earliest of all political buttons.

Pair of Garfield-Hancock pin-back eagle-crested pins; ca. 1881; $425–500 the pair. These are rare and choice items.

McKinley and Bryan buttons, with attached ribbons; 1896; $350–400 the pair.

Reverse of the Honest Dollar badge, showing slogan and platform.

Left: Tillman ("Pitchfork Ben") spear; $55–75. *Center:* McKinley gold bug; $150–210. *Right:* Parker and Davis watch fob; $45–60. All, early 1900s.

Extra-large gold-colored metal badge stamped "McKinley"; 1896; $75–115. The so-called Honest Dollar badge.

Teddy Roosevelt rabbit's-foot badge issued at the time he was campaigning for governor of New York; 1898; $70–110.

Rare Teddy Roosevelt vice-presidential button, celluloid; 1900; $375–475.

Jugate buttons with ribbons. *Left:* Teddy Roosevelt and Fairbanks. *Right:* Parker and Davis. $1,000–1,500 the pair.

McKinley and Teddy Roosevelt jugate button; 1900; $250–300. Double photo buttons are more valuable in most cases.

Unique Franklin D. Roosevelt-Garner jugate; issued by Slovak Democratic Clubs; $650–900.

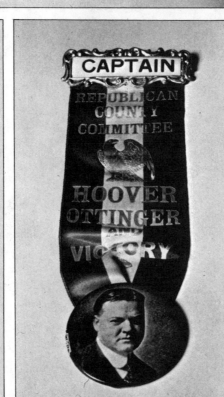

Captain's badge, Coolidge; 1924; $175–215. Captain's badge, Hoover; 1928; $70–105.

Socialist Labor Party buttons; 1924. *Left to right:* $7–11; $15–20; $25–35.

Communist Party buttons; 1936. *Left:* Browder-Ford; $65–95. *Right:* $15–25.

Left: Truman button; $10–15. *Center:* Henry A. Wallace; $7–12. *Right:* Dewey-Warren jugate; $10–15. All, ca. 1948.

Rare George McGovern button with pictures of rock superstars; 1927; $85–115.

Slogan buttons. *Left:* Anti-Nixon; 1964; $7–12. *Right:* Anti-Goldwater; 1964; $17–25.

Ford buttons. *Left:* Presidential; 1976; $2–5. *Right:* Vice-presidential; 1964; $45–70.

Satirical figure of a "suffragette,"
polychrome white earthenware; late 19th-
early 20th century; $165–235.

Eisenhower paper and wood fan; 1952; $12–
18.

Paper matches. *Left:* Robert Taft; 1952; $4–
7. *Center:* Wendell Willkie; 1940; $15–20.
Right: John Kennedy; 1960; $4–8.

372

Top: Rare Eugene McCarthy bandanna; 1968; $25–40. *Bottom:* Barry Goldwater bumper sticker; 1964; $4–7.

Two Nixon miniatures; 1972. *Left:* $7–15. *Right:* $10–18.

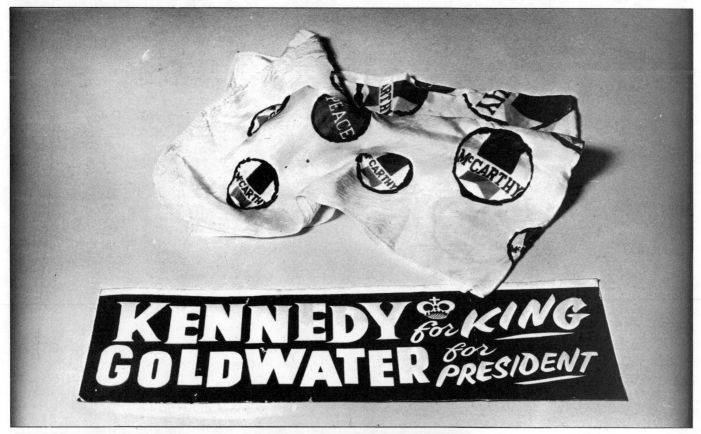

John Kennedy paper hat; 1960; $12–22.

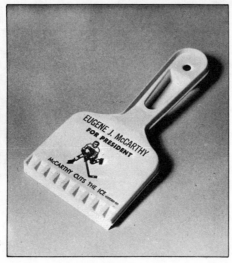

Eugene McCarthy plastic ice scraper; 1968; $8–15.

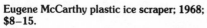

373

BIBLIOGRAPHY

Suggestions for further reading

FURNITURE

Bjerkee, Ethel Hall. *The Cabinet Makers of America.* New York: Bonanza Books, 1957.

Lockwood, Luke Vincent. *Colonial Furniture in America.* New York: Charles Scribner's Sons, 1957.

Morse, John D. *Country Cabinetwork and Simple City Furniture.* Charlottesville, Va.: University of Virginia Press, 1969.

Nutting, Wallace. *Furniture of the Pilgrim Century.* New York: Dover Publications, 1965.

Ormsbee, Thomas H. *Field Guide to American Victorian Furniture.* New York: Bonanza Books, 1951.

Smith, Nancy A. *Old Furniture: Understanding the Craftsman's Art.* Boston: Little, Brown & Co., 1976.

Williams, Henry L. *Country Furniture of Early America.* Cranbury, N.J.: A. S. Barnes & Co., 1963.

PAINTING AND SCULPTURE

Christensen, Erwin O. *Early American Wood Carving.* New York: Dover Publications, 1972.

Ebert, Katherine, and Ebert, John. *American Folk Painters.* New York: Charles Scribner's Sons, 1975.

Klamkin, Marian, and Klamkin, Charles. *Woodcarvings, North American Folk Sculpture.* New York: Hawthorn Books, 1974.

Lipman, Jean. *American Primitive Painting.* New York: Dover Publications, 1972.

Lipman, Jean, and Winchester, Alice. *The Flowering of American Folk Art.* New York: The Viking Press, 1974.

Montgomery, Charles, and Kane, Patricia. *American Art, 1750–1800.* New York: New York Graphic Society, 1975.

Wilmerding, John. *American Art.* New York: Penguin Books, 1976.

GLASS

Coppen-Gardner, Sylvia. *Background for Glass Collectors.* Levittown, N.Y.: Transatlantic Arts, 1976.

Daniel, Dorothy. *Cut and Engraved Glass.* New York: M. Barrows & Co., 1950.

Ketchum, William C., Jr. *A Treasury of American Bottles.* Indianapolis, Ind.: The Bobbs-Merrill Co., 1975.

McKearin, Helen, and McKearin, George S. *American Glass.* New York: Crown Publishers, 1941.

McKearin, Helen, and McKearin, George S. *Two Hundred Years of American Blown Glass.* New York: Crown Publishers, 1949.

Polak, Ada. *Glass: Its Traditions and Its Makers.* New York: G. P. Putnam's Sons, 1975.

Wilson, Kenneth M. *New England Glass and Glassmaking.* New York: Thomas Y. Crowell Co., 1972.

POTTERY

Barret, Richard Carter. *Bennington Pottery and Porcelain.* New York: Bonanza Books, 1968.

Bivins, John, Jr. *The Moravian Potters in North Carolina.* Chapel Hill, N.C.: University of North Carolina Press, 1972.

Guilland, Harold F. *Early American Folk Pottery.* Radnor, Pa.: Chilton Book Co., 1971.

Ketchum, William C., Jr. *Early Potters and Potteries of New York State.* New York: Funk & Wagnalls, 1970.

Ketchum, William C., Jr. *The Pottery and Porcelain Collector's Handbook.* New York: Funk & Wagnalls, 1971.

Watkins, Lura. *Early New England Potters and Their Wares.* Hamden, Conn.: The Shoe String Press, 1968.

Webster, Donald B. *Decorated Stoneware Pottery of North America.* Rutland, Vt.: Charles E. Tuttle Co., 1970.

SILVER AND PEWTER

Ebert, Katherine. *Collecting American Pewter.* New York: Charles Scribner's Sons, 1976.

Fales, Martha G. *Early American Silver.* New York: Funk & Wagnalls, 1970.

Kauffman, Henry J. *The Colonial Silversmith.* Nashville, Tenn.: Thomas Nelson, 1969.

Kerfoot, John Barrett. *American Pewter.* Detroit, Mich.: Gale Research Co., 1975.

Rainwater, Dorothy T. *Encyclopedia of American Silver Manufacturers.* Hanover, Pa.: Everybody's Press, 1974.

Schwartz, Marvin D. *Collector's Guide to Antique American Silver.* New York: Doubleday & Co., 1975.

Thomas, John C., ed. *American and British Pewter: An Historical Survey.* New York: Antiques Magazine Library, 1976.

COPPER AND BRASS

Fuller, A. S. *The Art of Coppersmithing.* David Williams Co., 1911.

Kauffman, Henry J. *Early American Copper, Tin and Brass.* Medill McBride, 1950.

IRON AND TIN

Coffin, Margaret. *American Country Tinware.* New York: Galahad Books, 1968.

Curtis, Will, and Curtis, Jane. *Antique Wood Stoves: Artistry in Iron.* Ashville, Maine: Cobblesmith, 1976.

Geerlings, Gerald Kenneth. *Wrought Iron in Architecture.* New York: Charles Scribner's Sons, 1971.

Gould, Mary E. *Antique Tin and Tole Ware: Its History and Romance.* Rutland, Vt.: Charles E. Tuttle Co., 1957.

Kauffman, Henry J. *Early American Copper, Tin and Brass.* Medill McBride, 1950.

Kauffman, Henry J. *Early American Ironware, Cast and Wrought.* Rutland, Vt.: Charles E. Tuttle Co., 1966.

Mercer, Henry C. *The Bible in Iron.* Doylestown, Pa.: Bucks County Historical Society, 1941.

Sonn, M. E. *Early American Wrought Iron.* New York: Charles Scribner's Sons, 1928.

TEXTILES

Bishop, Robert. *New Discoveries in American Quilts.* New York: E. P. Dutton & Co., 1975.

Bogdonoff, Nancy D. *Handwoven Textiles of Early New England.* Harrisburg, Pa.: Stackpole Books, 1975.

Ketchum, William C., Jr. *Hooked Rugs: A Historical Collector's Guide—How to Make Your Own.* New York: Harcourt Brace Jovanovich, 1976.

Kopp, Kate, and Kopp, Joel. *American Hooked and Sewn Rugs: Folk Art Underfoot.* New York: E. P. Dutton & Co., 1975.

Landon, Mary T., and Swan, Susan B. *American Crewel Work.* New York: Macmillan, 1970.

Safford, Carleton, and Bishop, Robert. *America's Quilts and Coverlets.* New York: E. P. Dutton & Co., 1972.

Swan, Susan B. *A Winterthur Guide to American Needlework.* New York: Crown Publishers, 1976.

WOODENWARE

Earle, Alice M. *Home Life in Colonial Days.* Stockbridge, Mass.: Berkshire Traveller, 1974.

Franklin, Linda C. *From Hearth to Cookstove: Kitchen Collectibles, 1700–1930.* Florence, Ala.: House of Collectibles, 1976.

Gould, Mary E. *Early American Wooden Ware.* Rutland, Vt.: Charles E. Tuttle Co., 1962.

Ketchum, William C., Jr. *American Basketry and Woodenware: A Collector's Guide.* New York: Macmillan, 1974.

Norwak, Mary. *Kitchen Antiques.* New York: Praeger

Publishers, 1975.

Powell, Elizabeth A. *Pennsylvania Butter: Tools and Processes.* Doylestown, Pa.: Bucks County Historical Society, 1974.

Toller, Jane. *Turned Woodware for Collectors: Treen and Other Objects.* Cranbury, N.J.: A.S. Barnes & Co., 1976.

BASKETRY

Bobart, Henry H. *Basketwork Through the Ages.* Oxford, England: Oxford University Press, 1936.

Ketchum, William C., Jr. *American Basketry and Woodenware: A Collector's Guide.* New York: Macmillan, 1974.

Reinert, R. P. *Pennsylvania German Splint and Straw Basketry.* Keyser, 1946.

Seeler, W. T. *Nantucket Lightship Baskets.* Cambridge, Mass.: Deermouse Press, 1972.

Woodstock, A. S. *Basketry.* Independence, Mo.: Herald House, 1960.

LIGHTING DEVICES

Cooke, Lawrence S., ed. *Lighting in America.* New York: Main Street Press/Universe Books, 1976.

Curtis, R. C. *Lamp Collectors Hand Book.* 1975.

Hayward, Arthur H. *Colonial and Early American Lighting.* New York: Dover Publications, 1962.

Rimalover, S. T. *Antique American Wall Match Holders.* Stonybrook, Long Island, N.Y.: Stonybrook Press, 1976.

Smith, Frank R., and Smith, Ruth E. *Miniature Lamps.* Huntertown, Indiana: R. J. Beck, 1974.

TOOLS

Bealer, Alex. *The Tools That Built America.* Barre, Mass.: Barre Publishing Co., 1975.

Blandford, Percy W. *Old Farm Tools and Machinery.* Detroit, Mich.: Gale Research Co., 1976.

Mercer, Henry C. *Ancient Carpenter's Tools.* New York: Horizon Press, 1976.

Rawson, Marion N. *Handwrought Ancestors.* New York: E. P. Dutton & Co., 1936.

Sloane, Eric. *Museum of Early American Tools.* New York: Funk & Wagnalls, 1964.

TOYS

Coleman, Dorothy S. et al. *The Collector's Book of Doll Clothes.* New York: Crown Publishers, 1975.

Eaton, W. M. *Dolls in Color.* New York: Macmillan, 1975.

Hertz, Louis H. *The Toy Collector.* New York: Funk & Wagnalls, 1969.

Jacobs, Flora G. *A History of Dolls' Houses.* New York: Charles Scribner's Sons, 1965.

Jacobs, Flora G. *Dolls' Houses in America.* New York: Charles Scribner's Sons, 1974.

McClinton, Katherine M. *Antiques of American Childhood.* New York: Clarkson N. Potter, 1970.

Pressland, David. *The Art of the Tin Toy.* New York: Crown Publishers, 1976.

DECOYS

Barber, Joel. *Wild Fowl Decoys.* Miami, Fla.: Windward House, 1934.

Mackey, William J., Jr. *American Bird Decoys.* New York: E. P. Dutton & Co., 1970.

Smith, T. M. *American Wild Life Decoys, From Folk Art to Factory.* Lebanon, Pa.: Applied Arts Publishers, 1974.

Starr, George. *Decoys of the Atlantic Flyway.* New York: Winchester Press, 1974.

WEATHERVANES

Kaye, Myrna. *Yankee Weathervanes.* New York: E. P. Dutton & Co., 1975.

Klamkin, Charles. *Weather Vanes: The History Manufacture, & Design of an American Folk Art.* New York: Hawthorn Books, 1973.

Lynch, Kenneth. *Weathervanes and Cupolas.* New York: Canterbury Press, 1975.

TRAMP ART

Fendelman, Helaine. *Tramp Art.* New York: E. P. Dutton & Co., 1975.

SCRIMSHAW

Dow, George F. *Whale Ships and Whaling.* New York: Argosy Publishers, 1967.

Flayderman, Norman E. *Scrimshaw and Scrimshanders: Whales and Whalemen.* (Privately published, 1973)

Klamkin, Marian. *Marine Antiques.* New York: Dodd, Mead & Co., 1975.

Kranz, Jacqueline L. *American Nautical Art and Antiques.* New York: Crown Publishers, 1975.

Ritchie, Carson I. *Bone and Horn Carving: A Pictorial History.* Cranbury, N.J.: A. S. Barnes & Co., 1975.

Stackpole, Edouard A. *The Sea-Hunters.* Philadelphia: J. B. Lippincott Co., 1953.

ADVERTISING MEMORABILIA

Davis, Marvin, and Davis, Helen. *Collector's Price Guide to Bottles, Tobacco Tins and Relics.* New York: A & W Visual Library, 1975.

Grossholz, Roselyn. *The Collectible Classics from Commerce.* Erie, Pa.: Tole House, 1976.

Hornung, Clarence P. *Handbook of Early Advertising Art.* New York: Dover Publications, 1956.

Kaduck, Mildred. *Advertising Trade Cards.* Des Moines, Iowa: Wallace-Homestead Book Co, 1975.

Larson, Henrietta M. *Guide to Business History: Materials for the Study of American Business History and Suggestions for Their Use.* Cambridge, Mass.: Harvard University Press, 1950.

Martells, Jack. *Beer Can Collector's Bible.* Matteson, Ill.: Greatlakes Living Press, 1976.

Mebane, John. *The Poor Man's Guide to Trivia Collecting.* New York: Doubleday & Co., 1975.

PHOTOGRAPHIC MEMORABILIA

Auer, Michel. *The Illustrated History of the Camera.* New York: New York Graphic Society, 1975.

Gilbert, George. *Collecting Photographica.* New York: Hawthorn Books, 1976.

Smith, R.C. *Antique Cameras.* N. Pomfret, Vt.: David & Charles, 1976.

Welling, William B. *Collector's Guide to Nineteenth Century Photographs.* New York: Macmillan, 1976.

Wolf, D. S. *Blue Book Price Guide to Collectible Cameras.* (Privately published, 1976)

Wolfe, S. T. *Directory of Collectible Cameras.* Photographic Memorabilia, 1975.

PAPER

Buchsbaum, Ann. *Practical Guide to Print Collecting.* New York: Van Nostrand Reinhold Co., 1975.

Comstock, Helen. *American Lithographs.* New York: M. Burrows & Co., 1950.

Lee, Ruth W. *A History of Valentines.* Wellesley Hills, Mass.: Lee Publications, 1962.

Margolin, Victor. *American Poster Renaissance.* New York: Watson-Guptill Publications, 1975.

Newman, Ewell L., and McMillan, Ladd. *A Guide to Collecting Currier & Ives.* New York: Pyramid Books, 1975.

Theofiles, George. *American Posters of World War One.* Des Moines, Iowa: Wallace-Homestead Book Co., 1975.

Welsch, Roger L. *Tall-Tale Postcards: A Pictorial History.* Cranbury, N.J.: A. S. Barnes & Co., 1976.

POLITICAL MEMORABILIA

Bristow, S. R. *Illustrated Political Buttons.* (Privately published, 1971)

Halse, W. T. *Encyclopedia of Political Buttons.* Old Bethpage, N.Y.: Dafran House Publishers, 1973.

Kahler, R. B. *Hail to the Chief.* Princeton, N.J.: Pyne Press, 1972.

INDEX

ACKNOWLEDGMENTS

The author wishes to extend his appreciation to Mimi Koren for her invaluable advice and assistance in the editing of the book. Grateful acknowledgment is made for the assistance and photographic permissions kindly provided by the following individuals and institutions: Joyce and Zane Anderson, Providence, Rhode Island; Richard and Nancy Pettibone, New York City; Ivan and Marilynn Karp, New York City; Doug and Fran Faulkner, New Kingston, New York; Rachael Ketchum, New York City; Helaine and Burton Fendelman, Scarsdale, New York; Noreen Lewandowski, New York City; William C. Ketchum, Sr., Burlington, Vermont; Confetti Iman, Cherryfield, Maine; Helene and Foster Pollack, New York City; Linda Campbell Franklin, New York City; Edward and Jacquie Atkins, Jefferson, New York; Lib Walsh, Machias, Maine; Jim Whetzel, Jim's Bottle Shop, Ardsley, New York; New York State Historical Association, Cooperstown, New York; Old Museum Village of Smith's Clove, Monroe, New York; Ruggles House Association, Columbia Falls, Maine; Hancock County Trustees of Public Restorations, Ellsworth, Maine; Hannah Weston Chapter, Daughters of the American Revolution, Machias, Maine; Halm-Tyson Antiques, New York City; America Hurrah Antiques, New York City; Montgomery-Ecklund Antiques, Stamford, New York; Stonehouse Antiques, Lexington, New York; Axtell Antiques, Deposit, New York; Jonesport Wood Company, Jonesport, Maine; Farmrest Antiques, Goldsboro, Maine; Old Salt House Antiques, West Goldsboro, Maine; Red House Antiques, Machias, Maine; Woodshed Antiques, Hall's Mills, Maine; Better Times Antiques, New York City; Nelson's Folly Antiques, New York City; Brandon Memorabilia, Inc., New York City; Blue Door Antiques, Harrington, Maine; Poster America, New York City.